Collins easy learning

Italian
Verbs

Cosa dicevo?

Non preoccuparti!

Published by Collins
An imprint of HarperCollins Publishers
Westerhill Road
Bishopbriggs
Glasgow G64 2QT

HarperCollinsPublishers
Macken House, 39/40 Mayor Street Upper,
Dublin 1, D01 C9W8, Ireland

Third edition 2016

ISBN 978-0-00-815844-6

10 9 8

© HarperCollins Publishers 2006, 2011,
2016

Collins® is a registered trademark of
HarperCollins Publishers Limited

www.collinsdictionary.com
www.collins.co.uk/languagesupport

Typeset by Davidson Publishing
Solutions, Glasgow

Printed and bound in the UK using 100%
Renewable Electricity at CPI Group (UK) Ltd

All rights reserved. No part of this book
may be reproduced, stored in a retrieval
system, or transmitted in any form or
by any means, electronic, mechanical,
photocopying, recording or otherwise,
without the prior permission in writing
of the Publisher. This book is sold subject
to the conditions that it shall not, by
way of trade or otherwise, be lent,
re-sold, hired out or otherwise circulated
without the Publisher's prior consent
in any form of binding or cover other
than that in which it is published and
without a similar condition including
this condition being imposed on the
subsequent purchaser.

Entered words that we have reason to
believe constitute trademarks have
been designated as such. However,
neither the presence nor absence of
such designation should be regarded
as affecting the legal status of any
trademark.

The contents of this publication are
believed correct at the time of printing.
Nevertheless the Publisher can accept
no responsibility for errors or omissions,
changes in the detail given or for any
expense or loss thereby caused.

HarperCollins does not warrant that
any website mentioned in this title will
be provided uninterrupted, that any
website will be error free, that defects
will be corrected, or that the website or
the server that makes it available are
free of viruses or bugs. For full terms and
conditions please refer to the site terms
provided on the website.

A catalogue record for this book is
available from the British Library.

If you would like to comment on any
aspect of this book, please contact us at
the given address or online.
E-mail: dictionaries@harpercollins.co.uk
www.facebook.com/collinsdictionary
@collinsdict

Acknowledgements
We would like to thank those authors
and publishers who kindly gave
permission for copyright material to be
used in the Collins Corpus. We would
also like to thank Times Newspapers Ltd
for providing valuable data.

MANAGING EDITOR
Maree Airlie

CONTRIBUTORS
Francesca Logi
Janice McNeillie
Maggie Seaton
FOR THE PUBLISHER
Gerry Breslin
Craig Balfour

MIX
Paper | Supporting
responsible forestry
FSC™ C007454

This book is produced from independently certified FSC™
paper to ensure responsible forest management .
For more information visit: www.harpercollins.co.uk/green

Contents

Introduction

The *Easy Learning Italian Verbs* is designed for both young and adult learners. Whether you are starting to learn Italian for the very first time, brushing up your language skills or revising for exams, the *Easy Learning Italian Verbs* and its companion volume, the *Easy Learning Italian Grammar*, are here to help.

Newcomers can sometimes struggle with the technical terms they come across when they start to explore the grammar of a new language. The *Easy Learning Italian Verbs* contains a glossary which explains verb grammar terms using simple language and cutting out jargon.

The text is divided into sections to help you become confident in using and understanding Italian verbs. The first section looks at verb formation. Written in clear language, with numerous examples in real Italian, this section helps you to understand the rules which are used to form verb tenses. In addition, this book marks which vowel is stressed in some Italian words by putting those vowels into italic.

The next section of text looks at certain common prepositions which are used with a number of verbs. Each combination of verb plus preposition is shown with a simple example of real Italian to show exactly how it is used.

The **Verb Tables** contain 120 important Italian verbs (both regular and irregular) which are given in full for various tenses. Examples show how to use these verbs in your own work. If you are unsure how a verb goes in Italian, you can look up the Verb Index at the back of the book to find either the conjugation of the verb itself, or a cross-reference to a model verb, which will show you the patterns that verb follows.

The *Easy Learning Italian Grammar* takes you a step further in your language learning. It supplements the information given in the *Easy Learning Italian Verbs* by offering even more guidance on the usage and meaning of verbs, as well as looking at the most important aspects of Italian grammar. Together, or individually, the *Easy Learning* titles offer you all the help you need when learning Italian.

6 Glossary

Glossary of Verb Grammar Terms

ACTIVE a form of the verb that is used when the subject of the sentence does the action, for example, *A dog bit him* (subject: *a dog*; active verb: *bit*). Compare with **passive**.

ADVERB a word used with verbs to give information on where, when or how an action takes place, for example, *here, today, quickly*. An adverb can also add information to adjectives and other adverbs, for example, *extremely quick, very quickly*.

AGREEMENT the matching of words or word endings to the person or thing they refer to. For example, the verb *to be* has different forms for *I, you* and *he*: *I am, you are, he is*. In Italian you use verbs in the form appropriate to the person doing the action, and articles and adjectives have masculine, feminine and plural forms to match (or agree with) the noun they go with.

ARTICLE a word such as *the, a,* and *an* which goes with nouns: *the sun, a happy boy, an orange*. See also **definite article**, **indefinite article**.

AUXILIARY VERB a verb such as *be, have* and *do* that is used with a main verb to form tenses, negatives and questions.

BASE FORM the form of the verb that has no ending added to it, for example, *walk, have, be, go*. Compare with **infinitive**.

CLAUSE a group of words containing a verb.

CONDITIONAL a verb form used to talk about things that would happen or would be true under certain conditions, for example, *I would help you if I could*. It is also used in requests and offers, for example, *Could you lend me some money?; I could give you a lift*.

CONJUGATE (to) to give a verb different endings depending on whether its subject is *I, you, he* and so on, and depending on whether you are referring to the present, past or future, for example, *I have, she has, they listened*.

CONJUGATION a group of verbs that has a particular pattern of endings.

CONTINUOUS TENSE a verb form made up of *to be* and the *–ing* form, for example, *I'm thinking; They were quarrelling*. Italian continuous tenses are made with **stare** and the gerund.

DEFINITE ARTICLE the word *the*. Compare with **indefinite article**.

DEMONSTRATIVE PRONOUN a word used instead of a noun to point out people or things, for example, *That's my brother*. In English the demonstrative pronouns are *this, that, these* and *those*.

DIRECT OBJECT a noun or pronoun used to show who or what is affected by the verb. For example, in the sentence *He sent flowers*, the subject of the verb is *He* (the person who did the sending) and the direct object of the verb is *flowers* (what he sent). Compare with **indirect object**.

DIRECT OBJECT PRONOUN a word such as *me, him, us* and *them* used instead of a noun to show who or what is affected by the action of the verb, for example, *His friends helped him*. Compare with **indirect object pronoun**.

ENDING something added to the end of a word. In English nouns have plural endings, for example, boy → boys, child → children and verbs have the endings *–s, –ed* and –*ing*, for example, *walk* → *walks, walked, walking*. In Italian there are plural endings for nouns, verb endings, and masculine, feminine and plural endings for adjectives and pronouns.

FEMININE a noun, pronoun, article or form of adjective used to refer to a living being, thing or idea that is not classed as masculine. For example, **una** (feminine indefinite article) **bella** (adjective with a feminine ending) **casa** (feminine noun).

FUTURE a tense used to talk about something that will happen, or be true in the future, for example, *He'll be here soon; I'll give you a call; It will be sunny tomorrow.*

GERUND in English, a verb form ending in –*ing*, for example, *eating, sleeping*. In Italian the gerund ends in **–ando** or **–endo**. Compare with **present participle**.

IMPERATIVE a form of the verb used to give orders and instructions, for example, *Sit down!; Don't go!; Let's start!*

IMPERFECT a tense used to say what was happening, what used to happen and what things were like in the past, for example, *It was sunny at the weekend; They weren't listening; They used to live in Spain.*

IMPERSONAL VERB a verb with the subject *it*, where '*it*' does not refer to any specific thing; for example, *It's going to rain; It's nine o'clock.*

INDEFINITE ARTICLE the word *a* or *an*. Compare with **definite article**.

INDEFINITE PRONOUN a word like *everything, nobody* and *something* which is used to refer to people or things in a non-specific way.

INDIRECT OBJECT a noun or pronoun used to show who benefits or suffers from an action. For example, in the sentence

He sent Claire flowers, the <u>direct</u> object (what was sent) is *flowers* and the <u>indirect</u> object is *Claire* (the person the flowers were sent to). An indirect object often has *to* in front of it: *He told lies to everyone; He told everyone lies.* In both these sentences the direct object is *lies* and the indirect object is *everyone*. Compare with **direct object**.

INDIRECT OBJECT PRONOUN a pronoun such as *to me* (or *me*), *to you* (or *you*) and *to her* (or *her*). In the sentence *He gave the chocolates <u>to me</u> and the flowers <u>to her</u>*, the direct objects are *the chocolates* and *the flowers* (what he gave), and the <u>indirect object pronouns</u> are *to me* and *to her* (who he gave them to). In the sentence *He gave me the chocolates and her the flowers*, the indirect object pronouns are *me* and *her*. Compare with **direct object pronoun**.

INDIRECT QUESTION a more roundabout way of asking a question, for example, instead of *Where are you going?* you can say *Tell me where you are going*, or *I'd like to know where you are going*.

INFINITIVE the base form of the verb, for example, *walk, see, hear*. It is used after other verbs such as *should, must* and *can*. The infinitive is often used with *to*: *to speak, to eat, to live*. Compare with **base form**.

INTRANSITIVE VERB a verb used without a direct object, for example, *The shop is closing; Nothing grows here*. Compare with **transitive verb**.

IRREGULAR VERB In Italian, a verb whose forms do not follow one of the three main patterns. Compare with **regular verb**.

MASCULINE a noun, pronoun, article or form of adjective used to refer to a living being, thing or idea that is not classed as feminine. For example, **il** (masculine definite article) **primo** (adjective with a masculine ending) **treno** (masculine noun).

NEGATIVE a question or statement which contains a word such as *not, never* or *nothing*: *Isn't he here?*; *I never eat meat*; *She's doing nothing about it*. Compare with **positive**.

NOUN a naming word for a living being, thing or idea, for example, *woman, Andrew, desk, happiness*.

NUMBER in grammar a verb agrees in number with its subject by being singular with a singular subject and plural with a plural subject, for example, *I am a teacher*; *They are teachers*.

OBJECT a noun or pronoun that, in English, usually comes after the verb and shows who or what is affected by it, for example, *I* (subject) *want* (verb) *a new car* (object); *They* (subject) *phoned* (verb) *him* (object). Compare with **direct object**, **indirect object** and **subject**.

OBJECT PRONOUN one of the following: *me, you, him, her, it, us, them*. They are used instead of nouns after prepositions, for example, *for me, with us* and as the object of verbs, for example, *The company sacked him*; *You'll enjoy it*. Compare with **subject pronoun**.

PART OF SPEECH a word with a particular grammatical function, for example, *noun, adjective, verb, preposition, pronoun*.

PASSIVE a verb form that is used when the subject of the verb is the person or thing the action is done to, for example, *Shaun was bitten by a dog. Shaun* is the subject of the sentence, but he did not do the action. Compare with **active**.

PAST PARTICIPLE a verb form usually ending *–ed*, for example, *lived, worked*. Some past participles are irregular, for example, *gone, sat, broken*. Past participles are used to make the perfect, pluperfect

and passive, for example, *They've gone; They hadn't noticed me; Nobody was hurt*. Past participles are also used as adjectives, for example, *a boiled egg*.

PAST PERFECT see **pluperfect**.

PERFECT a tense used in English to talk about what has or hasn't happened, for example, *We've won; I haven't touched it*. Compare with **simple past**.

PERSON in grammar one of the following: the first person (*I, we*), the second person (*you*) or the third person (*he, she, it, they*).

PERSONAL PRONOUN a word such as *I, you, he, she, us, them*, which makes it clear who you are talking about or talking to.

PLUPERFECT a tense used to talk about what had happened or had been true at a point in the past, for example, *I'd forgotten to send her a card*. Also called **past perfect**.

PLURAL the form of a word which is used to refer to more than one person or thing. In Italian, nouns, adjectives, articles, pronouns and verbs can be plural. Compare with **singular**.

POSITIVE a positive sentence does not contain a negative word such as *not*. Compare with **negative**.

PREPOSITION a word such as *at, for, with, into* or *from*, or a phrase such as *in front of* or *near to*. Prepositions are usually followed by a noun or a pronoun and show how people and things relate to the rest of the sentence, for example, *She's at home*; *It's for you*; *You'll get into trouble*; *It's in front of you*.

PRESENT a verb form used to talk about what is true at the moment, what generally happens and what is happening now; for example, *I'm a student*; *I travel to college by train*; *The phone's ringing*.

PRESENT PARTICIPLE a verb form ending in –ing, for example, *eating, sleeping*. Compare with **gerund**.

PRONOUN a word you use instead of a noun, when you do not need or want to name someone or something directly, for example, *it, you, somebody*.

PROPER NOUN the name of a person, place or organization. Proper nouns are always written with a capital letter, for example, *Kate, New York, the Forestry Commission*.

REFLEXIVE PRONOUN a word ending in –self or –selves, such as *myself* and *ourselves*, that is used as the object of a verb, for example, *I surprised myself; We're going to treat ourselves*.

REFLEXIVE VERB a verb where the subject and object are the same, and which uses reflexive pronouns such as *myself, yourself* and *themselves*, for example, *I've hurt myself; Look after yourself!; They're enjoying themselves*.

REGULAR VERB in Italian, a verb whose forms follow one of the three main patterns. Compare with **irregular verb**.

SIMPLE TENSE a verb form made up of one word, for example, *She lives here; They arrived late*. Compare with **continuous tense** and **perfect tense**.

SIMPLE PAST a tense used in English to say when exactly something happened, for example, *We met last summer; I ate it last night; It rained a lot yesterday*. In Italian the perfect tense is used in this kind of sentence.

SINGULAR the form of a word used to refer to one person or thing. Compare with **plural**.

STEM what is left of an Italian verb when you take away the **–are**, **–ere** or **–ire** ending of the infinitive.

STRESSED PRONOUN an object pronoun used in Italian after prepositions and when you want to stress the word for *me, him, them* and so on. Compare with **unstressed pronoun**.

SUBJECT a noun or pronoun that refers to the person or thing doing the action or being in the state described by the verb, for example, *Pat likes climbing; The bus is late*. Compare with **object**.

SUBJECT PRONOUN a word such as *I, he, she* and *they* used for the person or thing carrying out the action described by the verb. Pronouns replace nouns when it is clear who is being talked about, for example, *My brother's not here at the moment. He'll be back in an hour*. Compare with **object pronoun**.

SUBJUNCTIVE a verb form often used in Italian to express wishes, thoughts and suppositions. In English the subjunctive is only used occasionally, for example, *If I were you...; So be it; He asked that they be removed*.

TENSE a particular form of the verb. It shows whether you are referring to the present, past or future.

TRANSITIVE VERB a verb used with a direct object, for example, *Close the door!; They grow wheat*. Compare with **intransitive verb**.

UNSTRESSED PRONOUN an object pronoun used in Italian when you don't want to put any special emphasis on the word for *me, him, them* and so on. Compare with **stressed pronoun**.

VERB a word that describes what somebody or something does, what they are, or what happens to them, for example, *play, be, disappear*.

Introduction to Verb Formation

Verbs are frequently used with a noun, with somebody's name, or, particularly in English, with a pronoun such as *I, you* or *she*. They can relate to the present, the past or the future; this is called their <u>tense</u>.

Verbs are either:

> <u>regular</u>; their forms follow the normal rules.
> <u>irregular</u>; their forms do not follow normal rules.

Almost all verbs have a form called the <u>infinitive</u> that isn't present, past or future, (for example, *walk, see, hear*). It is used after other verbs, for example, *You should* <u>*walk*</u>; *You can <u>see</u>; Kirsty wants <u>to come</u>*.

In English, the infinitive is usually shown with the word *to*, for example, *to speak, to eat, to live.*

In Italian, the infinitive is always one word that in most cases ends in **–are**, **–ere** or **–ire**: for example, **parl<u>are</u>** (meaning *to speak*), **cred<u>ere</u>** (meaning *to believe*) and **dorm<u>ire</u>** (meaning *to sleep*).

Regular English verbs can add three endings to the infinitive: *–s* (*walks*), *–ing* (*walking*) and *–ed* (*walked*).

Italian verbs add many different endings to the verb <u>stem</u>, which is what is left of the verb when you take away the **–are**, **–ere** or **–ire** ending of the infinitive. This means the stem of **parlare** is **parl-**, the stem of **credere** is **cred-**, and the stem of **dormire** is **dorm-**.

Italian verb endings change according to who or what is doing the action. The person or thing that does the action is called the <u>subject</u> of the verb.

Verb formation

In English, you nearly always put a noun or a pronoun in front of a verb to show who is doing the action, for example, _Jack speaks Italian; She's playing tennis._
In Italian, <u>nouns</u> are used as the subject of verbs just as they are in English, but <u>pronouns</u> are used much less often. This is because the ending of an Italian verb often shows you who the subject is.

> **<u>Mia sorella</u> gioca a tennis.** My sister is playing tennis.
> **<u>Gioca</u> bene.** She plays well.

Italian verb forms also change depending on whether you are talking about the present, past or future: **cred<u>o</u>** means _I believe_, **cred<u>evo</u>** means _I believed_ and **cred<u>erò</u>** means _I will believe._

In English, some verbs are <u>irregular</u>: you do not add _–ed_ to _speak, go,_ or _see_ to make the past tense. In the same way some Italian verbs do not follow the usual patterns. These irregular verbs include some very important and common verbs such as **andare** (meaning _to go_), **essere** (meaning _to be_), **fare** (meaning _to do_ or _to make_).

The following sections give you all the help you need on how to make the different verb tenses used in Italian. If you would like even more information on how Italian verbs are used, the _Easy Learning Italian Grammar_ shows you when and how numerous different verbs are used when writing and speaking modern Italian.

Present simple

The present simple tense

Making the present simple tense of regular –are verbs

Verbs that have an infinitive ending in **–are**, such as **parlare**, **abitare** and **studiare** have a particular pattern of endings.

To make the present simple tense of regular **–are** verbs take off the **–are** ending to get the <u>stem</u> of the verb.

Infinitive	Meaning	Stem (without –are)
parlare	*to speak*	**parl-**
abitare	*to live*	**abit-**
studiare	*to study*	**studi-**

Then add the correct ending for the person you're talking about.

Here are the present simple endings for regular **–are** verbs:

Present simple endings	Present simple of parlare	Meaning: *to speak*
-o	**(io) parlo**	I speak/am speaking
-i	**(tu) parli**	you speak/are speaking
-a	**(lui/lei) parla**	he/she/it speaks/is speaking
	(Lei) parla	you speak/are speaking
-iamo	**(noi) parliamo**	we speak/are speaking
-ate	**(voi) parlate**	you speak/are speaking
-ano	**(loro) parlano**	they speak/are speaking

For further explanation of grammatical terms, please see 6–9.

Note that **lei** means *she*, and is also the more formal equivalent of **tu**. The same form of the verb is used for both meanings.

Parlo italiano. I speak Italian.

Dove lavori? Where do you work?

Carla studia medicina. Carla is studying medicine.

Il cane mangia molto. The dog eats a lot.

Parla italiano, signora? Do you speak Italian madam?

Vedi l'*au*tobus? – Sì, arriva. Can you see the bus? – Yes, it's coming.

Parcheggiamo sempre lì. We always park there.

Cercate qualcosa? Are you looking for something?

Vuole queste? – No, costano troppo.

Do you want these? – No, they cost too much.

Present simple

Making the present simple tense of regular –ere verbs

Verbs that have an infinitive ending in **–ere**, such as **credere, ricevere** and **ripetere** have their own pattern of endings.

To make the present simple tense of regular **–ere** verbs, take off the **–ere** ending to get the <u>stem</u> and then add the correct ending for the person you're talking about.

Infinitive	Meaning	Stem (without –ere)
credere	*to believe*	**cred-**
ricevere	*to receive*	**ricev-**
ripetere	*to repeat*	**ripet-**

The **io**, **tu** and **noi** endings you add to the stem of **–ere** verbs are the same as **–are** verb endings. The other endings are different.

Here are the present simple endings for regular **–ere** verbs:

Present simple endings	Present simple of **credere**	Meaning: *to believe*
-o	**(io) credo**	I believe
-i	**(tu) credi**	you believe
-e	**(lui/lei) crede**	he/she believes
	(Lei) crede	you believe
-iamo	**(noi) crediamo**	we believe
-ete	**(voi) credete**	you believe
-ono	**(loro) credono**	they believe

For further explanation of grammatical terms, please see 6–9.

Present simple

Non ci credo. I don't believe it.

Credi ai fantasmi? Do you believe in ghosts?

Lo credono tutti. They all believe it.

Dipende. It depends.

Perdiamo tempo. We're wasting time.

Making the present simple tense of regular –ire verbs

Most verbs that have an infinitive ending in **–ire**, such as **finire** (meaning *to finish*), **pulire** (meaning *to clean*) and **capire** (meaning *to understand*) follow one pattern of endings in the present. Some common verbs such as **dormire** and **servire** have a different pattern.

To make the present simple tense of <u>all</u> **–ire** verbs, take off the **–ire** ending to get the <u>stem</u> of the verb.

Infinitive	Meaning	Stem (without –ire)
finire	*to finish*	**fin-**
pulire	*to clean*	**pul-**
capire	*to understand*	**cap-**
dormire	*to sleep*	**dorm-**
servire	*to serve*	**serv-**

Here are the present simple endings for regular **–ire** verbs:

Present simple endings	Present simple of finire	Meaning: *to finish*
-isco	**(io) finisco**	I finish/am finishing
-isci	**(tu) finisci**	you finish/are finishing
-isce	**(lui/lei) finisce**	he/she/it finishes/is finishing
	(Lei) finisce	you finish/are finishing
-iamo	**(noi) finiamo**	we finish/are finishing
-ite	**(voi) finite**	you finish/are finishing
-iscono	**(loro) finiscono**	they finish/are finishing

Il film fin*isce* alle dieci. The film finishes at ten.

Fin*iscono* il lavoro. They're finishing the work.

Non pul*isco* mai la macchina. I never clean the car.

Prefer*isci* l'altro? Do you prefer the other one?

Non cap*iscono*. They don't understand.

Some common **–ire** verbs do not add **–isc** to the stem. The most important ones are **dormire** (meaning *to sleep*), **servire** (meaning *to serve*), **aprire** (meaning *to open*), **partire** (meaning *to leave*), **sentire** (meaning *to hear*) and **soffrire** (meaning *to suffer*).

The endings of these verbs are as follows:

Present simple endings	Present simple of dormire	Meaning: *to sleep*
-o	(io) dorm*o*	I sleep/am sleeping
-i	(tu) dorm*i*	you sleep/are sleeping
-e	(lui/lei) dorm*e*	he/she/it sleeps/is sleeping
	(Lei) dorm*e*	you sleep/are sleeping
-iamo	(noi) dorm*iamo*	we sleep/are sleeping
-ite	(voi) dorm*ite*	you sleep/are sleeping
-ono	(loro) dorm*ono*	they sleep/are sleeping

Note that these endings are the same as **–ere** verb endings, except for the second person plural (**voi**).

Dorm*o* sempre bene. I always sleep well.

A che cosa serv*e*? What's it for?

Quando part*ite*? When are you leaving?

Soffr*ono* molto. They are suffering a lot.

Present simple

Infinitives that end in –rre

All regular verbs have infinitives ending in **–are**, **–ere**, or **–ire**.

A few common irregular verbs have infinitives ending in **–rre**. For example:

comporre	to compose	**condurre**	to lead
porre	to put	**produrre**	to produce
proporre	to propose	**ridurre**	to reduce
supporre	to suppose	**tradurre**	to translate

Here are the present simple forms of **comporre**:

	Present simple of comporre	Meaning: *to compose*
(io)	compongo	I compose/I am composing
(tu)	componi	you compose/you are composing
(lui/lei)	compone	he/she/it composes/is composing
(Lei)	compone	you compose/are composing
(noi)	componiamo	we compose/are composing
(voi)	componete	you compose/are composing
(loro)	compongono	they compose/are composing

Here are the present simple forms of **produrre**:

	Present simple of produrre	Meaning: *to produce*
(io)	**produco**	I produce/I am producing
(tu)	**produci**	you produce/you are producing
(lui/lei)	**produce**	he/she/it produces/is producing
(Lei)	**produce**	you produce/are producing
(noi)	**produciamo**	we produce/are producing
(voi)	**producete**	you produce/are producing
(loro)	**producono**	they produce/are producing

The present tense of all verbs ending in **–porre** follow the pattern of **comporre**, and all verbs ending in **–durre** follow the pattern of **produrre**.

All the most important irregular verbs are shown in full at the end of the book.

Italic letters in Italian words show where stress does not follow the usual rules.

The present continuous tense

The Italian present continuous is made with the present tense of **stare** and the gerund of the verb. The gerund is a verb form that ends in **–ando** (for **–are** verbs), or **–endo** (for **–ere** and **–ire** verbs) and is the same as the *–ing* form of the verb in English, for example, *walking*, *swimming*.

> **<u>Sto cercando</u> il mio passaporto.** I'm looking for my passport.
> **<u>Sta scrivendo</u>.** He's writing.
> **<u>Stanno dormendo</u>.** They're sleeping.
> **Cosa <u>stai facendo</u>?** What are you doing?

To make the gerund of an **–are** verb, take off the **–are** ending of the infinitive and add **–ando**:

Infinitive	Meaning	Stem	Gerund	Meaning
parlare	to speak	**parl-**	**parlando**	speaking
mangiare	to eat	**mangi-**	**mangiando**	eating

> **A chi <u>stai pensando</u>?** Who are you thinking about?
> **Tutti <u>stanno mangiando</u>.** Everyone's eating.

To make the gerund of an **–ere** or **–ire** verb, take off the **–ere** or **–ire** ending of the infinitive and add **–endo**:

Infinitive	Meaning	Stem	Gerund	Meaning
scrivere	to write	**scriv-**	**scrivendo**	writing
partire	to leave	**part-**	**partendo**	leaving

> **<u>Sto scrivendo</u> una lettera.** I'm writing a letter.
> **<u>Stanno partendo</u>?** Are they leaving?

For further explanation of grammatical terms, please see 6–9.

The imperative

Making the imperative: instructions to do something

You make the imperative of regular verbs by adding endings to the verb <u>stem</u>. There are different endings for **–are**, **-ere** and **–ire** verbs.

The endings for **–are** verb imperatives are **–a** (**tu** form), **–i** (**Lei** form), **–iamo** (let's), **–ate** (**voi** form) and **–ino** (polite plural).

Imperative of aspettare	Example	Meaning: *to wait*
aspett<u>a</u>	**Aspetta Marco!**	Wait, Marco!
aspett<u>i</u>	**Aspetti signore!**	Wait, Sir!
aspett<u>iamo</u>	**Aspettiamo qui!**	Let's wait here.
aspett<u>ate</u>	**Aspettate ragazzi!**	Wait, children!
aspett<u>ino</u>	**Asp*e*ttino un *attimo* signori!**	Wait a moment, ladies and gentlemen!

The endings for **–ere** verb imperatives are **–i** (**tu** form), **–a** (**lei/Lei** form), **–iamo** (let's), **–ete** (**voi** form) and **–ano** (polite plural).

Imperative of prendere	Example	Meaning: *to take*
prend<u>i</u>	**Prendi quello, Marco!**	Take that one, Marco!
prend<u>a</u>	**Prenda quello, signore!**	Take that one, Sir!
prend<u>iamo</u>	**Prendiamo quello!**	Let's take that one.
prend<u>ete</u>	**Prendete quelli, ragazzi!**	Take those, children!
prend<u>ano</u>	**Pr*e*ndano quelli, signori!**	Take those, ladies and gentlemen!

Italic letters in Italian words show where stress does not follow the usual rules.

22 Imperative

The endings for most **–ire** verb imperatives are **–isci** (**tu** form), **–isca** (**Lei** form), **–iamo** (let's), **–ite** (**voi** form) and **–iscano** (polite plural).

Note that **sci** is pronounced *she*; **sca** is pronounced *ska*.

Imperative of		
finire	Example	Meaning: *to finish*
fin*isci*	**Finisci l'esercizio, Marco!**	Finish the exercise, Marco!
fin*isca*	**Finisca tutto, signore!**	Finish it all, Sir!
fin*iamo*	**Finiamo tutto!**	Let's finish it all.
fin*ite*	**Finite i compiti, ragazzi!**	Finish your homework, children!
fin*iscano*	**Finiscano tutto, signori!**	Finish it all, ladies and gentlemen!

The endings for verbs that do not add **–isc** to the stem, such as **partire** (meaning *to leave*), **dormire** (meaning *to sleep*), **aprire** (meaning *to open*) and **sentire** (meaning *to listen*) are **–i**, **–a**, **–iamo**, **–ite** and **–ano**.

> **Dormi Giulia!** Go to sleep, Giulia!
> **Senta, signora.** Listen, madam.
> **Partiamo.** Let's go.

Some of the most common verbs in Italian have irregular imperative forms. Here are the forms for some important verbs:

	dare	dire	essere	fare	andare
(tu)	da'! or dai!	di'!	sii!	fa'! or fai!	va'! or vai!
(Lei)	dia!	dica!	sia!	faccia!	vada!
(noi)	diamo!	diciamo!	siamo!	facciamo!	andiamo!
(voi)	date!	dite!	siate!	fate!	andate!
(loro)	diano!	dicano!	siano!	facciano!	vadano!

For further explanation of grammatical terms, please see 6–9.

Sii bravo, Paolo! Be good, Paolo!
Faccia pure, signore! Carry on, Sir!
Dite la verità, ragazzi! Tell the truth, children!

Where pronouns go

Pronouns come <u>after</u> the imperative in the **tu** and **voi** forms.

The pronoun joins with the imperative to make one word:

Guardami, mamma! Look at me, mum!
Aspettateli! Wait for them!

When the imperative is only one syllable **mi** becomes **mmi**, **ti** becomes **tti**, **lo** becomes **llo** and so on.

Dimmi! Tell me!
Fallo subito! Do it immediately!

When the pronouns **mi**, **ti**, **ci** and **vi** are followed by another pronoun they become **me-**, **te-**, **ce-** and **ve-**, and **gli** and **le** become **glie-**.

Mandameli. Send me them.
Daglielo. Give it to him.

In Italian you <u>always</u> put the indirect object pronoun first.

Pronouns also come <u>after</u> the **–iamo** form of the imperative, joining onto it to make one word.

Proviamolo! Let's try it!
Mandiamogliela! Let's send it to them.

Pronouns come <u>before</u> the **Lei** form of the imperative and the polite plural form.

Italic letters in Italian words show where stress does not follow the usual rules.

Mi dia un chilo d'uva, per favore. Give me a kilo of grapes, please.
La prenda, signore. Take it, Sir.
Ne assaggino un po', signori! Try a bit, ladies and gentlemen!
Si accomodi! Take a seat!

How to tell someone not to do something

When you are telling someone you call **tu** not to do something:

- use non with the <u>infinitive</u> of the verb

    Non <u>dire</u> bugie, Andrea! Don't tell lies, Andrea!
    Non <u>dimenticare</u>! Don't forget!

- join pronouns onto the infinitive, or put them in front

    Non toccar<u>lo</u>! OR
    Non <u>lo</u> toccare! Don't touch it!

    Non dir<u>glielo</u>! OR
    Non <u>glielo</u> dire! Don't tell him about it!

    Non far<u>mi</u> ridere! OR
    Non <u>mi</u> far ridere! Don't make me laugh!

    Non preoccupar<u>ti</u>! OR
    Non <u>ti</u> preoccupare! Don't worry!

    Non bagnar<u>ti</u>! OR
    Non <u>ti</u> bagnare! Don't get wet!

Note that the infinitive usually drops the final **e** when followed by a pronoun.

For further explanation of grammatical terms, please see 6–9.

In all other cases, to tell someone not to do something:

- use **non** with the imperative

    Non dimenticate, ragazzi. Don't forget, children.
    Non abbia paura, signora. Don't be afraid, madam.
    Non esageriamo! Don't let's go too far!

- join pronouns onto the **voi** and **–iamo** forms of the imperative

    Non guardateli! Don't look at them.
    Non ditemelo! Don't say it to me!

    Non mangiamoli tutti. Don't let's eat them all.
    Non diamoglielo. Don't let's give it to them.

- put pronouns in front of the **Lei** and polite plural forms of the imperative

    Non li guardi, signora. Don't look at them, madam.
    Non si preoccupino, signori. Don't worry, ladies and gentlemen.

Italic letters in Italian words show where stress does not follow the usual rules.

Reflexive

Reflexive verbs

Making the present tense of reflexive verbs

The present tense forms of a reflexive verb are just the same as those of an ordinary verb, except for the addition of the reflexive pronoun in front of the verb.

The following table shows the reflexive verb **divertirsi** (meaning *to enjoy oneself*) in full.

Subject pronoun	Reflexive pronoun	Present tense	Meaning
(io)	mi	**diverto**	I'm enjoying myself
(tu)	ti	**diverti**	you're enjoying yourself
(lui)	si	**diverte**	he is enjoying himself
(lei)	si	**diverte**	she is enjoying herself
(Lei)	si	**diverte**	you are enjoying yourself
(noi)	ci	**divertiamo**	we're enjoying ourselves
(voi)	vi	**divertite**	you're enjoying yourselves
(loro)	si	**divertono**	they're enjoying themselves

Where to put reflexive pronouns

The reflexive pronoun usually goes in front of the verb, but there are some exceptions. The pronoun goes <u>in front</u> if the verb is:

• an ordinary tense, such as the present simple:

Si diverte, signora? Are you enjoying yourself, madam?
Mi abituo al lavoro. I'm getting used to the work.

- the polite imperative:

    Si avvicini, signore. Come closer, sir.

- an imperative telling someone NOT to do something:

    Non vi avvicinate troppo, ragazzi. Don't come too close, children.
    Non si lamenti, dottore. Don't complain, doctor.

The pronoun comes <u>after</u> the verb if it is the **tu** or **voi** form of the imperative, used positively:

    Svegliati! Wake up!
    Divertitevi! Enjoy yourselves!

In the case of the infinitive, used with **non** to tell someone NOT to do something, the pronoun can either:

- go <u>in front of</u> the infinitive

    OR

- join onto the end of the infinitive

    Non ti bruciare! or **Non bruciarti!** Don't burn yourself!
    Non ti preoccupare! or **Non preoccuparti!** Don't worry!

Note that, when telling someone not to do something, you use **non** with the <u>infinitive</u> for people you call **tu**.

There are also two options when you use the infinitive of a reflexive verb after a verb such as *want, must, should* or *can't*. The pronoun can either:

- go <u>in front of</u> the main verb

    OR

- join onto the end of the infinitive

Italic letters in Italian words show where stress does not follow the usual rules.

28 Reflexive

<u>Mi</u> voglio abbronzare. or **Voglio abbronzar<u>mi</u>.** I want to get a tan.
<u>Ti</u> devi alzare. or **Devi alzar<u>ti</u>.** You must get up.
<u>Vi</u> dovreste preparare. or **Dovreste prepara<u>rvi</u>.** You ought to get ready.
Non <u>mi</u> posso fermare molto. or **Non posso ferma<u>rmi</u> molto.**
I can't stop for long.

In the same way, in <u>continuous tenses</u>, the reflexive pronoun can either:

- go <u>in front of</u> the verb **stare**

  OR

- join onto the gerund

  <u>Ti</u> stai annoiando? or **Stai annoiando<u>ti</u>?** Are you getting bored?
  <u>Si</u> stanno alzando? or **Stanno alzando<u>si</u>?** Are they getting up?

Note that the pronoun is always joined onto the gerund when it is not used in a continuous tense.

Incontrando<u>ci</u> per caso, abbiamo parlato molto.
Meeting by chance, we had a long talk.
Pettinando<u>mi</u> ho trovato un capello bianco.
When I combed my hair, I found a white hair.

For further explanation of grammatical terms, please see 6–9.

The future tense

Making the future tense

To make the future of regular **–are** and **–ere** verbs take the <u>stem</u> and add the following endings:

- **erò, erai, erà, eremo, erete, eranno**

The following table shows the future tenses of **parlare** (meaning *to speak*) and **credere** (meaning *to believe*).

Pronoun	Future tense of **parlare**	Meaning: *to speak*
(io)	parl<u>erò</u>	I'll speak
(tu)	parl<u>erai</u>	you'll speak
(lui/lei) (Lei)	parl<u>erà</u>	he/she'll speak you'll speak
(noi)	parl<u>eremo</u>	we'll speak
(voi)	parl<u>erete</u>	you'll speak
(loro)	parl<u>eranno</u>	they'll speak

Gli <u>parlerò</u> domani. I'll speak to him tomorrow.

Pronoun	Future tense of **credere**	Meaning: *to speak*
(io)	cred<u>erò</u>	I'll believe
(tu)	cred<u>erai</u>	you'll believe
(lui/lei) (Lei)	cred<u>erà</u>	he/she'll believe
(noi)	cred<u>eremo</u>	we'll believe
(voi)	cred<u>erete</u>	you'll believe
(loro)	cred<u>eranno</u>	they'll believe

Non ti <u>crederanno</u>. They won't believe you.

Italic letters in Italian words show where stress does not follow the usual rules.

30 Future

Note that there are accents on the first and third person singular forms, to show that you put the stress on the last syllable.

To make the future of regular **–ire** verbs take the <u>stem</u> and add the following endings:

- **irò**, **irai**, **irà**, **iremo**, **irete**, **iranno**

The following table shows the future tense of **finire** (meaning *to finish*).

Pronoun	Future tense of finire	Meaning: *to finish*
(io)	fin**irò**	I'll finish
(tu)	fin**irai**	you'll finish
(lui/lei) **(Lei)**	fin**irà**	he/she'll finish you'll finish
(noi)	fin**iremo**	we'll finish
(voi)	fin**irete**	you'll finish
(loro)	fin**iranno**	they'll finish

Quando <u>finirai</u> il lavoro? When will you finish the work?

For further explanation of grammatical terms, please see 6–9.

Irregular future forms

Some common verbs do not have a vowel before the **r** of the future ending.
These endings are: **–rό**, **–rai**, **–rά**, **–remo**, **–rete**, **–ranno**:

Verb	Meaning	io	tu	lui/lei/Lei	noi	voi	loro
andare	to go	andrò	andrai	andrà	andremo	andrete	andranno
cadere	to fall	cadrò	cadrai	cadrà	cadremo	cadrete	cadranno
dire	to say	dirò	dirai	dirà	diremo	direte	diranno
dovere	to have to	dovrò	dovrai	dovrà	dovremo	dovrete	dovranno
fare	to do/make	farò	farai	farà	faremo	farete	faranno
potere	to be able	potrò	potrai	potrà	potremo	potrete	potranno
sapere	to know	saprò	saprai	saprà	sapremo	saprete	sapranno
vedere	to see	vedrò	vedrai	vedrà	vedremo	vedrete	vedranno
vivere	to live	vivrò	vivrai	vivrà	vivremo	vivrete	vivranno

Andrò con loro. I'll go with them.
Pensi che diranno la verità? Do you think they'll tell the truth?
Non credo che farà bel tempo. I don't think the weather will be nice.
Lo sapremo domani. We'll know tomorrow.

Some verbs have no vowel before the future ending, and change their stem:

Verb	Meaning	io	tu	lui/lei/Lei	noi	voi	loro
rimanere	to remain	rimarrò	rimarrai	rimarrà	rimarremo	rimarrete	rimarranno
tenere	to hold	terrò	terrai	terrà	terremo	terrete	terranno
venire	to come	verrò	verrai	verrà	verremo	verrete	verranno
volere	to want	vorrò	vorrai	vorrà	vorremo	vorrete	vorranno

Italic letters in Italian words show where stress does not follow the usual rules.

Verbs with infinitives that end in **–ciare** and **–giare**, for example, **parcheggiare** (meaning *to park*), **cominciare** (meaning *to start*), **mangiare** (meaning *to eat*) and **viaggiare** (meaning *to travel*) drop the **i** in the future.

> **Comincerò domani.** I'll start tomorrow.
> **Mangeranno alle otto.** They'll eat at eight o'clock.

Verbs with infinitives that end in **–care** and **–gare**, for example **cercare** (meaning *to look for, to try*), **seccare** (meaning *to annoy*), **pagare** (meaning *to pay*) and **spiegare** (meaning *to explain*) add an **h** in the future.

> **Cercherò di aiutarvi.** I'll try to help you.
> **Mi pagheranno sabato.** They'll pay me on Saturday.

The future tense of *essere* and *avere*

essere (meaning *to be*) and **avere** (meaning *to have*) have irregular future forms.

Pronoun	Future tense of *essere*	Meaning	Future tense of *avere*	Meaning
(io)	sarò	I'll be	avrò	I'll have
(tu)	sarai	you'll be	avrai	you'll have
(lui/lei) (Lei)	sarà	he/she/it will be you'll be	avrà	he/she/it will have you'll have
(noi)	saremo	we'll be	avremo	we'll have
(voi)	sarete	you'll be	avrete	you'll have
(loro)	saranno	they'll be	avranno	they'll have

> **Sarà difficile.** It'll be difficult.
> **Non ne sarai deluso.** You won't be disappointed by it.
> **Non avrò tempo.** I won't have time.
> **Lo avrai domani.** You'll have it tomorrow.

For further explanation of grammatical terms, please see 6–9.

The conditional

Making the conditional

To make the conditional of regular **–are** and **–ere** verbs take the <u>stem</u> and add the following endings: **–erei**, **–eresti**, **–erebbe**, **–eremmo**, **–ereste**, **–er*e*bbero**.

The following table shows the conditional of **parlare** (meaning *to speak*) and **credere** (meaning *to believe*).

	Conditional of parlare	Meaning	Conditional of credere	Meaning
(io)	parl<u>erei</u>	I'd speak	cred<u>erei</u>	I'd believe
(tu)	parl<u>eresti</u>	you'd speak	cred<u>eresti</u>	you'd believe
(lui/lei)	parl<u>erebbe</u>	he/she'd speak	cred<u>erebbe</u>	he/she'd believe
(Lei)	parl<u>erebbe</u>	you'd speak	cred<u>erebbe</u>	you'd believe
(noi)	parl<u>eremmo</u>	we'd speak	cred<u>eremmo</u>	we'd believe
(voi)	parl<u>ereste</u>	you'd speak	cred<u>ereste</u>	you'd believe
(loro)	parl<u>erebbero</u>	they'd speak	cred<u>erebbero</u>	they'd believe

Con chi <u>parleresti</u>? Who would you speak to?
Non ti <u>crederebbe</u>. He wouldn't believe you.

To make the conditional of regular **–ire** verbs take the <u>stem</u> and add the following endings: **–irei**, **–iresti**, **–irebbe**, **–iremmo**, **–ireste**, **-ir*e*bbero**.

Italic letters in Italian words show where stress does not follow the usual rules.

34 Conditional

The following table shows the conditional of **finire** (meaning *to finish*).

(io)	**fin<u>i</u>rei**	I'd finish
(tu)	**fin<u>i</u>resti**	you'd finish
(lui/lei)	**fin<u>i</u>rebbe**	he/she'd finish
(Lei)	**fin<u>i</u>rebbe**	you'd finish
(noi)	**fin<u>i</u>remmo**	we'd finish
(voi)	**fin<u>i</u>reste**	you'd finish
(loro)	**fin<u>i</u>rebbero**	they'd finish

Non <u>finiremmo</u> in tempo. We wouldn't finish in time.

The conditionals of volere, potere and dovere

The conditionals of **volere** (meaning *to want*), **potere** (meaning *to be able*) and **dovere** (meaning *to have to*) are as follows:

(io)	**vorrei**	I'd like
(tu)	**vorresti**	you'd like
(lui/lei) **(Lei)**	**vorrebbe**	he/she'd like you'd like
(noi)	**vorremmo**	we'd like
(voi)	**vorreste**	you'd like
(loro)	**vorrebbero**	they'd like

<u>**Vorrei**</u> **un'insalata.** I'd like a salad.
<u>**Vorrei**</u> **vedere quel film.** I'd like to see that film.
<u>**Vorremmo**</u> **venire con voi.** We'd like to come with you.
<u>**Vorrebbero**</u> **rimanere qui.** They'd like to stay here.

For further explanation of grammatical terms, please see 6–9.

(io)	potrei	I could
(tu)	potresti	you could
(lui/lei) (Lei)	potrebbe	he/she/it could you could
(noi)	potremmo	we could
(voi)	potreste	you could
(loro)	potrebbero	they could

Potresti avere ragione. You could be right.

Potrebbe *essere* vero. It could be true.

Potrebbero vendere la casa. They could sell the house.

Potresti chiudere la finestra? Could you close the window?

(io)	dovrei	I should
(tu)	dovresti	you should
(lui/lei) (Lei)	dovrebbe	he/she/it should you should
(noi)	dovremmo	we should
(voi)	dovreste	you should
(loro)	dovrebbero	they should

Dovrei fare un po' di ginnastica. I should do some exercise.

Dovresti telefonare ai tuoi. You should phone your parents.

Dovrebbe arrivare verso le dieci. He should arrive at around ten.

Dovrebbe *essere* bello. It should be good.

Italic letters in Italian words show where stress does not follow the usual rules.

Irregular conditional forms

Some common verbs do not have a vowel before the **r** of the conditional ending. Their endings are **–rei**, **–resti**, **–rebbe**, **–remmo**, **–reste**, **–rebbero**.

Verb	Meaning	io	tu	lui/lei/Lei	noi	voi	loro
andare	to go	andrei	andresti	andrebbe	andremmo	andreste	andrebbero
cadere	to fall	cadrei	cadresti	cadrebbe	cadremmo	cadreste	cadrebbero
dire	to say	direi	diresti	direbbe	diremmo	direste	direbbero
fare	to do/make	farei	faresti	farebbe	faremmo	fareste	farebbero
sapere	to know	saprei	sapresti	saprebbe	sapremmo	sapreste	saprebbero
vedere	to see	vedrei	vedresti	vedrebbe	vedremmo	vedreste	vedrebbero
vivere	to live	vivrei	vivresti	vivrebbe	vivremmo	vivreste	vivrebbero

Non so se <u>andrebbe</u> bene. I don't know if it would be okay.

Non <u>direi</u>. I wouldn't say that.

Cosa <u>faresti</u>? What would you do?

Some verbs have no vowel before the conditional ending, and change their stem:

Verb	Meaning	io	tu	lui/lei/Lei	noi	voi	loro
rimanere	to remain	rimarrei	rimarresti	rimarrebbe	rimarremmo	rimarreste	rimarrebbero
tenere	to hold	terrei	terresti	terrebbe	terremmo	terreste	terrebbero
venire	to come	verrei	verresti	verrebbe	verremmo	verreste	verrebbero

For further explanation of grammatical terms, please see 6–9.

Verbs such as **cominciare** (meaning *to start*) and **mangiare** (meaning *to eat*), which end in **–ciare** or **–giare**, and which drop the **i** in the future also drop the **i** in the conditional.

> **Quando <u>comincerebbe</u>?** When would it start?
> **<u>Mangeresti</u> quei funghi?** Would you eat those mushrooms?

Verbs such as **cercare** (meaning *to look for*) and **pagare** (meaning *to pay*), which end in **–care** or **–gare**, and which add an **h** in the future also add an **h** in the conditional.

> **Probabilmente <u>cercherebbe</u> una scusa.** He'd probably look for an excuse.
> **Quanto mi <u>pagheresti</u>?** How much would you pay me?

Reflexive verbs in the conditional

The conditional of reflexive verbs is formed in just the same way as for ordinary verbs, except that you have to remember to give the reflexive pronoun (**mi**, **ti**, **si**, **ci**, **vi**, **si**).

> **Ti divertiresti molto.** You'd have a very good time.

Italic letters in Italian words show where stress does not follow the usual rules.

The imperfect tense

Making the imperfect tense

You make the imperfect of regular **–are**, **–ere**, and **–ire** verbs by knocking off the **–re** from the infinitive and adding **–vo**, **–vi**, **–va**, **–vamo**, **–vate**, **–vano**.

The following tables show the imperfect of three regular verbs, **parlare** (meaning *to speak*), **credere** (meaning *to believe*) and **finire** (meaning *to finish*).

	Imperfect tense of parlare	Meaning	Imperfect tense of credere	Meaning
(io)	parlavo	I was speaking	credevo	I believed
(tu)	parlavi	you were speaking	credevi	you believed
(lui/lei) (Lei)	parlava	he/she was speaking you were speaking	credeva	he/she believed you believed
(noi)	parlavamo	we were speaking	credevamo	we believed
(voi)	parlavate	you were speaking	credevate	you believed
(loro)	parlavano	they were speaking	credevano	they believed

	Imperfect tense of finire	Meaning
(io)	finivo	I was finishing
(tu)	finivi	you were finishing
(lui/lei) (Lei)	finiva	he/she was finishing you were finishing
(noi)	finivamo	we were finishing
(voi)	finivate	you were finishing
(loro)	finivano	they were finishing

For further explanation of grammatical terms, please see 6–9.

Con chi <u>parlavi</u>? Who were you talking to?
Una volta <u>costava</u> di più. It used to cost more.
Mi <u>alzavo</u> sempre prima di lei. I always got up before she did.
<u>Credevamo</u> di aver vinto. We thought we'd won.
Loro si <u>divertivano</u> mentre io <u>lavoravo</u>. They had fun while I was working.

Verbs with an irregular imperfect tense

The imperfect of **essere** (meaning *to be*) is irregular:

(io)	ero	I was
(tu)	eri	you were
(lui/lei) (Lei)	era	he/she/it was you were
(noi)	eravamo	we were
(voi)	eravate	you were
(loro)	erano	they were

<u>Era</u> un ragazzo molto simpatico. He was a very nice boy
<u>Eravamo</u> in Italia. We were in Italy.
<u>Erano</u> le quattro. It was four o'clock.

bere (meaning *to drink*), **dire** (meaning *to say*), **fare** (meaning *to do, to make*) and **tradurre** (meaning *to translate*) are common verbs which have the normal imperfect endings added onto an irregular stem.

Verb	(io)	(tu)	(lui/lei/Lei)	(noi)	(voi)	(loro)
bere	bevevo	bevevi	beveva	bevevamo	bevevate	bevevano
dire	dicevo	dicevi	diceva	dicevamo	dicevate	dicevano
fare	facevo	facevi	faceva	facevamo	facevate	facevano
tradurre	traducevo	traducevi	traduceva	traducevamo	traducevate	traducevano

Italic letters in Italian words show where stress does not follow the usual rules.

40 Imperfect

Di solito <u>bevevano</u> solo acqua. They usually only drank water.

Cosa <u>dicevo</u>? What was I saying?

<u>Faceva</u> molto freddo. It was very cold.

<u>Traducevo</u> la lettera. I was translating the letter.

The perfect tense

Making the perfect tense

In Italian there are two ways of making the perfect tense:

- the present tense of **avere** (meaning *to have*) followed by a past participle.

- the present tense of **essere** (meaning *to be*) followed by a past participle.

Making the past participle

To make the past participle of regular **–are** verbs, take off the **–are** ending of the infinitive and add **–ato**.

parlare (*to speak*) → **parlato** (*spoken*)

To make the past participle of regular **–ere** verbs, take off the **–ere** ending of the infinitive and add **–uto.**

credere (to *believe*) → **creduto** (*believed*)

To make the past participle of regular **–ire** verbs, take off the **–ire** ending of the infinitive and add **–ito**.

finire (to *finish*) → **finito** (*finished*)

Making the perfect tense with avere

To make the perfect with **avere**:

- choose the present tense form of **avere** that matches the subject of the sentence.

- add the past participle. Do not change the ending of the participle to make it agree with the subject.

Italic letters in Italian words show where stress does not follow the usual rules.

42 Perfect

The perfect tense of **parlare** (meaning *to speak*) is as follows:

	Present tense of avere	Past participle	Meaning
(io)	ho	parlato	I spoke *or* have spoken
(tu)	hai	parlato	you spoke *or* have spoken
(lui/lei) (Lei)	ha	parlato	he/she spoke *or* has spoken you spoke *or* have spoken
(noi)	abbiamo	parlato	we spoke *or* have spoken
(voi)	avete	parlato	you spoke *or* have spoken
(loro)	hanno	parlato	they spoke *or* have spoken

Non gli <u>ho</u> mai <u>parlato</u>. I've never spoken to him.
Roberta gli <u>ha parlato</u> ieri. Roberta spoke to him yesterday.

Most verbs form their perfect tense with **avere**.

<u>Ho buttato</u> giù alcune idee. <u>I've put down</u> some ideas.
<u>Abbiamo comprato</u> una macchina. <u>We've bought</u> a car.
Dove <u>avete parcheggiato?</u> Where <u>did you park</u>?
Non <u>hanno voluto</u> aiutarmi. They <u>didn't want</u> to help me.

Verbs with irregular past participles

Some very common verbs have irregular past participles. These are some of the
most important ones.

> **aprire** (*to open*) → **aperto** (*opened*)
> ALSO **coprire** (*to cover*) → **coperto** (*covered*)
> **chiudere** (*to close*) → **chiuso** (*closed*)
> **decidere** (to *decide*) → **deciso** (*decided*)
> **dire** (*to say*) → **detto** (*said*)
> **fare** (*to do, to make*) → **fatto** (*done, made*)
> **friggere** (*to fry*) → **fritto** (*fried*)
> **leggere** (*to read*) → **letto** (*read*)
> **mettere** (*to put*) → **messo** (*put*)
> ALSO **promettere** (*to promise*) → **promesso** (*promised*)
> **morire** (*to die*) → **morto** (*died*)
> **offrire** (*to offer*) → **offerto** (*offered*)
> **prendere** (*to take*) → **preso** (*taken*)
> ALSO **sorprendere** (*to surprise*) → **sorpreso** (*surprised*)
> **rispondere** (*to reply*) → **risposto** (*replied*)
> **rompere** (*to break*) → **rotto** (*broken*)
> **scegliere** (*to choose*) → **scelto** (*chosen*)
> **scrivere** (*to write*) → **scritto** (*written*)
> **spendere** (*to spend*) → **speso** (*spent*)
> **vincere** (*to win*) → **vinto** (*won*)
> ALSO **convincere** (*to convince*) → **convinto** (*convinced*)
> **vedere** (*to see*) → **visto** (*seen*)

Ho preso il treno delle dieci. I got the ten o'clock train.
L'hai messo in frigo? Have you put it in the fridge?
Perché l'hai fatto? Why did you do it?
Carlo ha speso più di me. Carlo spent more than me.
Ha scelto, signore? Have you chosen, sir?

Italic letters in Italian words show where stress does not follow the usual rules.

Making the perfect tense with *essere*

The perfect tense of <u>some</u> verbs which do not take a direct object, and of <u>all</u> reflexive verbs is formed with **essere**.

To make the perfect with **essere**:

- choose the present tense form of **essere** that matches the subject of the sentence.

- add the past participle. Make the ending of the participle agree with the subject.

The perfect tense of **andare** (meaning *to go*) is as follows:

	Present tense of *essere*	Past participle	Meaning
(io)	sono	**andato** *or* **andata**	I went *or* have gone
(tu)	sei	**andato** *or* **andata**	you went *or* have gone
(lui)	è	**andato**	he/it went *or* has gone
(lei)	è	**andata**	she/it went *or* has gone
(Lei)	è	**andato** *or* **andata**	you went *or* have gone
(noi)	siamo	**andati** *or* **andate**	we went *or* have gone
(voi)	siete	**andati** *or* **andate**	you went *or* have gone
(loro)	sono	**andati** *or* **andate**	they went *or* have gone

The most important verbs that form their perfect tense with **essere** are:

andare	to go	**arrivare**	to arrive
entrare	to come in	**diventare**	to become
partire	to leave	**rimanere**	to stay
riuscire	to succeed, manage	**salire**	to go up, to get on
scendere	to go down	**succedere**	to happen
stare	to be	**tornare**	to come back
uscire	to go out	**venire**	to come

For further explanation of grammatical terms, please see 6–9.

È rimasta a casa tutto il giorno. She stayed at home all day.
Siamo riusciti a convincerla. We managed to persuade her.
Sei mai stata a Bologna, Tina? Have you ever been to Bologna, Tina?
Le tue amiche sono arrivate. Your friends have arrived.
Cos'è successo? What happened?

Note that **essere** is used to make the perfect of **piacere** (meaning literally *to please*). The past participle agrees with the subject of the Italian verb, and not with the subject of the English verb *to like*.

La musica ti è piaciuta, Roberto? Did you like the music, Robert?
I cioccolatini mi sono piaciuti molto. I liked the chocolates very much.
Le foto sono piaciute a tutti. Everyone liked the photos.

Use **essere** to make the perfect tense of all reflexive verbs, putting the reflexive pronoun in front of **sono**, **sei**, **è** and so on.

I miei fratelli si sono alzati tardi. My brothers got up late.
Le ragazze si sono alzate alle sei. The girls got up at six.
Mi sono fatta tagliare i capelli. I had my hair cut.
Ti sei fatto male? Have you hurt yourself?

Italic letters in Italian words show where stress does not follow the usual rules.

The pluperfect or past perfect tense

Making the pluperfect tense

In Italian there are two ways of making the pluperfect tense:

- the imperfect tense of **avere** (meaning *to have*) followed by a past participle.

- the imperfect tense of ***essere*** (meaning *to be*) followed by a past participle.

Making the pluperfect tense with avere

To make the pluperfect tense with **avere**:

- choose the <u>imperfect</u> form of **avere** that matches the subject of the sentence.

- add the past participle. <u>Do not</u> change the ending of the participle to make it agree with the subject.

Most verbs form their pluperfect tense with **avere**.

The pluperfect tense of **parlare** (meaning *to speak*) is as follows:

	Imperfect tense of avere	Past participle	Meaning
(io)	avevo	parlato	I had spoken
(tu)	avevi	parlato	you had spoken
(lui/lei) (Lei)	aveva	parlato	he/she had spoken / you had spoken
(noi)	avevamo	parlato	we had spoken
(voi)	avevate	parlato	you had spoken
(loro)	avevano	parlato	they had spoken

Non gli <u>avevo</u> mai <u>parlato</u> prima. I'd never spoken to him before.

Sara gli <u>aveva parlato</u> il giorno prima. Sara had spoken to him the day before.

Remember that some very common verbs have irregular past participles.

aprire (*to open*) → **aperto** (*opened*)
ALSO **coprire** (*to cover*) → **coperto** (*covered*)
chiudere (*to close*) → **chiuso** (*closed*)
decidere (*to decide*) → **deciso** (*decided*)
dire (*to say*) → **detto** (*said*)
fare (*to do, to make*) → **fatto** (*done, made*)
friggere (*to fry*) → **fritto** (*fried*)
leggere (*to read*) → **letto** (*read*)
mettere (*to put*) → **messo** (*put*)
ALSO **promettere** (*to promise*) → **promesso** (*promised*)
morire (*to die*) → **morto** (*died*)
offrire (*to offer*) → **offerto** (*offered*)
prendere (*to take*) → **preso** (*taken*)
ALSO **sorprendere** (*to surprise*) → **sorpreso** (*surprised*)
rispondere (*to reply*) → **risposto** (*replied*)
rompere (*to break*) → **rotto** (*broken*)
scegliere (*to choose*) → **scelto** (*chosen*)
scrivere (*to write*) → **scritto** (*written*)
spendere (*to spend*) → **speso** (*spent*)
vincere (*to win*) → **vinto** (*won*)
ALSO **convincere** (*to convince*) → **convinto** (*convinced*)
vedere (*to see*) → **visto** (*seen*)

Carlo <u>aveva speso</u> più di me. Carlo had spent more than me.
Non gli <u>avevo detto</u> niente. I hadn't said anything to him.

Pluperfect

Making the pluperfect tense with *essere*

Verbs that make their perfect tense with **essere** also make their pluperfect tense with **essere**.

To make the pluperfect tense with **essere**:

- choose the <u>imperfect</u> form of **essere** that matches the subject of the sentence.

- add the past participle. Make the ending of the participle <u>agree</u> with the subject.

The pluperfect tense of **andare** (meaning *to go*) is as follows:

	Imperfect tense of *essere*	Past participle	Meaning
(io)	ero	**andato** *or* **andata**	I had gone
(tu)	eri	**andato** *or* **andata**	you had gone
(lui)	era	**andato**	he/it had gone
(lei)	era	**andata**	she/it had gone
(Lei)	era	**andato** *or* **andata**	you had gone
(noi)	eravamo	**andati** *or* **andate**	we had gone
(voi)	eravate	**andati** *or* **andate**	you had gone
(loro)	erano	**andati** *or* **andate**	they had gone

Silvia era andata con loro. Silvia had gone with them.
Tutti i miei amici erano andati alla festa. All my friends had gone to the party.

Remember that **essere** is used to form the pluperfect of <u>all</u> reflexive verbs, and of <u>some</u> verbs that do not take a direct object, such as **andare** (meaning *to go*), **venire** (meaning *to come*), **riuscire** (meaning *to succeed*), **diventare** (meaning *to become*) and **piacere** (meaning *to like*).

Ovviamente non gli _erano piaciuti_ i quadri.

He obviously hadn't liked the pictures.

Sono arrivata alle cinque, ma _erano_ già _partiti_.

I arrived at five, but they'd already gone.

Fortunatamente non _si era fatta_ male. Luckily she hadn't hurt herself.

Dopo che _si erano resi_ conto del loro errore...

After they'd realized their mistake...

Note that the reflexive pronoun comes before **ero**, **eri**, **era**, **eravamo**, **eravate** and **erano** in the pluperfect of reflexive verbs.

The passive

Making the passive

In English we use the verb *to be* with a <u>past participle</u> (*is done, was bitten*) to make the passive. In Italian the passive is formed in exactly the same way, using **essere** (meaning *to be*) and a <u>past participle</u>. When you say who or what is responsible for the action you use **da** (meaning *by*).

> <u>**Siamo invitati**</u> **ad una festa a casa loro.**
> We're invited to a party at their house.
> **L'elettricità <u>è stata tagliata</u> ieri.** The electricity was cut off yesterday.
> **La partita <u>è stata rinviata</u>.** The match has been postponed.
> <u>**È stato costretto**</u> a ritirarsi dalla gara.
> He was forced to withdraw from the competition
> **I ladri <u>sono stati catturati</u> dalla polizia.**
> The thieves were caught by the police.

Note that the past participle agrees with the subject of the verb **essere** in the same way an adjective would.

Here is the perfect tense of the **–are** verb **invitare** (meaning *to invite*) in its passive form.

(Subject pronoun)		Perfect tense of *essere*	Past Participle	Meaning
(io)	– masculine	**sono stato**	**invitato**	I was *or* have been invited
	– feminine	**sono stata**	**invitata**	I was *or* have been invited
(tu)	– masculine	**sei stato**	**invitato**	you were *or* have been invited
	– feminine	**sei stata**	**invitata**	you were *or* have been invited
(lui)		**è stato**	**invitato**	he was *or* has been invited
(lei)		**è stata**	**invitata**	she was *or* has been invited
(Lei)	– masculine	**è stato**	**invitato**	you were *or* have been invited
	– feminine	**è stata**	**invitata**	you were *or* have been invited
(noi)	– masculine	**siamo stati**	**invitati**	we were *or* have been invited
	– feminine	**siamo state**	**invitate**	we were *or* have been invited
(voi)	– masculine	**siete stati**	**invitati**	you were *or* have been invited
	– feminine	**siete state**	**invitate**	you were *or* have been invited
(loro)	– masculine	**sono stati**	**invitati**	they were *or* have been invited
	– feminine	**sono state**	**invitate**	they were *or* have been invited

Change the tense of the verb ***essere*** to make whatever passive tense you want, for example:

Future: **Sarete tutti invitati.** You'll all be invited.
Conditional: **Non so se sarebbe invitata.** I don't know if she would be invited.

Irregular past participles are shown in the Verb Tables at the back of the book.

The gerund

Making the gerund

To make the gerund of **–are** verbs, take off the **–are** ending of the infinitive to get the stem, and add **–ando**.

Infinitive	Stem	Gerund
lavorare	lavor-	lavorando
andare	and-	andando
dare	d-	dando
stare	st-	stando

Note that the only **–are** verb that does not follow this rule is **fare**, and verbs made of **fare** with a prefix, such as **rifare** (meaning *to do again*) and **disfare** (meaning *to undo*). The gerund of **fare** is **facendo**.

To make the gerund of **–ere** and **–ire** verbs, take off the **–ere** or **–ire** ending of the infinitive to get the stem, and add **–endo**.

Infinitive	Stem	Gerund
credere	cred-	credendo
essere	ess-	essendo
dovere	dov-	dovendo
finire	fin-	finendo
dormire	dorm-	dormendo

Note that the only **–ire** verb that does not follow this rule is **dire** (and verbs made of **dire** with a prefix, such as **disdire** (meaning *to cancel*) and **contraddire** (meaning *to contradict*)). The gerund of **dire** is **dicendo**.

For further explanation of grammatical terms, please see 6–9.

Where to put pronouns used with the gerund

Pronouns are usually joined onto the end of the gerund.

Vedendoli è scoppiata in lacrime. When she saw them she burst into tears.
Ascoltandolo mi sono addormentato. Listening to him, I fell asleep.
Incontrandosi per caso sono andati al bar.
Meeting each other by chance, they went to a café.

When the gerund is part of a continuous tense the pronoun can either come before **stare** or be joined onto the gerund.

Ti sto parlando or **Sto parlandoti.** I'm talking to you.
Si sta vestendo or **Sta vestendosi.** He's getting dressed.
Me lo stavano mostrando or **Stavano mostrandomelo.**
They were showing me it.

The subjunctive

Making the present subjunctive

To make the present subjunctive of most verbs, take off the **–o** ending of the **io** form and add endings.

For **–are** verbs the endings are **–i**, **–i**, **–i**, **–iamo**, **–iate**, **–ino**.

For **–ere** and **–ire** verbs the endings are **–a**, **–a**, **–a**, **–iamo**, **–iate**, **–ano**.

Note that in the case of **–ire** verbs which add **–isc** in the **io** form, for example **finisco** (meaning *I finish*) and **pulisco** (meaning *I clean*), **–isc** is <u>not</u> added in the **noi** and **voi** forms.

The following table shows the present subjunctive of three regular verbs: **parlare** (meaning *to speak*), **credere** (meaning *to believe*) and **finire** (meaning *to finish*).

Infinitive	io, tu, lui, lei	noi	voi	loro
parlare	parli	parliamo	parliate	parlino
credere	creda	crediamo	crediate	credano
finire	finisca	finiamo	finiate	finiscano

Non voglio che mi <u>parlino</u>. I don't want them to speak to me.
Può darsi che non ti <u>creda</u>. Maybe she doesn't believe you.
È meglio che lo <u>finisca</u> io. It'll be best if I finish it.

Some common verbs that are irregular in the ordinary present tense also have irregular present subjunctives:

Infinitive	io, tu, lui, lei	noi	voi	loro
andare to go	vada	andiamo	andiate	vadano
avere to have	abbia	abbiamo	abbiate	abbiano
dare to give	dia	diamo	diate	diano
dire to say	dica	diciamo	diciate	dicano
dovere to have to	debba	dobbiamo	dobbiate	debbano
essere to be	sia	siamo	siate	siano
fare to do/make	faccia	facciamo	facciate	facciano
potere to be able	possa	possiamo	possiate	possano
scegliere to choose	scelga	scegliamo	scegliate	scelgano
stare to be	stia	stiamo	stiate	stiano
tenere to hold	tenga	teniamo	teniate	tengano
tradurre to translate	traduca	traduciamo	traduciate	traducano
uscire to go out	esca	usciamo	usciate	escano
venire to come	venga	veniamo	veniate	vengano
volere to want	voglia	vogliamo	vogliate	vogliano

È meglio che tu te ne <u>vada</u>. You'd better leave.

Vuoi che lo <u>traduca</u>? Do you want me to translate it?

È facile che <u>scelgano</u> quelli rossi. They'll probably choose those red ones.

Spero che tua madre <u>stia</u> meglio ora. I hope your mother is better now.

Credi che <u>possa</u> essere vero? Do you think it can be true?

Italic letters in Italian words show where stress does not follow the usual rules.

Making the perfect subjunctive

To make the perfect subjunctive you use the subjunctive of **avere** (meaning *to have*) or **essere** (meaning *to be*) with the past participle.

For example, **fare** (meaning *to make* or *to do*) makes its ordinary perfect tense and its perfect subjunctive with **avere**, while **essere** makes its ordinary perfect tense and its perfect subjunctive with **essere**.

		ordinary perfect	perfect subjunctive
fare	**io, tu, lui, lei, Lei**	ho fatto, hai fatto, ha fatto	*a*bbia fatto
to do/make	**noi**	abbiamo fatto	abbiamo fatto
	voi	avete fatto	abbiate fatto
	loro	hanno fatto	*a*bbiano fatto
essere	**io**	sono stato, sono stata	sia stato, sia stata
to be	**tu**	sei stato, sei stata	sia stato, sia stata
	lui	è stato	sia stato
	lei	è stata	sia stata
	Lei	è stato, è stata	sia stato, sia stata
	noi	siamo stati, siamo state	siamo stati, siamo state
	voi	siete stati, siete state	siate stati, siate state
	loro	sono stati, sono state	siano stati, siano state

Non credo che l'_abbiano fatto_ loro. I don't think they did it.

È possibile che _sia stato_ un errore. It might have been a mistake.

Making the imperfect subjunctive

The imperfect subjunctive is made by adding endings to the verb <u>stem</u>.

The endings for **–are** verbs are **–assi**, **–assi**, **–asse**, **–*assimo***, **–aste**, and **–*assero***; the endings for **–ere** verbs are **–essi**, **–essi**, **–esse**, **–*essimo***, **–este**, and **–*essero***; the endings for **–ire** verbs are **–issi**, **–issi**, **–isse**, **–issimo**, **–iste** and **–issero**.

The following table shows the imperfect subjunctive of three regular verbs: **parlare** (meaning *to speak*), **credere** (meaning *to believe*) and **finire** (meaning *to finish*).

	parlare	credere	finire
(io)	parlassi	credessi	finissi
(tu)	parlassi	credessi	finissi
(lui/lei)	parlasse	credesse	finisse
(Lei)	parlasse	credesse	finisse
(noi)	parlassimo	credessimo	finissimo
(voi)	parlaste	credeste	finiste
(loro)	parlassero	credessero	finissero

Volevano che <u>parlassi</u> con l'inquilino.
They wanted me to speak to the tenant.
Anche se mi <u>credesse</u>, non farebbe niente.
Even if he believed me he wouldn't do anything.
Se solo <u>finisse</u> prima delle otto! If only it finished before eight o'clock!

The imperfect subjunctive of **essere** is as follows:

(io)	**fossi**
(tu)	**fossi**
(lui/lei)	**fosse**
(Lei)	**fosse**
(noi)	**fossimo**
(voi)	**foste**
(loro)	**fossero**

Se <u>fossi</u> in te non lo pagherei. If I were you I wouldn't pay it.

Se <u>fosse</u> più furba verrebbe. If she had more sense she'd come.

The imperfect subjunctive of other important irregular verbs – **bere** (meaning *to drink*), **dare** (meaning *to give*), **dire** (meaning *to say*), **fare** (meaning *to make* or *to do*) and **stare** (meaning *to be*) – is as follows:

	(io)	(tu)	(lui/lei/Lei)	(noi)	(voi)	(loro)
bere	bevessi	bevessi	bevesse	bevessimo	beveste	bevessero
dare	dessi	dessi	desse	dessimo	deste	dessero
dire	dicessi	dicessi	dicesse	dicessimo	diceste	dicessero
fare	facessi	facessi	facesse	facessimo	faceste	facessero
stare	stessi	stessi	stesse	stessimo	steste	stessero

Se solo <u>bevesse</u> meno! If only he drank less!

Voleva che gli <u>dessero</u> il permesso.

He wanted them to give him permission.

Verb combinations

Many Italian verbs can be followed by the infinitive. In some cases the infinitive follows directly, in others a linking preposition is used.

Verbs followed by an infinitive with no preposition

The following important Italian verbs are followed directly by the infinitive:

- **dovere** (to have to, must)

    È dovuto partire. He had to leave.
    Dev'essere tardi. It must be late.

- **potere** (can, may)

    Non posso aiutarti. I can't help you.
    Potresti aprire la finestra? Could you open the window?
    Potrebbe essere vero. It might be true.

- **sapere** (to know how to, can)

    Sai farlo? Do you know how to do it?
    Non sapeva nuotare. He couldn't swim.

- **volere** (to want)

    Voglio comprare una macchina nuova. I want to buy a new car.

Note that **voler dire** is the Italian for *to mean*.
    Cosa vuol dire? What does it mean?

- verbs such as **piacere** (meaning *to like*), **dispiacere** (meaning *to be sorry*) and **convenire** (meaning *to be advisable*)

    Mi piace andare in bici. I like cycling.
    Ci dispiace andar via. We're sorry to be leaving.
    Ti conviene partire presto. You'd best set off early.

Italic letters in Italian words show where stress does not follow the usual rules.

60 Verb combinations

- **vedere** (meaning *to see*), **ascoltare** (meaning *to listen to*) and **sentire** (meaning *to hear*)

    Ci <u>ha visto arrivare</u>. He saw us arriving.
    Ti <u>ho sentito cantare</u>. I heard you singing.
    L'<u>abbiamo ascoltato parlare</u>. We listened to him talking.

- **fare** (meaning *to make*) and **lasciare** (meaning *to let*)

    Non mi <u>far ridere</u>! Don't make me laugh!
    <u>Lascia fare</u> a me. Let me do it.

Note that **far fare qualcosa** and **farsi fare qualcosa** both mean *to have something done*:

    <u>Ho fatto riparare</u> la macchina. I had the car repaired.
    Mi <u>sono fatta tagliare</u> i capelli. I had my hair cut.

The following common verbs are also followed directly by the infinitive:

- **bisognare** (to be necessary)

    <u>Bisogna prenotare</u>. You have to book.

- **desiderare** (to want)

    <u>Desiderava migliorare</u> il suo inglese. He wanted to improve his English.

- **odiare** (to hate)

    <u>Odio alzarmi</u> presto al mattino. I hate getting up early in the morning.

- **preferire** (to prefer)

    <u>Preferisco</u> non <u>parlarne</u>. I prefer not to talk about it.

Verbs followed by the preposition a and the infinitive

The following are the most common verbs that can be followed by **a** and the infinitive:

andare a fare qualcosa to go to do something
È andato a chiudere la porta. He went to shut the door.

venire a fare qualcosa to come to do something
Sono venuti a trovarci. They came to see us.

imparare a fare qualcosa to learn to do something
Sto imparando a suonare la chitarra. I'm learning to play the guitar.

cominciare a fare qualcosa to start to do or doing something
Hanno cominciato a ridere. They started laughing.

continuare a fare qualcosa to go on doing something
Ha continuato a dormire. He went on sleeping.

abituarsi a fare qualcosa to get used to doing something
Dovrò abituarmi ad alzarmi presto.
I'll have to get used to getting up early.

riuscire a fare qualcosa to manage to do something
Siamo riusciti a convincerla. We managed to persuade her.

Verbs followed by the preposition di and the infinitive

The following are the most common verbs that can be followed by **di** and the infinitive:

cercare di fare qualcosa to try to do something
Cerca di smettere di fumare. He's trying to stop smoking.

decidere di fare qualcosa to decide to do something
Ho deciso di non andarci. I decided not to go.

dimenticare di fare qualcosa to forget to do something
Ho dimenticato di prendere la chiave. I forgot to take my key.

smettere di fare qualcosa to stop doing something
Quando sono entrato hanno smesso di parlare.
When I came in they stopped talking.

ricordarsi di aver fatto qualcosa to remember doing something
Non mi ricordo di aver detto una cosa del genere.
I don't remember saying anything like that.

negare di aver fatto qualcosa to deny doing something
Ha negato di aver preso i soldi. He denied taking the money.

stufarsi di fare qualcosa to get fed up of doing something
Mi sono stufato di aspettarlo. I got fed up of waiting for him.

Verbs followed by a and an object

a is used with the indirect object of verbs such as **dire** (meaning *to say*) and **dare** (meaning *to give*).

dare qualcosa a qualcuno to give something to someone
Ho dato un libro a mia madre. I gave my mother a book.

dire qualcosa a qualcuno to say something to someone
Ha detto la veritá a Paolo. He told Paolo the truth.

mandare qualcosa a qualcuno to send something to someone
Manderò una cartolina a Loredana. I'll send Loredana a postcard.

mostrare qualcosa a qualcuno to show something to someone
Ho mostrato le foto a Daphne. I showed Daphne the photos.

scrivere qualcosa a qualcuno to write something to someone
Ho scritto una lettera a Luca. I wrote Luca a letter.

Here are some verbs taking **a** in Italian when you might not expect it, since the English equivalent either does not have the preposition *to* or has no preposition at all:

arrivare a (una cittá) to arrive at (*a town*)
Quando arrivi a Londra? When do you arrive in London?

avvicinarsi a qualcuno to approach someone
Matteo, non avvicinarti troppo a Chiara.
Matteo, don't go too close to Chiara.

chiedere qualcosa a qualcuno to ask someone for something
Chiedi a Lidia come si chiama il suo cane. Ask Lidia what her dog's called.

far male a qualcuno to hurt someone
Marcello ha fatto male a Paolo. Marcello hurt Paolo.

giocare a qualcosa to play something (*game/sport*)
Giochi a calcio? Do you play football?

insegnare qualcosa a qualcuno to teach somebody something
Ha insegnato ai bambini i nomi delle piante.
She taught the children the names of plants.

partecipare a qualcosa to take part in something
Parteciperai alla gara? Are you going to take part in the competition?

permettere a qualcuno di fare qualcosa to allow someone to do something
Non permette a Luca di uscire. She doesn't allow Luca to go out.

proibire a qualcuno di fare qualcosa to forbid someone to do something
Ha proibito ai bambini di uscire. She's forbidden the children to go out.

rispondere a qualcuno to answer someone
A me non ha risposto nessuno. Nobody answered me.

rivolgersi a qualcuno to ask someone
Dovrebbe rivolgersi all'impiegato laggiù.
You should go and ask the man over there.

rubare qualcosa a qualcuno to steal something from someone
Ha rubato i soldi alla madre. He stole the money from his mother.

somigliare a qualcuno to look like someone
Somiglio moltissimo a mia madre. I look very like my mother.

For further explanation of grammatical terms, please see 6–9.

Verbs followed by di and an object

Here are some verbs taking **di** in Italian when the English verb is not followed by *of*:

accorgersi di qualcosa to realize something
Si è accorto del furto solo il giorno dopo.
He only realized it had been stolen the next day.

aver bisogno di qualcosa to need something
Ho bisogno di soldi. I need money.

aver voglia di qualcosa to want something
Adesso non ho voglia di mangiare. I don't want to eat just now.

discutere di qualcosa to discuss something
Discutono spesso di politica. They often discuss politics.

fidarsi di qualcosa/qualcuno to trust something/someone
Non mi fido di lui. I don't trust him.

intendersi di qualcosa to know about something
Si intende di fotografia. She knows about photography.

interessarsi di qualcosa to be interested in something
Non mi interesso di politica. I'm not interested in politics.

lamentarsi di qualcosa to complain about something
Si sono lamentati del cibo. They complained about the food.

ricordarsi di qualcosa/qualcuno to remember something/someone
Ti ricordi di Laura? Do you remember Laura?

Italic letters in Italian words show where stress does not follow the usual rules.

ridere di qualcosa/qualcuno to laugh at something/someone
Hanno riso della sua proposta. They laughed at his suggestion.

stufarsi di qualcosa/qualcuno to get fed up with something/someone
Mi sono stufato di loro. I got fed up with them.

stupirsi di qualcosa to be amazed by something
Mi sono stupito del suo coraggio. I was amazed by his courage.

trattare di qualcosa to be about something
Di cosa tratta il libro? What's the book about?

vantarsi di qualcosa to boast about something
Si vanta sempre del proprio successo.
He's always boasting about his success.

For further explanation of grammatical terms, please see 6–9.

Verbs followed by da and an object

Here are some verbs taking **da** in Italian when the English verb is not followed by *from*:

dipendere <u>da</u> qualcosa/qualcuno to depend on something/someone
Dipende <u>dal</u> tempo. It depends on the weather.

giudicare <u>da</u> qualcosa to judge by something
A giudicare <u>da</u> quello che dice. Judging by what he says.

scendere <u>da</u> qualcosa to get off something (*bus, train, plane*)
Siamo tutti scesi <u>dall'</u>autobus. We all got off the bus.

sporgersi <u>da</u> qualcosa to lean out of something
Non sporgerti <u>dal</u> finestrino. Don't lean out of the window.

Verbs that are followed by a preposition in English but not in Italian

Although the English verb is followed by a preposition, you <u>don't</u> use a preposition with the following Italian verbs:

ascoltare qualcosa/qualcuno to listen to something/someone
Mi stai ascoltando? Are you listening to me?

aspettare qualcosa/qualcuno to wait for something/someone
Aspettami! Wait for me!

cercare qualcosa/qualcuno to look for something/someone
Sto cercando la chiave. I'm looking for my key.

chiedere qualcosa to ask for something
Ha chiesto qualcosa da mangiare. He asked for something to eat.

guardare qualcosa/qualcuno to look at something/someone
Guarda la sua faccia. Look at his face.

pagare qualcosa to pay for something
Ho già pagato il biglietto. I've already paid for my ticket.

Verb Tables

Introduction

The **Verb Tables** in the following section contain 120 tables of Italian verbs (some regular and some irregular) in alphabetical order. Each table shows you the following forms: **Present**, **Present Subjunctive**, **Perfect**, **Imperfect**, **Future**, **Conditional**, **Past Historic**, **Pluperfect**, **Imperative** and the **Past Participle** and **Gerund**. For more information on these tenses, how they are formed, when they are used and so on, you should look at the section on **Verb Formation** in the main text on pages 10–11. If you want to find out in more detail how verbs are used in different contexts, the Easy Learning Italian Grammar will give you additional information. ·

In order to help you use the verbs shown in the **Verb Tables** correctly, there are also a number of example phrases at the bottom of each page to show the verb as it is used in context.

In Italian there are **regular** verbs (their forms follow the regular patterns of **-are**, **-ere** or **-ire** verbs), and **irregular** verbs (their forms do not follow the normal rules). Examples of regular verbs in these tables are:

> **parlare** (regular **-are** verb, Verb Table 134)
> **credere** (regular **-ere** verb, Verb Table 52)
> **capire** (regular **-ire** verb, Verb Table 28)

Some irregular verbs are irregular in most of their forms, while others may only have a couple of irregular forms.

The **Verb Index** at the end of this section contains over 1000 verbs, each of which is cross-referred to one of the verbs given in the Verb Tables. The table shows the patterns that the verb listed in the index follows.

accadere (to happen)

PRESENT

io	–
tu	–
lui/lei/Lei	**accade**
noi	–
voi	–
loro	**accadono**

PRESENT SUBJUNCTIVE

io	–
tu	–
lui/lei/Lei	**accada**
noi	–
voi	–
loro	**accadano**

PERFECT

io	–
tu	–
lui/lei/Lei	**è accaduto/a**
noi	–
voi	–
loro	**sono accaduti/e**

IMPERFECT

io	–
tu	–
lui/lei/Lei	**accadeva**
noi	–
voi	–
loro	**accadevano**

GERUND
accadendo

PAST PARTICIPLE
accaduto

EXAMPLE PHRASES

All'epoca questo **accadeva** spesso. *At that time this often happened.*
Stanno **accadendo** molte cose strane. *A lot of strange things are happening.*

accadere

FUTURE

io	–
tu	–
lui/lei/Lei	**accadrà**
noi	–
voi	–
loro	**accadranno**

CONDITIONAL

io	–
tu	–
lui/lei/Lei	**accadrebbe**
noi	–
voi	–
loro	**accadrebbero**

PAST HISTORIC

io	–
tu	–
lui/lei/Lei	**accadde**
noi	–
voi	–
loro	**accaddero**

PLUPERFECT

io	–
tu	–
lui/lei/Lei	**era accaduto/a**
noi	–
voi	–
loro	**erano accaduti/e**

IMPERATIVE

–

EXAMPLE PHRASES

Che cosa ti **accadrà**? *What will happen to you?*

Non sappiamo cosa ci **accadrebbe**. *We don't know what would happen to us.*

Accadde un fatto meraviglioso. *A wonderful thing happened.*

Non capivamo ciò che **era accaduto**. *We couldn't understand what had happened.*

Italic letters in Italian words show where stress does not follow the usual rules.

accendere (to light)

PRESENT

io	**accendo**
tu	**accendi**
lui/lei/Lei	**accende**
noi	**accendiamo**
voi	**accendete**
loro	**accendono**

PRESENT SUBJUNCTIVE

io	**accenda**
tu	**accenda**
lui/lei/Lei	**accenda**
noi	**accendiamo**
voi	**accendiate**
loro	**accendano**

PERFECT

io	**ho acceso**
tu	**hai acceso**
lui/lei/Lei	**ha acceso**
noi	**abbiamo acceso**
voi	**avete acceso**
loro	**hanno acceso**

IMPERFECT

io	**accendevo**
tu	**accendevi**
lui/lei/Lei	**accendeva**
noi	**accendevamo**
voi	**accendevate**
loro	**accendevano**

GERUND

accendendo

PAST PARTICIPLE

acceso

EXAMPLE PHRASES

Abbiamo acceso le candeline. *We lit the candles.*

Appena entrava in casa **accendeva** sempre la radio. *He always switched on the radio as soon as he came into the house.*

Mi stavo **accendendo** una sigaretta quando è arrivato il bus. *I was lighting a cigarette when the bus arrived.*

Mi fai **accendere**? *Have you got a light?*

Remember that subject pronouns are not used very often in Italian.

accendere

FUTURE

io	**accenderò**
tu	**accenderai**
lui/lei/Lei	**accenderà**
noi	**accenderemo**
voi	**accenderete**
loro	**accenderanno**

CONDITIONAL

io	**accenderei**
tu	**accenderesti**
lui/lei/Lei	**accenderebbe**
noi	**accenderemmo**
voi	**accendereste**
loro	**accenderebbero**

PAST HISTORIC

io	**accesi**
tu	**accendesti**
lui/lei/Lei	**accese**
noi	**accendemmo**
voi	**accendeste**
loro	**accesero**

PLUPERFECT

io	**avevo acceso**
tu	**avevi acceso**
lui/lei/Lei	**aveva acceso**
noi	**avevamo acceso**
voi	**avevate acceso**
loro	**avevano acceso**

IMPERATIVE

accendi
accendiamo
accendete

EXAMPLE PHRASES

Appena arrivati **accenderemo** un fuoco. *We'll light a fire as soon as we arrive.*
Accendi la TV. *Turn on the TV.*
Accese una candela in chiesa. *She lit a candle in church.*

Italic letters in Italian words show where stress does not follow the usual rules.

accorgersi (to realize)

PRESENT

io	**mi accorgo**
tu	**ti accorgi**
lui/lei/Lei	**si accorge**
noi	**ci accorgiamo**
voi	**vi accorgete**
loro	**si accorgono**

PRESENT SUBJUNCTIVE

io	**mi accorga**
tu	**ti accorga**
lui/lei/Lei	**si accorga**
noi	**ci accorgiamo**
voi	**vi accorgiate**
loro	**si accorgano**

PERFECT

io	**mi sono accorto/a**
tu	**ti sei accorto/a**
lui/lei/Lei	**si è accorto/a**
noi	**ci siamo accorti/e**
voi	**vi siete accorti/e**
loro	**si sono accorti/e**

IMPERFECT

io	**mi accorgevo**
tu	**ti accorgevi**
lui/lei/Lei	**si accorgeva**
noi	**ci accorgevamo**
voi	**vi accorgevate**
loro	**si accorgevano**

GERUND
accorgendosi

PAST PARTICIPLE
accorto

EXAMPLE PHRASES

Avvisami se non **mi accorgo** che è tardi. *Warn me if I don't notice it's getting late.*

Mi sono accorto subito che qualcosa non andava. *I immediately realized something was wrong.*

Si è accorto del furto solo il giorno dopo. *He only noticed it had been stolen the next day.*

Remember that subject pronouns are not used very often in Italian.

accorgersi

FUTURE

io	**mi accorgerò**
tu	**ti accorgerai**
lui/lei/Lei	**si accorgerà**
noi	**ci accorgeremo**
voi	**vi accorgerete**
loro	**si accorgeranno**

CONDITIONAL

io	**mi accorgerei**
tu	**ti accorgeresti**
lui/lei/Lei	**si accorgerebbe**
noi	**ci accorgeremmo**
voi	**vi accorgereste**
loro	**si accorgerebbero**

PAST HISTORIC

io	**mi accorsi**
tu	**ti accorgesti**
lui/lei/Lei	**si accorse**
noi	**ci accorgemmo**
voi	**vi accorgeste**
loro	**si accorsero**

PLUPERFECT

io	**mi ero accorto/a**
tu	**ti eri accorto/a**
lui/lei/Lei	**si era accorto/a**
noi	**ci eravamo accorti/e**
voi	**vi eravate accorti/e**
loro	**si erano accorti/e**

IMPERATIVE

accorgiti
accorgiamoci
accorgetevi

EXAMPLE PHRASES

Un giorno si **accorgerà** di te. *Some day he'll notice you.*

Se tu mi ingannassi, **me ne accorgerei**. *If you were tricking me I'd notice.*

Era malato ma nessuno se ne **accorse**. *He was ill, but nobody noticed.*

Non si **erano accorti** che ero nella stanza. *They hadn't noticed that I was in the room.*

È difficile **accorgersi** degli errori di battitura. *It's difficult to notice typing errors.*

Italic letters in Italian words show where stress does not follow the usual rules.

addormentarsi (to go to sleep)

PRESENT

io	**mi addormento**
tu	**ti addormenti**
lui/lei/Lei	**si addormenta**
noi	**ci addormentiamo**
voi	**vi addormentate**
loro	**si addormentano**

PRESENT SUBJUNCTIVE

io	**mi addormenti**
tu	**ti addormenti**
lui/lei/Lei	**si addormenti**
noi	**ci addormentiamo**
voi	**vi addormentiate**
loro	**si addormentino**

PERFECT

io	**mi sono addormentato/a**
tu	**ti sei addormentato/a**
lui/lei/Lei	**si è addormentato/a**
noi	**ci siamo addormentati/e**
voi	**vi siete addormentati/e**
loro	**si sono addormentati/e**

IMPERFECT

io	**mi addormentavo**
tu	**ti addormentavi**
lui/lei/Lei	**si addormentava**
noi	**ci addormentavamo**
voi	**vi addormentavate**
loro	**si addormentavano**

GERUND
addormentando

PAST PARTICIPLE
addormentato

EXAMPLE PHRASES

Mio padre **si addormenta** sempre davanti alla TV. *My father always goes to sleep in front of the TV.*

Mi **si è addormentato** un piede. *My foot has gone to sleep.*

Non riesco ad **addormentarmi**. *I can't get to sleep.*

Non voleva **addormentarsi**. *He didn't want to go to sleep.*

addormentarsi

FUTURE

io	**mi addormenterò**
tu	**ti addormenterai**
lui/lei/Lei	**si addormenterà**
noi	**ci addormenteremo**
voi	**vi addormenterete**
loro	**si addormenteranno**

CONDITIONAL

io	**mi addormenterei**
tu	**ti addormenteresti**
lui/lei/Lei	**si addormenterebbe**
noi	**ci addormenteremmo**
voi	**vi addormentereste**
loro	**si addormenterebbero**

PAST HISTORIC

io	**mi addormentai**
tu	**ti addormentasti**
lui/lei/Lei	**si addormentò**
noi	**ci addormentammo**
voi	**vi addormentaste**
loro	**si addormentarono**

PLUPERFECT

io	**mi ero addormentato/a**
tu	**ti eri addormentato/a**
lui/lei/Lei	**si era addormentato/a**
noi	**ci eravamo addormentati/e**
voi	**vi eravate addormentati/e**
loro	**si erano addormentati/e**

IMPERATIVE

addormentati
addormentiamoci
addormentatevi

EXAMPLE PHRASES

Leggo sempre prima di **addormentarmi**. *I always read before I go to sleep.*

Sono stanco: stasera **mi addormenterò** subito. *I'm tired: I'll go to sleep immediately tonight.*

Non mi accorsi che **si era addormentata**. *I didn't realize she'd gone to sleep.*

Italic letters in Italian words show where stress does not follow the usual rules.

andare (to go)

PRESENT

io	**vado**
tu	**vai**
lui/lei/Lei	**va**
noi	**andiamo**
voi	**andate**
loro	**vanno**

PRESENT SUBJUNCTIVE

io	**vada**
tu	**vada**
lui/lei/Lei	**vada**
noi	**andiamo**
voi	**andiate**
loro	**vadano**

PERFECT

io	**sono andato/a**
tu	**sei andato/a**
lui/lei/Lei	**è andato/a**
noi	**siamo andati/e**
voi	**siete andati/e**
loro	**sono andati/e**

IMPERFECT

io	**andavo**
tu	**andavi**
lui/lei/Lei	**andava**
noi	**andavamo**
voi	**andavate**
loro	**andavano**

GERUND

andando

PAST PARTICIPLE

andato

EXAMPLE PHRASES

Su, **andiamo**! *Come on, let's go!*

Come **va**? – Bene, grazie! *How are you? – Fine, thanks!*

La mamma vuole che tu **vada** a fare la spesa. *Mum wants you to go and do the shopping.*

Questo mese non **sono** ancora **andata** al cinema. *I haven't been to the cinema yet this month.*

Com'**è andata**? *How did it go?*

L'anno scorso **andavo** sempre a dormire tardi. *Last year I always went to bed late.*

Remember that subject pronouns are not used very often in Italian.

andare

FUTURE

io	**andrò**
tu	**andrai**
lui/lei/Lei	**andrà**
noi	**andremo**
voi	**andrete**
loro	**andranno**

CONDITIONAL

io	**andrei**
tu	**andresti**
lui/lei/Lei	**andrebbe**
noi	**andremmo**
voi	**andreste**
loro	**andrebbero**

PAST HISTORIC

io	**andai**
tu	**andasti**
lui/lei/Lei	**andò**
noi	**andammo**
voi	**andaste**
loro	**andarono**

PLUPERFECT

io	**ero andato/a**
tu	**eri andato/a**
lui/lei/Lei	**era andato/a**
noi	**eravamo andati/e**
voi	**eravate andati/e**
loro	**erano andati/e**

IMPERATIVE
vai
andiamo
andate

EXAMPLE PHRASES

Andremo in Grecia quest'estate. *We're going to Greece this summer.*
Stasera **andrei** volentieri al ristorante. *I'd like to go to a restaurant this evening.*
Andarono a trovare la nonna. *They went to see their grandmother.*
Era **andato** in biblioteca per l'accesso gratuito al wifi. *He'd gone to the library for the free wifi access.*

Italic letters in Italian words show where stress does not follow the usual rules.

apparire (to appear)

PRESENT

io	**appaio**
tu	**appari**
lui/lei/Lei	**appare**
noi	**appariamo**
voi	**apparite**
loro	**appaiono**

PRESENT SUBJUNCTIVE

io	**appaia**
tu	**appaia**
lui/lei/Lei	**appaia**
noi	**appaiamo**
voi	**appaiate**
loro	**appaiano**

PERFECT

io	**sono apparso/a**
tu	**sei apparso/a**
lui/lei/Lei	**è apparso/a**
noi	**siamo apparsi/e**
voi	**siete apparsi/e**
loro	**sono apparsi/e**

IMPERFECT

io	**apparivo**
tu	**apparivi**
lui/lei/Lei	**appariva**
noi	**apparivamo**
voi	**apparivate**
loro	**apparivano**

GERUND

apparendo

PAST PARTICIPLE

apparso

EXAMPLE PHRASES

Oggi Mario **appare** turbato. *Mario seems upset today.*

Aspettiamo che **appaia** la luce del faro. *Let's wait until we see the beam of the lighthouse.*

Il fantasma **appariva** ogni sera a mezzanotte. *The ghost appeared every night at twelve o'clock.*

Finalmente una nave **apparve** all'orizzonte. *At last a ship appeared on the horizon.*

Remember that subject pronouns are not used very often in Italian.

apparire

FUTURE

io	**apparirò**
tu	**apparirai**
lui/lei/Lei	**apparirà**
noi	**appariremo**
voi	**apparirete**
loro	**appariranno**

CONDITIONAL

io	**apparirei**
tu	**appariresti**
lui/lei/Lei	**apparirebbe**
noi	**appariremmo**
voi	**apparireste**
loro	**apparirebbero**

PAST HISTORIC

io	**apparvi**
tu	**apparisti**
lui/lei/Lei	**apparve**
noi	**apparimmo**
voi	**appariste**
loro	**apparvero**

PLUPERFECT

io	**ero apparso/a**
tu	**eri apparso/a**
lui/lei/Lei	**era apparso/a**
noi	**eravamo apparsi/e**
voi	**eravate apparsi/e**
loro	**erano apparsi/e**

IMPERATIVE
appari
appariamo
apparite

EXAMPLE PHRASES

Tra poco il sole **apparirà** in cielo. *The sun will soon appear in the sky.*
Con quel vestito **appariresti** ridicolo. *You'd look silly in that suit.*
I soldati si fermarono: i banditi **erano apparsi** tra le rocce. *The soldiers halted: the bandits had appeared from among the rocks.*
Non vorrei **apparire** maleducato. *I wouldn't want to seem rude.*

Italic letters in Italian words show where stress does not follow the usual rules.

aprire (to open)

PRESENT	
io	**apro**
tu	**apri**
lui/lei/Lei	**apre**
noi	**apriamo**
voi	**aprite**
loro	*aprono*

PRESENT SUBJUNCTIVE	
io	**apra**
tu	**apra**
lui/lei/Lei	**apra**
noi	**apriamo**
voi	**apriate**
loro	*aprano*

PERFECT	
io	**ho aperto**
tu	**hai aperto**
lui/lei/Lei	**ha aperto**
noi	**abbiamo aperto**
voi	**avete aperto**
loro	**hanno aperto**

IMPERFECT	
io	**aprivo**
tu	**aprivi**
lui/lei/Lei	**apriva**
noi	**aprivamo**
voi	**aprivate**
loro	**aprivano**

GERUND

aprendo

PAST PARTICIPLE

aperto

EXAMPLE PHRASES

Posso **aprire** la finestra? *Can I open the window?*

Dai, non **apri** il pacco? *Come on, aren't you going to open the package?*

Non **ha aperto** bocca. *She didn't say a word.*

Non voglio che **apriate** i regali prima di Natale. *I don't want you to open your presents before Christmas.*

Si **è** tagliato **aprendo** una scatola di tonno. *He cut himself opening a tin of tuna.*

Remember that subject pronouns are not used very often in Italian.

aprire

FUTURE

io	**aprirò**
tu	**aprirai**
lui/lei/Lei	**aprirà**
noi	**apriremo**
voi	**aprirete**
loro	**apriranno**

CONDITIONAL

io	**aprirei**
tu	**apriresti**
lui/lei/Lei	**aprirebbe**
noi	**apriremmo**
voi	**aprireste**
loro	**aprirebbero**

PAST HISTORIC

io	**aprii**
tu	**apristi**
lui/lei/Lei	**aprì**
noi	**aprimmo**
voi	**apriste**
loro	**aprirono**

PLUPERFECT

io	**avevo aperto**
tu	**avevi aperto**
lui/lei/Lei	**aveva aperto**
noi	**avevamo aperto**
voi	**avevate aperto**
loro	**avevano aperto**

IMPERATIVE

apri
apriamo
aprite

EXAMPLE PHRASES

Aprirono lo champagne e festeggiarono. *They opened the champagne and celebrated.*

Aveva aperto la busta per leggere la lettera. *She'd opened the envelope to read the letter.*

Apri il rubinetto e innaffia il giardino. *Turn on the tap and water the garden.*

Polizia! **Aprite** questa porta! *Police! Open the door!*

Italic letters in Italian words show where stress does not follow the usual rules.

arrivare (to arrive)

PRESENT

io	**arrivo**
tu	**arrivi**
lui/lei/Lei	**arriva**
noi	**arriviamo**
voi	**arrivate**
loro	**arrivano**

PRESENT SUBJUNCTIVE

io	**arrivi**
tu	**arrivi**
lui/lei/Lei	**arrivi**
noi	**arriviamo**
voi	**arriviate**
loro	**arrivino**

PERFECT

io	**sono arrivato/a**
tu	**sei arrivato/a**
lui/lei/Lei	**è arrivato/a**
noi	**siamo arrivati/e**
voi	**siete arrivati/e**
loro	**sono arrivati/e**

IMPERFECT

io	**arrivavo**
tu	**arrivavi**
lui/lei/Lei	**arrivava**
noi	**arrivavamo**
voi	**arrivavate**
loro	**arrivavano**

GERUND
arrivando

PAST PARTICIPLE
arrivato

EXAMPLE PHRASES

Come si **arriva** al castello? *How do you get to the castle?*
A che ora **arrivi** a scuola? *What time do you get to school?*
Sono arrivato a Londra alle sette. *I arrived in London at seven.*
È troppo in alto, non ci **arrivo**. *It's too high, I can't reach it.*
Non **arrivava** mai in orario. *He never arrived on time.*
Aspettami, sto **arrivando**! *Wait, I'm coming!*

Remember that subject pronouns are not used very often in Italian.

arrivare

FUTURE

io	**arriverò**
tu	**arriverai**
lui/lei/Lei	**arriverà**
noi	**arriveremo**
voi	**arriverete**
loro	**arriveranno**

CONDITIONAL

io	**arriverei**
tu	**arriveresti**
lui/lei/Lei	**arriverebbe**
noi	**arriveremmo**
voi	**arrivereste**
loro	**arriverebbero**

PAST HISTORIC

io	**arrivai**
tu	**arrivasti**
lui/lei/Lei	**arrivò**
noi	**arrivammo**
voi	**arrivaste**
loro	**arrivarono**

PLUPERFECT

io	**ero arrivato/a**
tu	**eri arrivato/a**
lui/lei/Lei	**era arrivato/a**
noi	**eravamo arrivati/e**
voi	**eravate arrivati/e**
loro	**erano arrivati/e**

IMPERATIVE

arriva
arriviamo
arrivate

EXAMPLE PHRASES

Arriveremo in ritardo per colpa del traffico. *We'll get there late because of the traffic.*

Arrivammo al rifugio molto stanchi. *We were very tired when we got to the mountain refuge.*

Dopo due giorni di viaggio **era** finalmente **arrivata**. *After two days' travelling he'd at last arrived.*

Italic letters in Italian words show where stress does not follow the usual rules.

assumere (to take on, to employ)

PRESENT

io	**assumo**
tu	**assumi**
lui/lei/Lei	**assume**
noi	**assumiamo**
voi	**assumete**
loro	**assumono**

PRESENT SUBJUNCTIVE

io	**assuma**
tu	**assuma**
lui/lei/Lei	**assuma**
noi	**assumiamo**
voi	**assumiate**
loro	**assumano**

PERFECT

io	**ho assunto**
tu	**hai assunto**
lui/lei/Lei	**ha assunto**
noi	**abbiamo assunto**
voi	**avete assunto**
loro	**hanno assunto**

IMPERFECT

io	**assumevo**
tu	**assumevi**
lui/lei/Lei	**assumeva**
noi	**assumevamo**
voi	**assumevate**
loro	**assumevano**

GERUND
assumendo

PAST PARTICIPLE
assunto

EXAMPLE PHRASES

La ditta **assumeva** e ho presentato il curriculum. *The company was taking on staff and I sent in my CV.*

Sua moglie vuole **assumere** una badante. *His wife wants to employ a carer.*

C'è troppo lavoro: **assumiamo** del personale. *There's too much work: let's take on some more staff.*

È stata **assunta** come programmatrice. *She's got a job as a programmer.*

Remember that subject pronouns are not used very often in Italian.

assumere

FUTURE

io	**assumerò**
tu	**assumerai**
lui/lei/Lei	**assumerà**
noi	**assumeremo**
voi	**assumerete**
loro	**assumeranno**

CONDITIONAL

io	**assumerei**
tu	**assumeresti**
lui/lei/Lei	**assumerebbe**
noi	**assumeremmo**
voi	**assumereste**
loro	**assumerebbero**

PAST HISTORIC

io	**assunsi**
tu	**assumesti**
lui/lei/Lei	**assunse**
noi	**assumemmo**
voi	**assumeste**
loro	**assunsero**

PLUPERFECT

io	**avevo assunto**
tu	**avevi assunto**
lui/lei/Lei	**aveva assunto**
noi	**avevamo assunto**
voi	**avevate assunto**
loro	**avevano assunto**

IMPERATIVE

assumi
assumiamo
assumete

EXAMPLE PHRASES

L'azienda **assumerà** due operai. *The company is going to take on two workers.*

Sei bravo: ti **assumerei** come assistente. *You're good: I'd give you a job as an assistant.*

Italic letters in Italian words show where stress does not follow the usual rules.

avere (to have)

PRESENT

io	**ho**
tu	**hai**
lui/lei/Lei	**ha**
noi	**abbiamo**
voi	**avete**
loro	**hanno**

PRESENT SUBJUNCTIVE

io	*abbia*
tu	*abbia*
lui/lei/Lei	*abbia*
noi	**abbiamo**
voi	**abbiate**
loro	*abbiano*

PERFECT

io	**ho avuto**
tu	**hai avuto**
lui/lei/Lei	**ha avuto**
noi	**abbiamo avuto**
voi	**avete avuto**
loro	**hanno avuto**

IMPERFECT

io	**avevo**
tu	**avevi**
lui/lei/Lei	**aveva**
noi	**avevamo**
voi	**avevate**
loro	**avevano**

GERUND
avendo

PAST PARTICIPLE
avuto

EXAMPLE PHRASES

All'inizio **ha avuto** un sacco di problemi. *He had a lot of problems at first.*

Ho glà mangiato. *I've already eaten.*

Ora **ha** uno smartphone. *Now she's got a smartphone.*

Non penso che tu **abbia** il coraggio necessario per farlo. *I don't think you're brave enough to do it.*

Quanti ne **abbiamo** oggi? *What's the date today?*

Aveva la mia età. *He was the same age as me.*

Remember that subject pronouns are not used very often in Italian.

avere

FUTURE

io	**avrò**
tu	avrai
lui/lei/Lei	**avrà**
noi	avremo
voi	avrete
loro	avranno

CONDITIONAL

io	**avrei**
tu	**avresti**
lui/lei/Lei	**avrebbe**
noi	**avremmo**
voi	**avreste**
loro	**avrebbero**

PAST HISTORIC

io	**ebbi**
tu	**avesti**
lui/lei/Lei	**ebbe**
noi	**avemmo**
voi	**aveste**
loro	**ebbero**

PLUPERFECT

io	**avevo avuto**
tu	**avevi avuto**
lui/lei/Lei	**aveva avuto**
noi	**avevamo avuto**
voi	**avevate avuto**
loro	**avevano avuto**

IMPERATIVE

abbi
abbiamo
abbiate

EXAMPLE PHRASES

Quanti anni **avrà**? *How old do you think she is?*

Quando **ebbe** fame, mangiò. *When he was hungry he had something to eat.*

Prima di atterrare **avevano avuto** veramente paura. *Before the plane landed they'd been really frightened.*

Abbi pazienza, non ho ancora finito! *Be patient, I've not finished yet!*

Italic letters in Italian words show where stress does not follow the usual rules.

bere (to drink)

PRESENT		PRESENT SUBJUNCTIVE	
io	**bevo**	io	**beva**
tu	**bevi**	tu	**beva**
lui/lei/Lei	**beve**	lui/lei/Lei	**beva**
noi	**beviamo**	noi	**beviamo**
voi	**bevete**	voi	**beviate**
loro	**bevono**	loro	**bevano**

PERFECT		IMPERFECT	
io	**ho bevuto**	io	**bevevo**
tu	**hai bevuto**	tu	**bevevi**
lui/lei/Lei	**ha bevuto**	lui/lei/Lei	**beveva**
noi	**abbiamo bevuto**	noi	**bevevamo**
voi	**avete bevuto**	voi	**bevevate**
loro	**hanno bevuto**	loro	**bevevano**

GERUND
bevendo

PAST PARTICIPLE
bevuto

EXAMPLE PHRASES

Vuoi **bere** qualcosa? *Would you like something to drink?*

Chi porta da **bere**? *Who's going to bring the drinks?*

Ho l'impressione che tu **beva** troppo. *I've a feeling you drink too much.*

Mai **bevuto** un vino così! *I've never tasted a wine like this!*

Beveva sei caffè al giorno, ma ora ha smesso. *He used to drink six cups of coffee a day, but he's stopped now.*

Bevendo così si ubriacherà di sicuro. *If he drinks like that he'll be bound to get drunk.*

Remember that subject pronouns are not used very often in Italian.

bere

FUTURE

io	**berrò**
tu	**berrai**
lui/lei/Lei	**berrà**
noi	**berremo**
voi	**berrete**
loro	**berranno**

CONDITIONAL

io	**berrei**
tu	**berresti**
lui/lei/Lei	**berrebbe**
noi	**berremmo**
voi	**berreste**
loro	**berrebbero**

PAST HISTORIC

io	**bevvi**
tu	**bevesti**
lui/lei/Lei	**bevve**
noi	**bevemmo**
voi	**beveste**
loro	**bevvero**

PLUPERFECT

io	**avevo bevuto**
tu	**avevi bevuto**
lui/lei/Lei	**aveva bevuto**
noi	**avevamo bevuto**
voi	**avevate bevuto**
loro	**avevano bevuto**

IMPERATIVE

bevi
beviamo
bevete

EXAMPLE PHRASES

Berrei volentieri un bicchiere di vino bianco. *I'd love a glass of white wine.*

Non sono potuti tornare in auto perché **avevano bevuto**. *They couldn't drive back because they'd been drinking.*

Beviamo alla salute degli sposi! *Let's drink to the health of the bride and groom!*

Italic letters in Italian words show where stress does not follow the usual rules.

cadere (to fall)

PRESENT		PRESENT SUBJUNCTIVE	
io	cado	io	cada
tu	cadi	tu	cada
lui/lei/Lei	cade	lui/lei/Lei	cada
noi	cadiamo	noi	cadiamo
voi	cadete	voi	cadiate
loro	cadono	loro	cadano

PERFECT		IMPERFECT	
io	sono caduto/a	io	cadevo
tu	sei caduto/a	tu	cadevi
lui/lei/Lei	è caduto/a	lui/lei/Lei	cadeva
noi	siamo caduti/e	noi	cadevamo
voi	siete caduti/e	voi	cadevate
loro	sono caduti/e	loro	cadevano

GERUND
cadendo

PAST PARTICIPLE
caduto

EXAMPLE PHRASES

Il mio compleanno **cade** di lunedì. *My birthday is on a Monday.*

Ti **è caduta** la sciarpa. *You've dropped your scarf.*

Ho inciampato e **sono caduta**. *I tripped and fell.*

È caduta la linea. *We were cut off.*

Attento che fai **cadere** il bicchiere. *Mind you don't knock over your glass.*

Ha fatto **cadere** il vassoio. *She dropped the tray.*

Si è fatta male **cadendo** con i pattini. *She fell and hurt herself when she was skating.*

Remember that subject pronouns are not used very often in Italian.

cadere

FUTURE

io	**cadrò**
tu	**cadrai**
lui/lei/Lei	**cadrà**
noi	**cadremo**
voi	**cadrete**
loro	**cadranno**

CONDITIONAL

io	**cadrei**
tu	**cadresti**
lui/lei/Lei	**cadrebbe**
noi	**cadremmo**
voi	**cadreste**
loro	**cadrebbero**

PAST HISTORIC

io	**caddi**
tu	**cadesti**
lui/lei/Lei	**cadde**
noi	**cademmo**
voi	**cadeste**
loro	**caddero**

PLUPERFECT

io	**ero caduto/a**
tu	**eri caduto/a**
lui/lei/Lei	**era caduto/a**
noi	**eravamo caduti/e**
voi	**eravate caduti/e**
loro	**erano caduti/e**

IMPERATIVE

cadi
cadiamo
cadete

EXAMPLE PHRASES

Quando glielo diremo **cadranno** dalle nuvole. *When we tell them they'll be amazed.*

Cadde dalla bicicletta. *She fell off her bike.*

Italic letters in Italian words show where stress does not follow the usual rules.

cambiare (to change)

PRESENT

io	**cambio**
tu	**cambi**
lui/lei/Lei	**cambia**
noi	**cambiamo**
voi	**cambiate**
loro	**cambiano**

PRESENT SUBJUNCTIVE

io	**cambi**
tu	**cambi**
lui/lei/Lei	**cambi**
noi	**cambiamo**
voi	**cambiate**
loro	**cambino**

PERFECT

io	**ho cambiato**
tu	**hai cambiato**
lui/lei/Lei	**ha cambiato**
noi	**abbiamo cambiato**
voi	**avete cambiato**
loro	**hanno cambiato**

IMPERFECT

io	**cambiavo**
tu	**cambiavi**
lui/lei/Lei	**cambiava**
noi	**cambiavamo**
voi	**cambiavate**
loro	**cambiavano**

GERUND
cambiando

PAST PARTICIPLE
cambiato

EXAMPLE PHRASES

È necessario che **cambiate** atteggiamento. *You need to change your attitude.*

Era confuso e **cambiava** opinione in continuazione. *He was confused and kept changing his mind.*

Ultimamente è molto **cambiato**. *He's changed a lot recently.*

Vorrei **cambiare** questi euro in sterline. *I'd like to change these euros into pounds.*

Remember that subject pronouns are not used very often in Italian.

cambiare

FUTURE

io	**cambierò**
tu	**cambierai**
lui/lei/Lei	**cambierà**
noi	**cambieremo**
voi	**cambierete**
loro	**cambieranno**

CONDITIONAL

io	**cambierei**
tu	**cambieresti**
lui/lei/Lei	**cambierebbe**
noi	**cambieremmo**
voi	**cambiereste**
loro	**cambierebbero**

PAST HISTORIC

io	**cambiai**
tu	**cambiasti**
lui/lei/Lei	**cambiò**
noi	**cambiammo**
voi	**cambiaste**
loro	**cambiarono**

PLUPERFECT

io	**avevo cambiato**
tu	**avevi cambiato**
lui/lei/Lei	**aveva cambiato**
noi	**avevamo cambiato**
voi	**avevate cambiato**
loro	**avevano cambiato**

IMPERATIVE

cambia
cambiamo
cambiate

EXAMPLE PHRASES

Cambieremo casa il mese prossimo. *We're moving house next month.*

Cambiammo idea e prendemmo quell'altro. *We changed our mind and took the other one.*

Ci **cambiammo** prima di uscire. *We got changed before we went out.*

Aveva cambiato l'auto poco prima del furto. *She'd changed the car shortly before it was stolen.*

Cambiamo argomento. *Let's change the subject.*

Italic letters in Italian words show where stress does not follow the usual rules.

capire (to understand)

PRESENT

io	**capisco**
tu	**capisci**
lui/lei/Lei	**capisce**
noi	**capiamo**
voi	**capite**
loro	**capiscono**

PRESENT SUBJUNCTIVE

io	**capisca**
tu	**capisca**
lui/lei/Lei	**capisca**
noi	**capiamo**
voi	**capiate**
loro	**capiscano**

PERFECT

io	**ho capito**
tu	**hai capito**
lui/lei/Lei	**ha capito**
noi	**abbiamo capito**
voi	**avete capito**
loro	**hanno capito**

IMPERFECT

io	**capivo**
tu	**capivi**
lui/lei/Lei	**capiva**
noi	**capivamo**
voi	**capivate**
loro	**capivano**

GERUND

capendo

PAST PARTICIPLE

capito

EXAMPLE PHRASES

Va bene, **capisco**. *OK, I understand.*

È necessario che **capiate** bene le istruzioni. *You've got to understand the instructions properly.*

Non **ho capito** una parola. *I didn't understand a word.*

Non **ho capito**, puoi ripetere? *I don't understand, could you say it again?*

Fammi **capire**... *Let me get this straight...*

Capivamo le sue ragioni, ma aveva torto. *We understood his motives, but he was wrong.*

Remember that subject pronouns are not used very often in Italian.

capire

FUTURE

io	**capirò**
tu	**capirai**
lui/lei/Lei	**capirà**
noi	**capiremo**
voi	**capirete**
loro	**capiranno**

CONDITIONAL

io	**capirei**
tu	**capiresti**
lui/lei/Lei	**capirebbe**
noi	**capiremmo**
voi	**capireste**
loro	**capirebbero**

PAST HISTORIC

io	**capii**
tu	**capisti**
lui/lei/Lei	**capì**
noi	**capimmo**
voi	**capiste**
loro	**capirono**

PLUPERFECT

io	**avevo capito**
tu	**avevi capito**
lui/lei/Lei	**aveva capito**
noi	**avevamo capito**
voi	**avevate capito**
loro	**avevano capito**

IMPERATIVE

capisci

capiamo

capite

EXAMPLE PHRASES

Non ti **capirò** mai. *I'll never understand you.*

Se mi volessi bene, mi **capiresti**. *If you loved me, you'd understand me.*

Capirono che era ora di andarsene. *They realized it was time to go.*

Avevamo capito male le sue intenzioni. *We'd misunderstood his intentions.*

Italic letters in Italian words show where stress does not follow the usual rules.

cercare (to look for)

PRESENT

io	**cerco**
tu	**cerchi**
lui/lei/Lei	**cerca**
noi	**cerchiamo**
voi	**cercate**
loro	**cercano**

PRESENT SUBJUNCTIVE

io	**cerchi**
tu	**cerchi**
lui/lei/Lei	**cerchi**
noi	**cerchiamo**
voi	**cerchiate**
loro	**cerchino**

PERFECT

io	**ho cercato**
tu	**hai cercato**
lui/lei/Lei	**ha cercato**
noi	**abbiamo cercato**
voi	**avete cercato**
loro	**hanno cercato**

IMPERFECT

io	**cercavo**
tu	**cercavi**
lui/lei/Lei	**cercava**
noi	**cercavamo**
voi	**cercavate**
loro	**cercavano**

GERUND
cercando

PAST PARTICIPLE
cercato

EXAMPLE PHRASES

Io non **cerco** guai. *I'm not looking for trouble.*

È bene che **cerchiate** di essere puntuali. *You'd do well to try to be punctual.*

Le **ho cercate** dappertutto. *I've looked for them everywhere.*

Stai **cercando** lavoro? *Are you looking for a job?*

Sta **cercando** di imparare l'inglese. *He's trying to learn English.*

Remember that subject pronouns are not used very often in Italian.

cercare

FUTURE

io	**cercherò**
tu	**cercherai**
lui/lei/Lei	**cercherà**
noi	**cercheremo**
voi	**cercherete**
loro	**cercheranno**

CONDITIONAL

io	**cercherei**
tu	**cercheresti**
lui/lei/Lei	**cercherebbe**
noi	**cercheremmo**
voi	**cerchereste**
loro	**cercherebbero**

PAST HISTORIC

io	**cercai**
tu	**cercasti**
lui/lei/Lei	**cercò**
noi	**cercammo**
voi	**cercaste**
loro	**cercarono**

PLUPERFECT

io	**avevo cercato**
tu	**avevi cercato**
lui/lei/Lei	**aveva cercato**
noi	**avevamo cercato**
voi	**avevate cercato**
loro	**avevano cercato**

IMPERATIVE

cerca
cerchiamo
cercate

EXAMPLE PHRASES

Mi **cercheresti** il suo numero nell'agenda? *Would you look for his number in your diary?*

Cercammo di spiegargli il motivo. *We tried to explain the reason to him.*

Cerca di non fare tardi. *Try not to be late.*

Italic letters in Italian words show where stress does not follow the usual rules.

chiedere (to ask)

PRESENT

io	**chiedo**
tu	**chiedi**
lui/lei/Lei	**chiede**
noi	**chiediamo**
voi	**chiedete**
loro	**chiedono**

PRESENT SUBJUNCTIVE

io	**chieda**
tu	**chieda**
lui/lei/Lei	**chieda**
noi	**chiediamo**
voi	**chiediate**
loro	**chiedano**

PERFECT

io	**ho chiesto**
tu	**hai chiesto**
lui/lei/Lei	**ha chiesto**
noi	**abbiamo chiesto**
voi	**avete chiesto**
loro	**hanno chiesto**

IMPERFECT

io	**chiedevo**
tu	**chiedevi**
lui/lei/Lei	**chiedeva**
noi	**chiedevamo**
voi	**chiedevate**
loro	**chiedevano**

GERUND
chiedendo

PAST PARTICIPLE
chiesto

EXAMPLE PHRASES

Non **chiedo** mai favori a nessuno. *I never ask anyone for favours.*
Mi **ha chiesto** l'ora. *He asked me the time.*
Se non lo sai, basta **chiedere**. *If you don't know, just ask.*

Remember that subject pronouns are not used very often in Italian.

chiedere

FUTURE

io	**chiederò**
tu	**chiederai**
lui/lei/Lei	**chiederà**
noi	**chiederemo**
voi	**chiederete**
loro	**chiederanno**

CONDITIONAL

io	**chiederei**
tu	**chiederesti**
lui/lei/Lei	**chiederebbe**
noi	**chiederemmo**
voi	**chiedereste**
loro	**chiederebbero**

PAST HISTORIC

io	**chiesi**
tu	**chiedesti**
lui/lei/Lei	**chiese**
noi	**chiedemmo**
voi	**chiedeste**
loro	**chiesero**

PLUPERFECT

io	**avevo chiesto**
tu	**avevi chiesto**
lui/lei/Lei	**aveva chiesto**
noi	**avevamo chiesto**
voi	**avevate chiesto**
loro	**avevano chiesto**

IMPERATIVE

chiedi
chiediamo
chiedete

EXAMPLE PHRASES

Chiederemo agli amici di ospitarci. *We'll ask our friends to put us up.*
Chiederesti a Giulia di spostarsi un po'? *Would you ask Giulia to move a bit?*
Chiedemmo la strada per la stazione. *We asked the way to the station.*
Avevo chiesto il conto al cameriere, ma è sparito. *I'd asked the waiter for the bill, but he disappeared.*
Chiedi a Lidia come si chiama il suo cane. *Ask Lidia what her dog's called.*

Italic letters in Italian words show where stress does not follow the usual rules.

chiudere (to close)

PRESENT

io	**chiudo**
tu	**chiudi**
lui/lei/Lei	**chiude**
noi	**chiudiamo**
voi	**chiudete**
loro	**chiudono**

PRESENT SUBJUNCTIVE

io	**chiuda**
tu	**chiuda**
lui/lei/Lei	**chiuda**
noi	**chiudiamo**
voi	**chiudiate**
loro	**chiudano**

PERFECT

io	**ho chiuso**
tu	**hai chiuso**
lui/lei/Lei	**ha chiuso**
noi	**abbiamo chiuso**
voi	**avete chiuso**
loro	**hanno chiuso**

IMPERFECT

io	**chiudevo**
tu	**chiudevi**
lui/lei/Lei	**chiudeva**
noi	**chiudevamo**
voi	**chiudevate**
loro	**chiudevano**

GERUND
chiudendo

PAST PARTICIPLE
chiuso

EXAMPLE PHRASES

Un momento! **Chiudo** casa e scendo. *I'll just be a minute. I'll lock the door and come down.*

È meglio che tu **chiuda** a chiave. *You'd better lock the door.*

La fabbrica **ha chiuso** due anni fa. *The factory closed two years ago.*

Con lui **ho chiuso**. *I've finished with him.*

Remember that subject pronouns are not used very often in Italian.

chiudere

FUTURE

io	**chiuderò**
tu	**chiuderai**
lui/lei/Lei	**chiuderà**
noi	**chiuderemo**
voi	**chiuderete**
loro	**chiuderanno**

CONDITIONAL

io	**chiuderei**
tu	**chiuderesti**
lui/lei/Lei	**chiuderebbe**
noi	**chiuderemmo**
voi	**chiudereste**
loro	**chiuderebbero**

PAST HISTORIC

io	**chiusi**
tu	**chiudesti**
lui/lei/Lei	**chiuse**
noi	**chiudemmo**
voi	**chiudeste**
loro	**chiusero**

PLUPERFECT

io	**avevo chiuso**
tu	**avevi chiuso**
lui/lei/Lei	**aveva chiuso**
noi	**avevamo chiuso**
voi	**avevate chiuso**
loro	**avevano chiuso**

IMPERATIVE

chiudi
chiudiamo
chiudete

EXAMPLE PHRASES

A che ora **chiuderà** il negozio? *What time will the shop shut?*

La porta si **chiuse**. *The door closed.*

L'ho sgridato perché non **aveva chiuso** il gas. *I told him off because he'd not turned the gas off.*

Chiudi bene il rubinetto. *Turn the tap off properly.*

Italic letters in Italian words show where stress does not follow the usual rules.

cogliere (to pick)

PRESENT

io	**colgo**
tu	**cogli**
lui/lei/Lei	**coglie**
noi	**cogliamo**
voi	**cogliete**
loro	**colgono**

PRESENT SUBJUNCTIVE

io	**colga**
tu	**colga**
lui/lei/Lei	**colga**
noi	**cogliamo**
voi	**cogliate**
loro	**colgano**

PERFECT

io	**ho colto**
tu	**hai colto**
lui/lei/Lei	**ha colto**
noi	**abbiamo colto**
voi	**avete colto**
loro	**hanno colto**

IMPERFECT

io	**coglievo**
tu	**coglievi**
lui/lei/Lei	**coglieva**
noi	**coglievamo**
voi	**coglievate**
loro	**coglievano**

GERUND
cogliendo

PAST PARTICIPLE
colto

EXAMPLE PHRASES

Colgo l'occasione per augurarvi buon Natale. *May I take this opportunity to wish you a happy Christmas.*

L'**ho colto** sul fatto. *I caught him red-handed.*

Stavamo **cogliendo** dei fiori quando arrivò il temporale. *We were picking flowers when the storm started.*

Remember that subject pronouns are not used very often in Italian.

cogliere

FUTURE

io	**coglierò**
tu	**coglierai**
lui/lei/Lei	**coglierà**
noi	**coglieremo**
voi	**coglierete**
loro	**coglieranno**

CONDITIONAL

io	**coglierei**
tu	**coglieresti**
lui/lei/Lei	**coglierebbe**
noi	**coglieremmo**
voi	**cogliereste**
loro	**coglierebbero**

PAST HISTORIC

io	**colsi**
tu	**cogliesti**
lui/lei/Lei	**colse**
noi	**cogliemmo**
voi	**coglieste**
loro	**colsero**

PLUPERFECT

io	**avevo colto**
tu	**avevi colto**
lui/lei/Lei	**aveva colto**
noi	**avevamo colto**
voi	**avevate colto**
loro	**avevano colto**

IMPERATIVE

cogli
cogliamo
cogliete

EXAMPLE PHRASES

Tra qualche giorno **coglieranno** le fragole. *In a few days' time they'll be picking the strawberries.*

Colsi una mela dall'albero. *I picked an apple off the tree.*

Andiamo in campagna a **cogliere** la frutta. *Let's go into the countryside and pick some fruit.*

Italic letters in Italian words show where stress does not follow the usual rules.

cominciare (to start)

PRESENT

io	**comincio**
tu	**cominci**
lui/lei/Lei	**comincia**
noi	**cominciamo**
voi	**cominciate**
loro	**cominciano**

PRESENT SUBJUNCTIVE

io	**cominci**
tu	**cominci**
lui/lei/Lei	**cominci**
noi	**cominciamo**
voi	**cominciate**
loro	**comincino**

PERFECT

io	**ho cominciato**
tu	**hai cominciato**
lui/lei/Lei	**ha cominciato**
noi	**abbiamo cominciato**
voi	**avete cominciato**
loro	**hanno cominciato**

IMPERFECT

io	**cominciavo**
tu	**cominciavi**
lui/lei/Lei	**cominciava**
noi	**cominciavamo**
voi	**cominciavate**
loro	**cominciavano**

GERUND
cominciando

PAST PARTICIPLE
cominciato

EXAMPLE PHRASES

Il film **comincia** con un'esplosione. *The film starts with an explosion.*

Hai cominciato il libro che ti ho prestato? *Have you started the book I lent you?*

Faceva freddo e **cominciava** a nevicare. *It was cold and starting to snow.*

Cominciando oggi, dovrei finire lunedì. *If I start today I should finish on Monday.*

Remember that subject pronouns are not used very often in Italian.

cominciare

FUTURE

io	**comincerò**
tu	**comincerai**
lui/lei/Lei	**comincerà**
noi	**cominceremo**
voi	**comincerete**
loro	**cominceranno**

CONDITIONAL

io	**comincerei**
tu	**cominceresti**
lui/lei/Lei	**comincerebbe**
noi	**cominceremmo**
voi	**comincereste**
loro	**comincerebbero**

PAST HISTORIC

io	**cominciai**
tu	**cominciasti**
lui/lei/Lei	**cominciò**
noi	**cominciammo**
voi	**cominciaste**
loro	**cominciarono**

PLUPERFECT

io	**avevo cominciato**
tu	**avevi cominciato**
lui/lei/Lei	**aveva cominciato**
noi	**avevamo cominciato**
voi	**avevate cominciato**
loro	**avevano cominciato**

IMPERATIVE

comincia
cominciamo
cominciate

EXAMPLE PHRASES

Adesso **cominceranno** di sicuro a lamentarsi. *Now they're sure to start complaining.*

Cominciarono tutti a ridere. *They all started to laugh.*

Non **avevo** ancora **cominciato** che lui mi interruppe. *I hadn't even started and he interrupted me.*

Cominciamo bene! *This is a fine start!*

Italic letters in Italian words show where stress does not follow the usual rules.

compiere (to complete)

PRESENT

io	**compio**
tu	**compi**
lui/lei/Lei	**compie**
noi	**compiamo**
voi	**compite**
loro	**compiono**

PRESENT SUBJUNCTIVE

io	**compia**
tu	**compia**
lui/lei/Lei	**compia**
noi	**compiamo**
voi	**compiate**
loro	**compiano**

PERFECT

io	**ho compiuto**
tu	**hai compiuto**
lui/lei/Lei	**ha compiuto**
noi	**abbiamo compiuto**
voi	**avete compiuto**
loro	**hanno compiuto**

IMPERFECT

io	**compivo**
tu	**compivi**
lui/lei/Lei	**compiva**
noi	**compivamo**
voi	**compivate**
loro	**compivano**

GERUND
compiendo

PAST PARTICIPLE
compiuto

EXAMPLE PHRASES

Quando **compi** gli anni? *When is your birthday?*

Quanti anni **compi**? *How old will you be?*

Ho compiuto sedici anni il mese scorso. *I was sixteen last month.*

Per essere maggiorenne devi **compiere** 18 anni. *To be of age you have to be 18.*

Remember that subject pronouns are not used very often in Italian.

compiere

FUTURE

io	**compirò**
tu	**compirai**
lui/lei/Lei	**compirà**
noi	**compiremo**
voi	**compirete**
loro	**compiranno**

CONDITIONAL

io	**compirei**
tu	**compiresti**
lui/lei/Lei	**compirebbe**
noi	**compiremmo**
voi	**compireste**
loro	**compirebbero**

PAST HISTORIC

io	**compii**
tu	**compisti**
lui/lei/Lei	**compì**
noi	**compimmo**
voi	**compiste**
loro	**compirono**

PLUPERFECT

io	**avevo compiuto**
tu	**avevi compiuto**
lui/lei/Lei	**aveva compiuto**
noi	**avevamo compiuto**
voi	**avevate compiuto**
loro	**avevano compiuto**

IMPERATIVE

compi
compiamo
compite

EXAMPLE PHRASES

Quando **compirai** gli anni faremo una bella festa. *When it's your birthday we'll have a great party.*

Aveva compiuto 18 anni e gli regalarono l'auto. *He was 18 and they gave him a car.*

Italic letters in Italian words show where stress does not follow the usual rules.

confondere (to mix up)

PRESENT

io	**confondo**
tu	**confondi**
lui/lei/Lei	**confonde**
noi	**confondiamo**
voi	**confondete**
loro	**confondono**

PRESENT SUBJUNCTIVE

io	**confonda**
tu	**confonda**
lui/lei/Lei	**confonda**
noi	**confondiamo**
voi	**confondiate**
loro	**confondano**

PERFECT

io	**ho confuso**
tu	**hai confuso**
lui/lei/Lei	**ha confuso**
noi	**abbiamo confuso**
voi	**avete confuso**
loro	**hanno confuso**

IMPERFECT

io	**confondevo**
tu	**confondevi**
lui/lei/Lei	**confondeva**
noi	**confondevamo**
voi	**confondevate**
loro	**confondevano**

GERUND
confondendo

PAST PARTICIPLE
confuso

EXAMPLE PHRASES

Ho confuso le date. *I mixed up the dates.*

No, scusa, mi **sono confuso**: era ieri. *No, sorry, I've got mixed up: it was yesterday.*

Maria **confondeva** sempre i sogni e la realtà. *Maria always mixed up dreams and reality.*

Tutti questi discorsi mi **confondono** le idee. *All this talk is getting me confused.*

Non starai **confondendo** i nomi? *You're not mixing up the names, are you?*

Remember that subject pronouns are not used very often in Italian.

confondere

FUTURE

io	**confonderò**
tu	**confonderai**
lui/lei/Lei	**confonderà**
noi	**confonderemo**
voi	**confonderete**
loro	**confonderanno**

CONDITIONAL

io	**confonderei**
tu	**confonderesti**
lui/lei/Lei	**confonderebbe**
noi	**confonderemmo**
voi	**confondereste**
loro	**confonderebbero**

PAST HISTORIC

io	**confusi**
tu	**confondesti**
lui/lei/Lei	**confuse**
noi	**confondemmo**
voi	**confondeste**
loro	**confusero**

PLUPERFECT

io	**avevo confuso**
tu	**avevi confuso**
lui/lei/Lei	**aveva confuso**
noi	**avevamo confuso**
voi	**avevate confuso**
loro	**avevano confuso**

IMPERATIVE

confondi
confondiamo
confondete

EXAMPLE PHRASES

All'esame di storia **confonderò** di certo le date. *In the history exam I'm sure to mix up the dates.*

Se fossi stanca come me, ti **confonderesti** anche tu. *If you were as tired as I am, you'd get mixed up too.*

Avevate confuso i dati e l'esperimento è fallito. *You had got the data mixed up and the experiment was a failure.*

Italic letters in Italian words show where stress does not follow the usual rules.

connettere (to connect)

PRESENT

io	**connetto**
tu	**connetti**
lui/lei/Lei	**connette**
noi	**connettiamo**
voi	**connettete**
loro	**connettono**

PRESENT SUBJUNCTIVE

io	**connetta**
tu	**connetta**
lui/lei/Lei	**connetta**
noi	**connettiamo**
voi	**connettiate**
loro	**connettano**

PERFECT

io	**ho connesso**
tu	**hai connesso**
lui/lei/Lei	**ha connesso**
noi	**abbiamo connesso**
voi	**avete connesso**
loro	**hanno connesso**

IMPERFECT

io	**connettevo**
tu	**connettevi**
lui/lei/Lei	**connetteva**
noi	**connettevamo**
voi	**connettevate**
loro	**connettevano**

GERUND

connettendo

PAST PARTICIPLE

connesso

EXAMPLE PHRASES

Non **connetti** più: hai bisogno di un caffè. *You're not thinking straight: you need a coffee.*

Non **hanno connesso** il suo buon umore con l'arrivo di Carla. *They didn't make the connection between his good mood and Carla's arrival.*

Sta **connettendo** il computer alla presa elettrica. *She's plugging the computer into the socket.*

La mattina non riesco a **connettere**. *I can't think straight in the morning.*

Remember that subject pronouns are not used very often in Italian.

connettere

FUTURE

io	**connetterò**
tu	**connetterai**
lui/lei/Lei	**connetterà**
noi	**connetteremo**
voi	**connetterete**
loro	**connetteranno**

CONDITIONAL

io	**connetterei**
tu	**connetteresti**
lui/lei/Lei	**connetterebbe**
noi	**connetteremmo**
voi	**connettereste**
loro	**connetterebbero**

PAST HISTORIC

io	**connettei**
tu	**connettesti**
lui/lei/Lei	**connetté**
noi	**connettemmo**
voi	**connetteste**
loro	**connetterono**

PLUPERFECT

io	**avevo connesso**
tu	**avevi connesso**
lui/lei/Lei	**aveva connesso**
noi	**avevamo connesso**
voi	**avevate connesso**
loro	**avevano connesso**

IMPERATIVE

connetti
connettiamo
connettete

EXAMPLE PHRASES

Attento ai cortocircuiti quando **connetterai** la batteria. *Mind you don't get a short-circuit when you connect the battery.*

Non **avevo connesso** i due fatti. *I hadn't connected the two facts.*

Italic letters in Italian words show where stress does not follow the usual rules.

conoscere (to know)

PRESENT

io	**conosco**
tu	**conosci**
lui/lei/Lei	**conosce**
noi	**conosciamo**
voi	**conoscete**
loro	**conoscono**

PRESENT SUBJUNCTIVE

io	**conosca**
tu	**conosca**
lui/lei/Lei	**conosca**
noi	**conosciamo**
voi	**conosciate**
loro	**conoscano**

PERFECT

io	**ho conosciuto**
tu	**hai conosciuto**
lui/lei/Lei	**ha conosciuto**
noi	**abbiamo conosciuto**
voi	**avete conosciuto**
loro	**hanno conosciuto**

IMPERFECT

io	**conoscevo**
tu	**conoscevi**
lui/lei/Lei	**conosceva**
noi	**conoscevamo**
voi	**conoscevate**
loro	**conoscevano**

GERUND

conoscendo

PAST PARTICIPLE

conosciuto

EXAMPLE PHRASES

Non **conosco** bene la città. *I don't know the town well.*

Ci **conosciamo** da poco tempo. *We haven't known each other long.*

Voglio che tu **conosca** i miei. *I'd like you to meet my parents.*

Ci siamo **conosciuti** a Firenze. *We first met in Florence.*

Lo **conoscevamo** solo di vista. *We only knew him by sight.*

Remember that subject pronouns are not used very often in Italian.

conoscere

FUTURE

io	**conoscerò**
tu	**conoscerai**
lui/lei/Lei	**conoscerà**
noi	**conosceremo**
voi	**conoscerete**
loro	**conosceranno**

CONDITIONAL

io	**conoscerei**
tu	**conosceresti**
lui/lei/Lei	**conoscerebbe**
noi	**conosceremmo**
voi	**conoscereste**
loro	**conoscerebbero**

PAST HISTORIC

io	**conobbi**
tu	**conoscesti**
lui/lei/Lei	**conobbe**
noi	**conoscemmo**
voi	**conosceste**
loro	**conobbero**

PLUPERFECT

io	**avevo conosciuto**
tu	**avevi conosciuto**
lui/lei/Lei	**aveva conosciuto**
noi	**avevamo conosciuto**
voi	**avevate conosciuto**
loro	**avevano conosciuto**

IMPERATIVE

conosci
conosciamo
conoscete

EXAMPLE PHRASES

Viaggeremo e **conosceremo** posti nuovi. *We'll travel and get to know new places.*

Ci **conoscemmo** in vacanza. *We met on holiday.*

Conoscendoti, credo che farai la scelta giusta. *Knowing you, I think you'll make the right choice.*

Italic letters in Italian words show where stress does not follow the usual rules.

correggere (to correct)

PRESENT

io	**correggo**
tu	**correggi**
lui/lei/Lei	**corregge**
noi	**correggiamo**
voi	**correggete**
loro	**correggono**

PRESENT SUBJUNCTIVE

io	**corregga**
tu	**corregga**
lui/lei/Lei	**corregga**
noi	**correggiamo**
voi	**correggiate**
loro	**correggano**

PERFECT

io	**ho corretto**
tu	**hai corretto**
lui/lei/Lei	**ha corretto**
noi	**abbiamo corretto**
voi	**avete corretto**
loro	**hanno corretto**

IMPERFECT

io	**correggevo**
tu	**correggevi**
lui/lei/Lei	**correggeva**
noi	**correggevamo**
voi	**correggevate**
loro	**correggevano**

GERUND

correggendo

PAST PARTICIPLE

corretto

EXAMPLE PHRASES

Correggimi se faccio un errore. *Correct me if I make a mistake.*

Non **ha** ancora **corretto** i compiti di ieri. *She hasn't corrected yesterday's homework yet.*

Non **correggevano** mai gli errori del figlio. *They never corrected their son's mistakes.*

Si migliora **correggendo** i propri errori. *You improve by correcting your own mistakes.*

Remember that subject pronouns are not used very often in Italian.

correggere

FUTURE

io	**correggerò**
tu	**correggerai**
lui/lei/Lei	**correggerà**
noi	**correggeremo**
voi	**correggerete**
loro	**correggeranno**

CONDITIONAL

io	**correggerei**
tu	**correggeresti**
lui/lei/Lei	**correggerebbe**
noi	**correggeremmo**
voi	**correggereste**
loro	**correggerebbero**

PAST HISTORIC

io	**corressi**
tu	**correggesti**
lui/lei/Lei	**corresse**
noi	**correggemmo**
voi	**correggeste**
loro	**corressero**

PLUPERFECT

io	**avevo corretto**
tu	**avevi corretto**
lui/lei/Lei	**aveva corretto**
noi	**avevamo corretto**
voi	**avevate corretto**
loro	**avevano corretto**

IMPERATIVE

correggi
correggiamo
correggete

EXAMPLE PHRASES

Se non ti sforzi, non **correggerai** mai la tua pronuncia. *If you don't make an effort you'll never get your pronunciation right.*

Si è offeso perché lo **avevo corretto**. *He took offence because I'd corrected him.*

Se sbaglia, lo **correggiamo**. *If he makes a mistake we correct him.*

Italic letters in Italian words show where stress does not follow the usual rules.

correre (to run)

PRESENT

io	**corro**
tu	**corri**
lui/lei/Lei	**corre**
noi	**corriamo**
voi	**correte**
loro	**corrono**

PRESENT SUBJUNCTIVE

io	**corra**
tu	**corra**
lui/lei/Lei	**corra**
noi	**corriamo**
voi	**corriate**
loro	**corrano**

PERFECT

io	**ho corso**
tu	**hai corso**
lui/lei/Lei	**ha corso**
noi	**abbiamo corso**
voi	**avete corso**
loro	**hanno corso**

IMPERFECT

io	**correvo**
tu	**correvi**
lui/lei/Lei	**correva**
noi	**correvamo**
voi	**correvate**
loro	**correvano**

GERUND

correndo

PAST PARTICIPLE

corso

EXAMPLE PHRASES

Corre troppo in macchina. *He drives too fast.*

Non voglio che **corriate** dei rischi. *I don't want you to take risks.*

Abbiamo corso come pazzi per non perdere il treno. *We ran like mad to catch the train.*

Sono inciampato mentre **correvo**. *I tripped when I was running.*

Sono corso subito fuori. *I immediately rushed outside.*

Remember that subject pronouns are not used very often in Italian.

correre

FUTURE

io	**correrò**
tu	**correrai**
lui/lei/Lei	**correrà**
noi	**correremo**
voi	**correrete**
loro	**correranno**

CONDITIONAL

io	**correrei**
tu	**correresti**
lui/lei/Lei	**correrebbe**
noi	**correremmo**
voi	**correreste**
loro	**correrebbero**

PAST HISTORIC

io	**corsi**
tu	**corresti**
lui/lei/Lei	**corse**
noi	**corremmo**
voi	**correste**
loro	**corsero**

PLUPERFECT

io	**avevo corso**
tu	**avevi corso**
lui/lei/Lei	**aveva corso**
noi	**avevamo corso**
voi	**avevate corso**
loro	**avevano corso**

IMPERATIVE

corri
corriamo
correte

EXAMPLE PHRASES

Paola **correrà** i cento metri. *Paola is going to run the hundred metres.*

È prudente: non **correrebbe** mai rischi inutili. *She's sensible: she'd never take unnecessary risks.*

Aveva corso e ansimava ancora. *He'd been running and was still out of breath.*

Corri o perdiamo l'autobus! *Run or we'll miss the bus!*

Italic letters in Italian words show where stress does not follow the usual rules.

credere (to believe)

PRESENT		PRESENT SUBJUNCTIVE	
io	**credo**	io	**creda**
tu	**credi**	tu	**creda**
lui/lei/Lei	**crede**	lui/lei/Lei	**creda**
noi	**crediamo**	noi	**crediamo**
voi	**credete**	voi	**crediate**
loro	**credono**	loro	**credano**

PERFECT		IMPERFECT	
io	**ho creduto**	io	**credevo**
tu	**hai creduto**	tu	**credevi**
lui/lei/Lei	**ha creduto**	lui/lei/Lei	**credeva**
noi	**abbiamo creduto**	noi	**credevamo**
voi	**avete creduto**	voi	**credevate**
loro	**hanno creduto**	loro	**credevano**

GERUND
credendo

PAST PARTICIPLE
creduto

EXAMPLE PHRASES

Non ci **credo**! *I don't believe it!*

Non dirmi che **credi** ai fantasmi! *Don't tell me you believe in ghosts!*

Non voglio che lei **creda** che sono un bugiardo. *I don't want her to think I'm a liar.*

Non **ha** mai **creduto** nell'astrologia. *She's never believed in astrology.*

Non **credeva** ai suoi occhi. *She couldn't believe her eyes.*

Remember that subject pronouns are not used very often in Italian.

credere

FUTURE

io	**crederò**
tu	**crederai**
lui/lei/Lei	**crederà**
noi	**crederemo**
voi	**crederete**
loro	**crederanno**

CONDITIONAL

io	**crederei**
tu	**crederesti**
lui/lei/Lei	**crederebbe**
noi	**crederemmo**
voi	**credereste**
loro	**crederebbero**

PAST HISTORIC

io	**credetti** *or* **credei**
tu	**credesti**
lui/lei/Lei	**credette**
noi	**credemmo**
voi	**credeste**
loro	**credettero**

PLUPERFECT

io	**avevo creduto**
tu	**avevi creduto**
lui/lei/Lei	**aveva creduto**
noi	**avevamo creduto**
voi	**avevate creduto**
loro	**avevano creduto**

IMPERATIVE

credi
crediamo
credete

EXAMPLE PHRASES

Non ti **crederò** mai più. *I'll never believe you again.*

Ci **credereste**? Ho comprato casa. *Would you believe it! I've bought a house.*

Stento a **crederci**! *I can hardly believe it!*

Credemmo di aver perso le chiavi. *We thought we'd lost our keys.*

Italic letters in Italian words show where stress does not follow the usual rules.

crescere (to grow)

PRESENT	**PRESENT SUBJUNCTIVE**
io **cresco**	io **cresca**
tu **cresci**	tu **cresca**
lui/lei/Lei **cresce**	lui/lei/Lei **cresca**
noi **cresciamo**	noi **cresciamo**
voi **crescete**	voi **cresciate**
loro **crescono**	loro **crescano**

PERFECT	**IMPERFECT**
io **sono cresciuto/a**	io **crescevo**
tu **sei cresciuto/a**	tu **crescevi**
lui/lei/Lei **è cresciuto/a**	lui/lei/Lei **cresceva**
noi **siamo cresciuti/e**	noi **crescevamo**
voi **siete cresciuti/e**	voi **crescevate**
loro **sono cresciuti/e**	loro **crescevano**

GERUND	**PAST PARTICIPLE**
crescendo	cresciuto

EXAMPLE PHRASES

Tuo figlio **cresce** a vista d'occhio. *Your son is growing very fast.*

Più lavora e più **cresce** la sua insoddisfazione. *The harder she works the more dissatisfied she becomes.*

Com'**è cresciuto** tuo fratello! *Hasn't your brother grown!*

È cresciuto in campagna. *He grew up in the country.*

Si sta facendo **crescere** i capelli. *She's growing her hair.*

Le tue piante stanno **crescendo** molto bene. *Your plants are growing very well.*

Remember that subject pronouns are not used very often in Italian.

crescere

FUTURE

io	**crescerò**
tu	**crescerai**
lui/lei/Lei	**crescerà**
noi	**cresceremo**
voi	**crescerete**
loro	**cresceranno**

CONDITIONAL

io	**crescerei**
tu	**cresceresti**
lui/lei/Lei	**crescerebbe**
noi	**cresceremmo**
voi	**crescereste**
loro	**crescerebbero**

PAST HISTORIC

io	**crebbi**
tu	**crescesti**
lui/lei/Lei	**crebbe**
noi	**crescemmo**
voi	**cresceste**
loro	**crebbero**

PLUPERFECT

io	**ero cresciuto/a**
tu	**eri cresciuto/a**
lui/lei/Lei	**era cresciuto/a**
noi	**eravamo cresciuti/e**
voi	**eravate cresciuti/e**
loro	**erano cresciuti/e**

IMPERATIVE

cresci
cresciamo
crescete

EXAMPLE PHRASES

I prezzi **cresceranno** durante le feste. *Prices will go up during the holiday season.*

Era molto **cresciuta** e non la riconoscevo. *She'd grown a lot and I didn't recognize her.*

Italic letters in Italian words show where stress does not follow the usual rules.

cucire (to sew)

PRESENT		PRESENT SUBJUNCTIVE	
io	**cucio**	io	**cucia**
tu	**cuci**	tu	**cucia**
lui/lei/Lei	**cuce**	lui/lei/Lei	**cucia**
noi	**cuciamo**	noi	**cuciamo**
voi	**cucite**	voi	**cuciate**
loro	**cuciono**	loro	**cuciano**

PERFECT		IMPERFECT	
io	**ho cucito**	io	**cucivo**
tu	**hai cucito**	tu	**cucivi**
lui/lei/Lei	**ha cucito**	lui/lei/Lei	**cuciva**
noi	**abbiamo cucito**	noi	**cucivamo**
voi	**avete cucito**	voi	**cucivate**
loro	**hanno cucito**	loro	**cucivano**

GERUND
cucendo

PAST PARTICIPLE
cucito

EXAMPLE PHRASES

Bisogna che entro domani **cucia** il vestito. *She has to finish sewing the dress by tomorrow.*

Mi piacciono le toppe che **hai cucito** sulla giacca. *I like the patches you've sewn on your jacket.*

Si è punta con l'ago mentre **cuciva**. *She pricked her finger with the needle while she was sewing.*

Sta **cucendo** uno strappo alla gonna. *She's mending a tear in her skirt.*

Remember that subject pronouns are not used very often in Italian.

cucire

FUTURE

io	**cucirò**
tu	**cucirai**
lui/lei/Lei	**cucirà**
noi	**cuciremo**
voi	**cucirete**
loro	**cuciranno**

CONDITIONAL

io	**cucirei**
tu	**cuciresti**
lui/lei/Lei	**cucirebbe**
noi	**cuciremmo**
voi	**cucireste**
loro	**cucirebbero**

PAST HISTORIC

io	**cucii**
tu	**cucisti**
lui/lei/Lei	**cucì**
noi	**cucimmo**
voi	**cuciste**
loro	**cucirono**

PLUPERFECT

io	**avevo cucito**
tu	**avevi cucito**
lui/lei/Lei	**aveva cucito**
noi	**avevamo cucito**
voi	**avevate cucito**
loro	**avevano cucito**

IMPERATIVE
cuci
cuciamo
cucite

EXAMPLE PHRASES

Domani **cucirò** i bottoni sul vestito. *I'll sew the buttons on the dress tomorrow.*
Non so **cucire**. *I can't sew.*

Italic letters in Italian words show where stress does not follow the usual rules.

cuocere (to cook)

PRESENT

io	**cuocio**
tu	**cuoci**
lui/lei/Lei	**cuoce**
noi	**cuociamo**
voi	**cuocete**
loro	**cuociono**

PRESENT SUBJUNCTIVE

io	**cuocia**
tu	**cuocia**
lui/lei/Lei	**cuocia**
noi	**cuociamo**
voi	**cuociate**
loro	**cuociano**

PERFECT

io	**ho cotto**
tu	**hai cotto**
lui/lei/Lei	**ha cotto**
noi	**abbiamo cotto**
voi	**avete cotto**
loro	**hanno cotto**

IMPERFECT

io	**cuocevo**
tu	**cuocevi**
lui/lei/Lei	**cuoceva**
noi	**cuocevamo**
voi	**cuocevate**
loro	**cuocevano**

GERUND
cuocendo

PAST PARTICIPLE
cotto

EXAMPLE PHRASES

Si è bruciato **cuocendo** la pizza. *He burnt himself when he was baking the pizza.*

La carne **cuoceva** sulla brace. *The meat was cooking on the barbecue.*

Mi piace la carne **cotta** sulla piastra. *I like meat cooked on the hotplate.*

cuocere

FUTURE

io	**cuocerò**
tu	**cuocerai**
lui/lei/Lei	**cuocerà**
noi	**cuoceremo**
voi	**cuocerete**
loro	**cuoceranno**

CONDITIONAL

io	**cuocerei**
tu	**cuoceresti**
lui/lei/Lei	**cuocerebbe**
noi	**cuoceremmo**
voi	**cuocereste**
loro	**cuocerebbero**

PAST HISTORIC

io	**cossi**
tu	**cuocesti**
lui/lei/Lei	**cosse**
noi	**cuocemmo**
voi	**cuoceste**
loro	**cossero**

PLUPERFECT

io	**avevo cotto**
tu	**avevi cotto**
lui/lei/Lei	**aveva cotto**
noi	**avevamo cotto**
voi	**avevate cotto**
loro	**avevano cotto**

IMPERATIVE

cuoci
cuociamo
cuocete

EXAMPLE PHRASES

Stasera, il pesce, lo **cuocerò** alla griglia. *This evening I'll grill the fish.*

Come lo **cuocerai**? *How are you going to cook it?*

Avevamo cotto troppo la torta: era immangiabile. *We'd left the cake in the oven too long: it was inedible.*

Cuocilo per mezz'ora. *Cook it for half an hour.*

Italic letters in Italian words show where stress does not follow the usual rules.

dare (to give)

PRESENT		PRESENT SUBJUNCTIVE	
io	**do**	io	**dia**
tu	**dai**	tu	**dia**
lui/lei/Lei	**dà**	lui/lei/Lei	**dia**
noi	**diamo**	noi	**diamo**
voi	**date**	voi	**diate**
loro	**danno**	loro	**diano**

PERFECT		IMPERFECT	
io	**ho dato**	io	**davo**
tu	**hai dato**	tu	**davi**
lui/lei/Lei	**ha dato**	lui/lei/Lei	**dava**
noi	**abbiamo dato**	noi	**davamo**
voi	**avete dato**	voi	**davate**
loro	**hanno dato**	loro	**davano**

GERUND
dando

PAST PARTICIPLE
dato

EXAMPLE PHRASES

Può **darsi** che sia malata. *She may be ill.*

La mia finestra **dà** sul giardino. *My window looks onto the garden.*

Gli **ho dato** un libro. *I gave him a book.*

Dandoti da fare, potresti ottenere molto di più. *If you exerted yourself you could achieve a lot more.*

Remember that subject pronouns are not used very often in Italian.

dare

FUTURE

io	**darò**
tu	**darai**
lui/lei/Lei	**darà**
noi	**daremo**
voi	**darete**
loro	**daranno**

CONDITIONAL

io	**darei**
tu	**daresti**
lui/lei/Lei	**darebbe**
noi	**daremmo**
voi	**dareste**
loro	**darebbero**

PAST HISTORIC

io	**diedi** or **detti**
tu	**desti**
lui/lei/Lei	**diede** or **dette**
noi	**demmo**
voi	**deste**
loro	**diedero** or **dettero**

PLUPERFECT

io	**avevo dato**
tu	**avevi dato**
lui/lei/Lei	**aveva dato**
noi	**avevamo dato**
voi	**avevate dato**
loro	**avevano dato**

IMPERATIVE

dai or **da'**
diamo
date

EXAMPLE PHRASES

Domani sera **daranno** un bel film in TV. *There's a good film on TV tomorrow evening.*

Quanti anni gli **daresti**? *How old would you say he was?*

Ci **diede** l'impressione di essere molto infelice. *We got the impression he was very unhappy.*

Lo ringraziai perché mi aveva **dato** una mano. *I thanked him for giving me a hand.*

Ricordami di **darti** la lista della spesa. *Remind me to give you the shopping list.*

Dammelo. *Give it to me.*

Italic letters in Italian words show where stress does not follow the usual rules.

decidere (to decide)

PRESENT

io	**decido**
tu	**decidi**
lui/lei/Lei	**decide**
noi	**decidiamo**
voi	**decidete**
loro	**decidono**

PRESENT SUBJUNCTIVE

io	**decida**
tu	**decida**
lui/lei/Lei	**decida**
noi	**decidiamo**
voi	**decidiate**
loro	**decidano**

PERFECT

io	**ho deciso**
tu	**hai deciso**
lui/lei/Lei	**ha deciso**
noi	**abbiamo deciso**
voi	**avete deciso**
loro	**hanno deciso**

IMPERFECT

io	**decidevo**
tu	**decidevi**
lui/lei/Lei	**decideva**
noi	**decidevamo**
voi	**decidevate**
loro	**decidevano**

GERUND

decidendo

PAST PARTICIPLE

deciso

EXAMPLE PHRASES

Quand'è che si **decidono** a venirci a trovare? *When will they decide to come and see us?*

Hai deciso? *Have you decided?*

Allora ci vai? – Non so, sto ancora **decidendo**. *So, are you going? – I don't know, I'm still trying to decide.*

Non so **decidermi**. *I can't decide.*

Remember that subject pronouns are not used very often in Italian.

decidere

FUTURE

io	**deciderò**
tu	**deciderai**
lui/lei/Lei	**deciderà**
noi	**decideremo**
voi	**deciderete**
loro	**decideranno**

CONDITIONAL

io	**deciderei**
tu	**decideresti**
lui/lei/Lei	**deciderebbe**
noi	**decideremmo**
voi	**decidereste**
loro	**deciderebbero**

PAST HISTORIC

io	**decisi**
tu	**decidesti**
lui/lei/Lei	**decise**
noi	**decidemmo**
voi	**decideste**
loro	**decisero**

PLUPERFECT

io	**avevo deciso**
tu	**avevi deciso**
lui/lei/Lei	**aveva deciso**
noi	**avevamo deciso**
voi	**avevate deciso**
loro	**avevano deciso**

IMPERATIVE
decidi
decidiamo
decidete

EXAMPLE PHRASES

Deciderai quando sarai sicura. *You'll decide when you're sure.*

Decidemmo di non andarci. *We decided not to go.*

Aveva deciso di smettere di fumare, ma non ce l'ha fatta. *She'd decided to stop smoking, but she didn't manage to.*

Non so scegliere: **decidi** tu al posto mio. *I don't know which to choose: you decide for me.*

Italic letters in Italian words show where stress does not follow the usual rules.

deludere (to disappoint)

PRESENT

io	**deludo**
tu	**deludi**
lui/lei/Lei	**delude**
noi	**deludiamo**
voi	**deludete**
loro	**deludono**

PRESENT SUBJUNCTIVE

io	**deluda**
tu	**deluda**
lui/lei/Lei	**deluda**
noi	**deludiamo**
voi	**deludiate**
loro	**deludano**

PERFECT

io	**ho deluso**
tu	**hai deluso**
lui/lei/Lei	**ha deluso**
noi	**abbiamo deluso**
voi	**avete deluso**
loro	**hanno deluso**

IMPERFECT

io	**deludevo**
tu	**deludevi**
lui/lei/Lei	**deludeva**
noi	**deludevamo**
voi	**deludevate**
loro	**deludevano**

GERUND
deludendo

PAST PARTICIPLE
deluso

EXAMPLE PHRASES

Spero proprio che tu non mi **deluda**. *I really hope you won't disappoint me.*

Il suo ultimo film mi **ha deluso**. *His last film was disappointing.*

Non vorrei **deluderti**, ma l'esame è andato male. *I hate to disappoint you, but the exam didn't go well.*

deludere

FUTURE

io	**deluderò**
tu	**deluderai**
lui/lei/Lei	**deluderà**
noi	**deluderemo**
voi	**deluderete**
loro	**deluderanno**

CONDITIONAL

io	**deluderei**
tu	**deluderesti**
lui/lei/Lei	**deluderebbe**
noi	**deluderemmo**
voi	**deludereste**
loro	**deluderebbero**

PAST HISTORIC

io	**delusi**
tu	**deludesti**
lui/lei/Lei	**deluse**
noi	**deludemmo**
voi	**deludeste**
loro	**delusero**

PLUPERFECT

io	**avevo deluso**
tu	**avevi deluso**
lui/lei/Lei	**aveva deluso**
noi	**avevamo deluso**
voi	**avevate deluso**
loro	**avevano deluso**

IMPERATIVE

deludi
deludiamo
deludete

EXAMPLE PHRASES

So che vi **deluderò**, ma ormai ho deciso. *I know you're going to be disappointed, but I've made up my mind.*

Se lo facessero mi **deluderebbero** molto. *If they did that I'd be very disappointed in them.*

Mi **deluse** molto. *It disappointed me very much.*

Ci **aveva deluso** e non gli parlammo più. *He'd let us down and we didn't speak to him any more.*

Italic letters in Italian words show where stress does not follow the usual rules.

dire (to say)

PRESENT

io	**dico**
tu	**dici**
lui/lei/Lei	**dice**
noi	**diciamo**
voi	**dite**
loro	**dicono**

PRESENT SUBJUNCTIVE

io	**dica**
tu	**dica**
lui/lei/Lei	**dica**
noi	**diciamo**
voi	**diciate**
loro	**dicano**

PERFECT

io	**ho detto**
tu	**hai detto**
lui/lei/Lei	**ha detto**
noi	**abbiamo detto**
voi	**avete detto**
loro	**hanno detto**

IMPERFECT

io	**dicevo**
tu	**dicevi**
lui/lei/Lei	**diceva**
noi	**dicevamo**
voi	**dicevate**
loro	**dicevano**

GERUND

dicendo

PAST PARTICIPLE

detto

EXAMPLE PHRASES

Come si **dice** "quadro" in inglese? *How do you say "quadro" in English?*

Ha detto che verrà. *He said he'll come.*

Era una persona generosa: **diceva** sempre di sì a tutti. *She was a generous person: she always said yes to everyone.*

Che ne **diresti** di farci un selfie? *Shall we take a selfie?*

Che cosa stai **dicendo**? *What are you saying?*

Remember that subject pronouns are not used very often in Italian.

dire

FUTURE

io	**dirò**
tu	**dirai**
lui/lei/Lei	**dirà**
noi	**diremo**
voi	**direte**
loro	**diranno**

CONDITIONAL

io	**direi**
tu	**diresti**
lui/lei/Lei	**direbbe**
noi	**diremmo**
voi	**direste**
loro	**direbbero**

PAST HISTORIC

io	**dissi**
tu	**dicesti**
lui/lei/Lei	**disse**
noi	**dicemmo**
voi	**diceste**
loro	**dissero**

PLUPERFECT

io	**avevo detto**
tu	**avevi detto**
lui/lei/Lei	**aveva detto**
noi	**avevamo detto**
voi	**avevate detto**
loro	**avevano detto**

IMPERATIVE

di'
diciamo
dite

EXAMPLE PHRASES

Ti **dirò** un segreto. *I'll tell you a secret.*

Non **disse** una parola. *She didn't say a word.*

Gli **avevo detto** di andarsene. *I'd told him to go away.*

Dimmi dov'è. *Tell me where it is.*

Dovete **dire** la verità. *You must tell the truth.*

Italic letters in Italian words show where stress does not follow the usual rules.

dirigere (to direct)

PRESENT		PRESENT SUBJUNCTIVE	
io	**dirigo**	io	**diriga**
tu	**dirigi**	tu	**diriga**
lui/lei/Lei	**dirige**	lui/lei/Lei	**diriga**
noi	**dirigiamo**	noi	**dirigiamo**
voi	**dirigete**	voi	**dirigiate**
loro	**dirigono**	loro	**dirigano**

PERFECT		IMPERFECT	
io	**ho diretto**	io	**dirigevo**
tu	**hai diretto**	tu	**dirigevi**
lui/lei/Lei	**ha diretto**	lui/lei/Lei	**dirigeva**
noi	**abbiamo diretto**	noi	**dirigevamo**
voi	**avete diretto**	voi	**dirigevate**
loro	**hanno diretto**	loro	**dirigevano**

GERUND	PAST PARTICIPLE
dirigendo	**diretto**

EXAMPLE PHRASES

I vigili **dirigono** il traffico. *The police are directing the traffic.*

Voglio che tu **diriga** il progetto. *I want you to manage the project.*

Ha diretto l'orchestra con grande abilità. *He conducted the orchestra with great skill.*

Si **è diretto** verso la porta. *He headed for the door.*

Prima **dirigeva** una ditta. *Before that he managed a company.*

Remember that subject pronouns are not used very often in Italian.

dirigere

FUTURE

io	**dirigerò**
tu	**dirigerai**
lui/lei/Lei	**dirigerà**
noi	**dirigeremo**
voi	**dirigerete**
loro	**dirigeranno**

CONDITIONAL

io	**dirigerei**
tu	**dirigeresti**
lui/lei/Lei	**dirigerebbe**
noi	**dirigeremmo**
voi	**dirigereste**
loro	**dirigerebbero**

PAST HISTORIC

io	**diressi**
tu	**dirigesti**
lui/lei/Lei	**diresse**
noi	**dirigemmo**
voi	**dirigeste**
loro	**diressero**

PLUPERFECT

io	**avevo diretto**
tu	**avevi diretto**
lui/lei/Lei	**aveva diretto**
noi	**avevamo diretto**
voi	**avevate diretto**
loro	**avevano diretto**

IMPERATIVE

dirigi
dirigiamo
dirigete

EXAMPLE PHRASES

Chi **dirigerà** i lavori? *Who'll be in charge of the work?*

Prima dell'incidente **erano diretti** a nord. *Before the accident they'd been heading north.*

Dirigiamoci verso sud. *Let's head south.*

Italic letters in Italian words show where stress does not follow the usual rules.

discutere (to discuss)

PRESENT

io **discuto**
tu **discuti**
lui/lei/Lei **discute**
noi **discutiamo**
voi **discutete**
loro **discutono**

PRESENT SUBJUNCTIVE

io **discuta**
tu **discuta**
lui/lei/Lei **discuta**
noi **discutiamo**
voi **discutiate**
loro **discutano**

PERFECT

io **ho discusso**
tu **hai discusso**
lui/lei/Lei **ha discusso**
noi **abbiamo discusso**
voi **avete discusso**
loro **hanno discusso**

IMPERFECT

io **discutevo**
tu **discutevi**
lui/lei/Lei **discuteva**
noi **discutevamo**
voi **discutevate**
loro **discutevano**

GERUND
discutendo

PAST PARTICIPLE
discusso

EXAMPLE PHRASES

Discutono spesso di politica. *They often discuss politics.*

Ho discusso a lungo con lui. *I had a long discussion with him.*

C'è stato un periodo in cui **discutevano** sempre. *There was a time when they argued constantly.*

Il problema non si risolverà solo **discutendo**. *Just talking about it won't solve the problem.*

Remember that subject pronouns are not used very often in Italian.

discutere

FUTURE

io	**discuterò**
tu	**discuterai**
lui/lei/Lei	**discuterà**
noi	**discuteremo**
voi	**discuterete**
loro	**discuteranno**

CONDITIONAL

io	**discuterei**
tu	**discuteresti**
lui/lei/Lei	**discuterebbe**
noi	**discuteremmo**
voi	**discutereste**
loro	**discuterebbero**

PAST HISTORIC

io	**discussi**
tu	**discutesti**
lui/lei/Lei	**discusse**
noi	**discutemmo**
voi	**discuteste**
loro	**discussero**

PLUPERFECT

io	**avevo discusso**
tu	**avevi discusso**
lui/lei/Lei	**aveva discusso**
noi	**avevamo discusso**
voi	**avevate discusso**
loro	**avevano discusso**

IMPERATIVE

discuti
discutiamo
discutete

EXAMPLE PHRASES

Discuteremo della questione più tardi. *We'll discuss the matter later.*

Discussero a fondo della possibilità di trasferirsi. *They had a detailed discussion about the possibility of moving.*

Mi ha ubbidito senza **discutere**. *He obeyed me without question.*

È inutile che **discutiamo**: ho ragione io. *There's no point arguing: I'm right.*

Italic letters in Italian words show where stress does not follow the usual rules.

distinguere (to see)

PRESENT		PRESENT SUBJUNCTIVE	
io	**distinguo**	io	**distingua**
tu	**distingui**	tu	**distingua**
lui/lei/Lei	**distingue**	lui/lei/Lei	**distingua**
noi	**distinguiamo**	noi	**distinguiamo**
voi	**distinguete**	voi	**distinguiate**
loro	**distinguono**	loro	**distinguano**

PERFECT		IMPERFECT	
io	**ho distinto**	io	**distinguevo**
tu	**hai distinto**	tu	**distinguevi**
lui/lei/Lei	**ha distinto**	lui/lei/Lei	**distingueva**
noi	**abbiamo distinto**	noi	**distinguevamo**
voi	**avete distinto**	voi	**distinguevate**
loro	**hanno distinto**	loro	**distinguevano**

GERUND	PAST PARTICIPLE
distinguendo	**distinto**

EXAMPLE PHRASES

Non li **distinguo** tra loro. *I can't tell the difference between them.*

Mi pare che tu non **distingua** bene i colori. *I think you have difficulty telling one colour from another.*

Non **distinguevo** il numero dell'autobus. *I couldn't see the number of the bus.*

Si è **distinto** per efficienza. *He's exceptionally efficient.*

distinguere

FUTURE
io	**distinguerò**
tu	**distinguerai**
lui/lei/Lei	**distinguerà**
noi	**distingueremo**
voi	**distinguerete**
loro	**distingueranno**

CONDITIONAL
io	**distinguerei**
tu	**distingueresti**
lui/lei/Lei	**distinguerebbe**
noi	**distingueremmo**
voi	**distinguereste**
loro	**distinguerebbero**

PAST HISTORIC
io	**distinsi**
tu	**distinguesti**
lui/lei/Lei	**distinse**
noi	**distinguemmo**
voi	**distingueste**
loro	**distinsero**

PLUPERFECT
io	**avevo distinto**
tu	**avevi distinto**
lui/lei/Lei	**aveva distinto**
noi	**avevamo distinto**
voi	**avevate distinto**
loro	**avevano distinto**

IMPERATIVE
distingui
distinguiamo
distinguete

EXAMPLE PHRASES

È una copia perfetta: non **distinguerei** il falso dall'originale. *It's a perfect copy: I couldn't tell the fake from the original.*

Distinguemmo nella nebbia la sagoma della nave. *Through the mist we could see the outline of the ship.*

Non sa **distinguere** sogni e realtà. *She can't tell the difference between dreams and reality.*

Italic letters in Italian words show where stress does not follow the usual rules.

dividere (to divide)

PRESENT

io	**divido**
tu	**dividi**
lui/lei/Lei	**divide**
noi	**dividiamo**
voi	**dividete**
loro	**dividono**

PRESENT SUBJUNCTIVE

io	**divida**
tu	**divida**
lui/lei/Lei	**divida**
noi	**dividiamo**
voi	**dividiate**
loro	**dividano**

PERFECT

io	**ho diviso**
tu	**hai diviso**
lui/lei/Lei	**ha diviso**
noi	**abbiamo diviso**
voi	**avete diviso**
loro	**hanno diviso**

IMPERFECT

io	**dividevo**
tu	**dividevi**
lui/lei/Lei	**divideva**
noi	**dividevamo**
voi	**dividevate**
loro	**dividevano**

GERUND
dividendo

PAST PARTICIPLE
diviso

EXAMPLE PHRASES

Il libro si **divide** in tre parti. *The book is divided into three parts.*

L'**ho diviso** in tre parti. *I've divided it into three parts.*

Abitavano insieme e **dividevano** le spese. *They lived together and shared expenses.*

Otto **diviso** quattro fa due. *Eight divided by four is two.*

Dividendo il lavoro, faremo prima. *If we share the work we'll get it done sooner.*

Remember that subject pronouns are not used very often in Italian.

dividere

FUTURE

io	**dividerò**
tu	**dividerai**
lui/lei/Lei	**dividerà**
noi	**divideremo**
voi	**dividerete**
loro	**divideranno**

CONDITIONAL

io	**dividerei**
tu	**divideresti**
lui/lei/Lei	**dividerebbe**
noi	**divideremmo**
voi	**dividereste**
loro	**dividerebbero**

PAST HISTORIC

io	**divisi**
tu	**dividesti**
lui/lei/Lei	**divise**
noi	**dividemmo**
voi	**divideste**
loro	**divisero**

PLUPERFECT

io	**avevo diviso**
tu	**avevi diviso**
lui/lei/Lei	**aveva diviso**
noi	**avevamo diviso**
voi	**avevate diviso**
loro	**avevano diviso**

IMPERATIVE

dividi
dividiamo
dividete

EXAMPLE PHRASES

È egoista e non **dividerebbe** mai nulla con nessuno. *He's selfish and would never share anything with anyone.*

Li **avevano divisi** perché litigavano sempre. *They had separated them because they quarrelled all the time.*

Dividi la cioccolata con tuo fratello. *Share the chocolate with your brother.*

Italic letters in Italian words show where stress does not follow the usual rules.

dormire (to sleep)

PRESENT

io	**dormo**
tu	**dormi**
lui/lei/Lei	**dorme**
noi	**dormiamo**
voi	**dormite**
loro	**dormono**

PRESENT SUBJUNCTIVE

io	**dorma**
tu	**dorma**
lui/lei/Lei	**dorma**
noi	**dormiamo**
voi	**dormiate**
loro	**dormano**

PERFECT

io	**ho dormito**
tu	**hai dormito**
lui/lei/Lei	**ha dormito**
noi	**abbiamo dormito**
voi	**avete dormito**
loro	**hanno dormito**

IMPERFECT

io	**dormivo**
tu	**dormivi**
lui/lei/Lei	**dormiva**
noi	**dormivamo**
voi	**dormivate**
loro	**dormivano**

GERUND
dormendo

PAST PARTICIPLE
dormito

EXAMPLE PHRASES

Era così stanco che **dormiva** in piedi. *He was so tired he was asleep on his feet.*

Dormivo e non ti ho sentita entrare. *I was asleep and didn't hear you come in.*

Sta **dormendo**. *She's sleeping.*

Vado a **dormire**. *I'm going to bed.*

Remember that subject pronouns are not used very often in Italian.

dormire

FUTURE

io	**dormirò**
tu	**dormirai**
lui/lei/Lei	**dormirà**
noi	**dormiremo**
voi	**dormirete**
loro	**dormiranno**

CONDITIONAL

io	**dormirei**
tu	**dormiresti**
lui/lei/Lei	**dormirebbe**
noi	**dormiremmo**
voi	**dormireste**
loro	**dormirebbero**

PAST HISTORIC

io	**dormii**
tu	**dormisti**
lui/lei/Lei	**dormì**
noi	**dormimmo**
voi	**dormiste**
loro	**dormirono**

PLUPERFECT

io	**avevo dormito**
tu	**avevi dormito**
lui/lei/Lei	**aveva dormito**
noi	**avevamo dormito**
voi	**avevate dormito**
loro	**avevano dormito**

IMPERATIVE

dormi
dormiamo
dormite

EXAMPLE PHRASES

Stanotte **dormirò** come un ghiro. *I'll sleep like a log tonight.*

Se potessi **dormirei** fino a tardi. *If I could I'd have a lie-in.*

Dormimmo profondamente e ci svegliammo riposati. *We slept soundly and woke up refreshed.*

Aveva dormito male ed era nervoso. *He hadn't slept well and was irritable.*

Italic letters in Italian words show where stress does not follow the usual rules.

dovere (to have to)

PRESENT

io	**devo**
tu	**devi**
lui/lei/Lei	**deve**
noi	**dobbiamo**
voi	**dovete**
loro	**devono**

PRESENT SUBJUNCTIVE

io	**debba**
tu	**debba**
lui/lei/Lei	**debba**
noi	**dobbiamo**
voi	**dobbiate**
loro	**debbano**

PERFECT

io	**ho dovuto**
tu	**hai dovuto**
lui/lei/Lei	**ha dovuto**
noi	**abbiamo dovuto**
voi	**avete dovuto**
loro	**hanno dovuto**

IMPERFECT

io	**dovevo**
tu	**dovevi**
lui/lei/Lei	**doveva**
noi	**dovevamo**
voi	**dovevate**
loro	**dovevano**

GERUND
dovendo

PAST PARTICIPLE
dovuto

EXAMPLE PHRASES

Ora **devo** proprio andare. *I've really got to go now.*

Devi finire i compiti prima di uscire. *You must finish your homework before you go out.*

Dev'essere tardi. *It must be late.*

Non è che si **debba** sempre dire la verità. *You don't always have to tell the truth.*

Gli **dovevo** 30 euro e così l'ho invitato a cena. *I owed him 30 euros so I took him out to dinner.*

È **dovuto** partire. *He had to leave.*

Remember that subject pronouns are not used very often in Italian.

dovere

FUTURE

io	**dovrò**
tu	**dovrai**
lui/lei/Lei	**dovrà**
noi	**dovremo**
voi	**dovrete**
loro	**dovranno**

CONDITIONAL

io	**dovrei**
tu	**dovresti**
lui/lei/Lei	**dovrebbe**
noi	**dovremmo**
voi	**dovreste**
loro	**dovrebbero**

PAST HISTORIC

io	**dovetti**
tu	**dovesti**
lui/lei/Lei	**dovette**
noi	**dovemmo**
voi	**doveste**
loro	**dovettero**

PLUPERFECT

io	**avevo dovuto**
tu	**avevi dovuto**
lui/lei/Lei	**aveva dovuto**
noi	**avevamo dovuto**
voi	**avevate dovuto**
loro	**avevano dovuto**

IMPERATIVE

–

EXAMPLE PHRASES

Per correre la maratona **dovranno** allenarsi molto. *They'll have to do a lot of training to run the marathon.*

Dovrebbe arrivare alle dieci. *He should arrive at ten.*

Dovemmo partire all'improvviso. *We had to leave unexpectedly.*

Dovendo scegliere, preferisco la giacca blu. *If I have to choose, I prefer the blue jacket.*

Italic letters in Italian words show where stress does not follow the usual rules.

escludere (to exclude)

PRESENT

io	**escludo**
tu	**escludi**
lui/lei/Lei	**esclude**
noi	**escludiamo**
voi	**escludete**
loro	**escludono**

PRESENT SUBJUNCTIVE

io	**escluda**
tu	**escluda**
lui/lei/Lei	**escluda**
noi	**escludiamo**
voi	**escludiate**
loro	**escludano**

PERFECT

io	**ho escluso**
tu	**hai escluso**
lui/lei/Lei	**ha escluso**
noi	**abbiamo escluso**
voi	**avete escluso**
loro	**hanno escluso**

IMPERFECT

io	**escludevo**
tu	**escludevi**
lui/lei/Lei	**escludeva**
noi	**escludevamo**
voi	**escludevate**
loro	**escludevano**

GERUND
escludendo

PAST PARTICIPLE
escluso

EXAMPLE PHRASES

Escludo che possa essere stato lui. *I certainly don't think it could have been him.*

Una cosa non **esclude** l'altra. *The one doesn't rule out the other.*

È stato **escluso** dalla gara. *He was excluded from the competition.*

Non conosceva nessuno e si sentiva **esclusa**. *She didn't know anyone and felt excluded.*

Escludendo il pesce, mangio di tutto. *Apart from fish, I eat everything.*

Remember that subject pronouns are not used very often in Italian.

escludere

FUTURE

io	**escluderò**
tu	**escluderai**
lui/lei/Lei	**escluderà**
noi	**escluderemo**
voi	**escluderete**
loro	**escluderanno**

CONDITIONAL

io	**escluderei**
tu	**escluderesti**
lui/lei/Lei	**escluderebbe**
noi	**escluderemmo**
voi	**escludereste**
loro	**escluderebbero**

PAST HISTORIC

io	**esclusi**
tu	**escludesti**
lui/lei/Lei	**escluse**
noi	**escludemmo**
voi	**escludeste**
loro	**esclusero**

PLUPERFECT

io	**avevo escluso**
tu	**avevi escluso**
lui/lei/Lei	**aveva escluso**
noi	**avevamo escluso**
voi	**avevate escluso**
loro	**avevano escluso**

IMPERATIVE

escludi
escludiamo
escludete

EXAMPLE PHRASES

Non **escluderei** questa possibilità. *I wouldn't rule out this possibility.*

Italic letters in Italian words show where stress does not follow the usual rules.

esigere (to require)

PRESENT

io	**esigo**
tu	**esigi**
lui/lei/Lei	**esige**
noi	**esigiamo**
voi	**esigete**
loro	**esigono**

PRESENT SUBJUNCTIVE

io	**esiga**
tu	**esiga**
lui/lei/Lei	**esiga**
noi	**esigiamo**
voi	**esigiate**
loro	**esigano**

PERFECT

io	–
tu	–
lui/lei/Lei	–
noi	–
voi	–
loro	–

IMPERFECT

io	**esigevo**
tu	**esigevi**
lui/lei/Lei	**esigeva**
noi	**esigevamo**
voi	**esigevate**
loro	**esigevano**

GERUND

esigendo

PAST PARTICIPLE

–

EXAMPLE PHRASES

Il proprietario **esige** il pagamento immediato. *The owner is demanding immediate payment.*

È un lavoro che **esige** molta concentrazione. *It's a job which demands a lot of concentration.*

Il capufficio **esigeva** sempre la perfezione. *The head clerk always demanded perfection.*

Remember that subject pronouns are not used very often in Italian.

esigere

FUTURE

io	**esigerò**
tu	**esigerai**
lui/lei/Lei	**esigerà**
noi	**esigeremo**
voi	**esigerete**
loro	**esigeranno**

CONDITIONAL

io	**esigerei**
tu	**esigeresti**
lui/lei/Lei	**esigerebbe**
noi	**esigeremmo**
voi	**esigereste**
loro	**esigerebbero**

PAST HISTORIC

io	**esigetti**
tu	**esigesti**
lui/lei/Lei	**esigette**
noi	**esigemmo**
voi	**esigeste**
loro	**esigettero**

PLUPERFECT

io	–
tu	–
lui/lei/Lei	–
noi	–
voi	–
loro	–

IMPERATIVE

esigi
esigiamo
esigete

EXAMPLE PHRASES

Esigerò sempre il massimo dagli studenti. *I'll always demand the maximum from my students.*

Devi **esigere** sempre rispetto dagli altri. *You must always demand respect from other people.*

Esigemmo una risposta immediata. *We demanded an immediate reply.*

Italic letters in Italian words show where stress does not follow the usual rules.

esistere (to exist)

PRESENT		PRESENT SUBJUNCTIVE	
io	**esisto**	io	**esista**
tu	**esisti**	tu	**esista**
lui/lei/Lei	**esiste**	lui/lei/Lei	**esista**
noi	**esistiamo**	noi	**esistiamo**
voi	**esistete**	voi	**esistiate**
loro	**esistono**	loro	**esistano**

PERFECT		IMPERFECT	
io	**sono esistito/a**	io	**esistevo**
tu	**sei esistito/a**	tu	**esistevi**
lui/lei/Lei	**è esistito/a**	lui/lei/Lei	**esisteva**
noi	**siamo esistiti/e**	noi	**esistevamo**
voi	**siete esistiti/e**	voi	**esistevate**
loro	**sono esistiti/e**	loro	**esistevano**

GERUND	PAST PARTICIPLE
esistèndo	**esistito**

EXAMPLE PHRASES

Babbo Natale non **esiste**. *Father Christmas doesn't exist.*

Non **esiste**! *No way!*

In Italia **esistono** molte tradizioni religiose. *There are many religious traditions in Italy.*

Non sappiamo se **esista** la vita su altri pianeti. *We do not know if life exists on other planets.*

Il 221b di Baker Street non **è** mai **esistito**. *There never was a 221b Baker Street.*

Un tempo qui **esisteva** una grande città. *At one time there was a great city here.*

Remember that subject pronouns are not used very often in Italian.

esistere

FUTURE

io	**esisterò**
tu	**esisterai**
lui/lei/Lei	**esisterà**
noi	**esisteremo**
voi	**esisterete**
loro	**esisteranno**

CONDITIONAL

io	**esisterei**
tu	**esisteresti**
lui/lei/Lei	**esisterebbe**
noi	**esisteremmo**
voi	**esistereste**
loro	**esisterebbero**

PAST HISTORIC

io	**esistei**
tu	**esistesti**
lui/lei/Lei	**esistette**
noi	**esistemmo**
voi	**esisteste**
loro	**esistettero**

PLUPERFECT

io	**ero esistito/a**
tu	**eri esistito/a**
lui/lei/Lei	**era esistito/a**
noi	**eravamo esistiti/e**
voi	**eravate esistiti/e**
loro	**erano esistiti/e**

IMPERATIVE

esisti
esistiamo
esistite

EXAMPLE PHRASES

Non disperare: **esisterà** pure una soluzione al problema! *Don't despair: there's sure to be a solution to the problem!*

Secondo alcuni **esisterebbe** una quarta dimensione. *Some people think there's a fourth dimension.*

Italic letters in Italian words show where stress does not follow the usual rules.

espellere (to expel)

PRESENT		PRESENT SUBJUNCTIVE	
io	**espello**	io	**espella**
tu	**espelli**	tu	**espella**
lui/lei/Lei	**espelle**	lui/lei/Lei	**espella**
noi	**espelliamo**	noi	**espelliamo**
voi	**espellete**	voi	**espelliate**
loro	**espellono**	loro	**espellano**

PERFECT		IMPERFECT	
io	**ho espulso**	io	**espellevo**
tu	**hai espulso**	tu	**espellevi**
lui/lei/Lei	**ha espulso**	lui/lei/Lei	**espelleva**
noi	**abbiamo espulso**	noi	**espellevamo**
voi	**avete espulso**	voi	**espellevate**
loro	**hanno espulso**	loro	**espellevano**

GERUND
espellendo

PAST PARTICIPLE
espulso

EXAMPLE PHRASES

Non va a scuola perché l'**hanno espulso**. *He doesn't go to school because he's been expelled.*

Tutt'e due i calciatori **sono** stati **espulsi**. *Both players were sent off.*

espellerre

FUTURE

io	**espellerò**
tu	**espellerai**
lui/lei/Lei	**espellerà**
noi	**espelleremo**
voi	**espellerete**
loro	**espelleranno**

CONDITIONAL

io	**espellerei**
tu	**espelleresti**
lui/lei/Lei	**espellerebbe**
noi	**espelleremmo**
voi	**espellereste**
loro	**espellerebbero**

PAST HISTORIC

io	**espulsi**
tu	**espellesti**
lui/lei/Lei	**espulse**
noi	**espellemmo**
voi	**espelleste**
loro	**espulsero**

PLUPERFECT

io	**avevo espulso**
tu	**avevi espulso**
lui/lei/Lei	**aveva espulso**
noi	**avevamo espulso**
voi	**avevate espulso**
loro	**avevano espulso**

IMPERATIVE

espelli
espelliamo
espellete

EXAMPLE PHRASES

Espellerò chi non rispetta la disciplina. *I will expel anyone who doesn't obey the rules.*

Se farai un altro fallo ti **espelleranno**. *If you commit another foul you'll be sent off.*

Lo **espulsero** dalla scuola. *He was expelled from the school.*

Dopo mezz'ora l'arbitro **aveva** già **espulso** due giocatori. *After half an hour the referee had already sent two players off.*

Italic letters in Italian words show where stress does not follow the usual rules.

esplodere (to explode)

PRESENT		PRESENT SUBJUNCTIVE	
io	**esplodo**	io	**esploda**
tu	**esplodi**	tu	**esploda**
lui/lei/Lei	**esplode**	lui/lei/Lei	**esploda**
noi	**esplodiamo**	noi	**esplodiamo**
voi	**esplodete**	voi	**esplodiate**
loro	**esplodono**	loro	**esplodano**

PERFECT		IMPERFECT	
io	**sono esploso/a**	io	**esplodevo**
tu	**sei esploso/a**	tu	**esplodevi**
lui/lei/Lei	**è esploso/a**	lui/lei/Lei	**esplodeva**
noi	**siamo esplosi/e**	noi	**esplodevamo**
voi	**siete esplosi/e**	voi	**esplodevate**
loro	**sono esplosi/e**	loro	**esplodevano**

GERUND
esplodendo

PAST PARTICIPLE
esploso

EXAMPLE PHRASES

La nitroglicerina **esplode** facilmente. *Nitroglycerin explodes easily.*

L'ordigno **è esploso** uccidendo tre persone. *The bomb exploded, killing three people.*

Tutt'intorno **esplodevano** i colpi di cannone. *Guns were firing on all sides.*

Remember that subject pronouns are not used very often in Italian.

esplodere

FUTURE

io	**esploderò**
tu	**esploderai**
lui/lei/Lei	**esploderà**
noi	**esploderemo**
voi	**esploderete**
loro	**esploderanno**

CONDITIONAL

io	**esploderei**
tu	**esploderesti**
lui/lei/Lei	**esploderebbe**
noi	**esploderemmo**
voi	**esplodereste**
loro	**esploderebbero**

PAST HISTORIC

io	**esplosi**
tu	**esplodesti**
lui/lei/Lei	**esplose**
noi	**esplodemmo**
voi	**esplodeste**
loro	**esplosero**

PLUPERFECT

io	**ero esploso/a**
tu	**eri esploso/a**
lui/lei/Lei	**era esploso/a**
noi	**eravamo esplosi/e**
voi	**eravate esplosi/e**
loro	**erano esplosi/e**

IMPERATIVE

esplodi
esplodiamo
esplodete

EXAMPLE PHRASES

Cerca di trattenersi, ma prima o poi **esploderà**. *He's trying to control himself, but sooner or later he'll explode.*

Una bomba **esplose** vicino alla trincea. *A bomb exploded near the trench.*

Le mina **era esplosa** senza ferire nessuno. *The mine exploded without injuring anyone.*

Italic letters in Italian words show where stress does not follow the usual rules.

esprimere (to express)

PRESENT		PRESENT SUBJUNCTIVE	
io	**esprimo**	io	**esprima**
tu	**esprimi**	tu	**esprima**
lui/lei/Lei	**esprime**	lui/lei/Lei	**esprima**
noi	**esprimiamo**	noi	**esprimiamo**
voi	**esprimete**	voi	**esprimiate**
loro	**esprimono**	loro	**esprimano**

PERFECT		IMPERFECT	
io	**ho espresso**	io	**esprimevo**
tu	**hai espresso**	tu	**esprimevi**
lui/lei/Lei	**ha espresso**	lui/lei/Lei	**esprimeva**
noi	**abbiamo espresso**	noi	**esprimevamo**
voi	**avete espresso**	voi	**esprimevate**
loro	**hanno espresso**	loro	**esprimevano**

GERUND
esprimendo

PAST PARTICIPLE
espresso

EXAMPLE PHRASES

Non **esprime** mai la sua opinione. *He never expresses his own opinion.*

Se non conosco la lingua, mi **esprimo** a gesti. *If I don't know the language, I use gestures.*

È meglio che tu non **esprima** le tue idee. *You'd better not express your ideas.*

Abbiamo espresso i nostri dubbi. *We expressed our doubts.*

Remember that subject pronouns are not used very often in Italian.

esprimere

FUTURE

io	**esprimerò**
tu	**esprimerai**
lui/lei/Lei	**esprimerà**
noi	**esprimeremo**
voi	**esprimerete**
loro	**esprimeranno**

CONDITIONAL

io	**esprimerei**
tu	**esprimeresti**
lui/lei/Lei	**esprimerebbe**
noi	**esprimeremmo**
voi	**esprimereste**
loro	**esprimerebbero**

PAST HISTORIC

io	**espressi**
tu	**esprimesti**
lui/lei/Lei	**espresse**
noi	**esprimemmo**
voi	**esprimeste**
loro	**espressero**

PLUPERFECT

io	**avevo espresso**
tu	**avevi espresso**
lui/lei/Lei	**aveva espresso**
noi	**avevamo espresso**
voi	**avevate espresso**
loro	**avevano espresso**

IMPERATIVE

esprimi
esprimiamo
esprimete

EXAMPLE PHRASES

Il Parlamento si **espresse** a favore della proposta di legge. *Parliament approved the legislation.*

Avevano espresso il desiderio di uscire. *They had expressed a desire to go out.*

Trovo difficile **esprimermi** in inglese. *I find it difficult to express myself in English.*

Dai, **esprimi** un desiderio! *Go on, make a wish!*

Italic letters in Italian words show where stress does not follow the usual rules.

essere (to be)

PRESENT

io	**sono**
tu	**sei**
lui/lei/Lei	**è**
noi	**siamo**
voi	**siete**
loro	**sono**

PRESENT SUBJUNCTIVE

io	**sia**
tu	**sia**
lui/lei/Lei	**sia**
noi	**siamo**
voi	**siate**
loro	**siano**

PERFECT

io	**sono stato/a**
tu	**sei stato/a**
lui/lei/Lei	**è stato/a**
noi	**siamo stati/e**
voi	**siete stati/e**
loro	**sono stati/e**

IMPERFECT

io	**ero**
tu	**eri**
lui/lei/Lei	**era**
noi	**eravamo**
voi	**eravate**
loro	**erano**

GERUND

essendo

PAST PARTICIPLE

stato

EXAMPLE PHRASES

Sono italiana. *I'm Italian.*

Mario **è** appena partito. *Mario has just left.*

Siete mai **stati** in Africa? *Have you ever been to Africa?*

Quando è arrivato **erano** le quattro. *When he arrived it was four o'clock.*

La foto **era** già virale. *The photo had already gone viral.*

Essendo così tardi, dubito che verranno. *As it's so late I doubt they'll be coming.*

Remember that subject pronouns are not used very often in Italian.

essere

FUTURE

io	**sarò**
tu	**sarai**
lui/lei/Lei	**sarà**
noi	**saremo**
voi	**sarete**
loro	**saranno**

CONDITIONAL

io	**sarei**
tu	**saresti**
lui/lei/Lei	**sarebbe**
noi	**saremmo**
voi	**sareste**
loro	**sarebbero**

PAST HISTORIC

io	**fui**
tu	**fosti**
lui/lei/Lei	**fu**
noi	**fummo**
voi	**foste**
loro	**furono**

PLUPERFECT

io	**ero stato/a**
tu	**eri stato/a**
lui/lei/Lei	**era stato/a**
noi	**eravamo stati/e**
voi	**eravate stati/e**
loro	**erano stati/e**

IMPERATIVE

sii
siamo
siate

EXAMPLE PHRASES

Alla festa ci **saranno** tutti i miei amici. *All my friends will be at the party.*

Saresti così gentile da aiutarmi? *Would you be kind enough to help me?*

Quando **fui** pronto, chiusi la valigia e partii. *When I was ready I fastened my case and left.*

Non **era** mai **stato** così preoccupato in vita sua. *He'd never been so worried in his life.*

Siate onesti, e ammettete il vostro errore. *Be honest and admit your mistake.*

Italic letters in Italian words show where stress does not follow the usual rules.

fare (to do, to make)

PRESENT

io	*faccio*
tu	**fai**
lui/lei/Lei	**fa**
noi	**facciamo**
voi	**fate**
loro	**fanno**

PRESENT SUBJUNCTIVE

io	*faccia*
tu	*faccia*
lui/lei/Lei	*faccia*
noi	**facciamo**
voi	**facciate**
loro	*facciano*

PERFECT

io	**ho fatto**
tu	**hai fatto**
lui/lei/Lei	**ha fatto**
noi	**abbiamo fatto**
voi	**avete fatto**
loro	**hanno fatto**

IMPERFECT

io	**facevo**
tu	**facevi**
lui/lei/Lei	**faceva**
noi	**facevamo**
voi	**facevate**
loro	**facevano**

GERUND

facendo

PAST PARTICIPLE

fatto

EXAMPLE PHRASES

Due più due **fa** quattro. *Two and two makes four.*

Fa il medico. *He is a doctor.*

Fa caldo. *It's hot.*

Ho fatto un errore. *I made a mistake.*

Cosa stai **facendo**? *What are you doing?*

Remember that subject pronouns are not used very often in Italian.

fare

FUTURE

io	**farò**
tu	**farai**
lui/lei/Lei	**farà**
noi	**faremo**
voi	**farete**
loro	**faranno**

CONDITIONAL

io	**farei**
tu	**faresti**
lui/lei/Lei	**farebbe**
noi	**faremmo**
voi	**fareste**
loro	**farebbero**

PAST HISTORIC

io	**feci**
tu	**facesti**
lui/lei/Lei	**fece**
noi	**facemmo**
voi	**faceste**
loro	**fecero**

PLUPERFECT

io	**avevo fatto**
tu	**avevi fatto**
lui/lei/Lei	**aveva fatto**
noi	**avevamo fatto**
voi	**avevate fatto**
loro	**avevano fatto**

IMPERATIVE

fai or **fa'**
facciamo
fate

EXAMPLE PHRASES

Domani si **farà** tagliare i capelli. *He's going to get his hair cut tomorrow.*

Mi **faresti** un piacere? *Would you do me a favour?*

Fecero una stupenda vacanza al mare. *They had a wonderful holiday at the seaside.*

Le **aveva fatto** male la testa tutto il pomeriggio. *She'd had a headache all afternoon.*

Fammi un favore, ti prego. *Please do me a favour.*

Italic letters in Italian words show where stress does not follow the usual rules.

fingere (to pretend)

PRESENT		PRESENT SUBJUNCTIVE	
io	**fingo**	io	**finga**
tu	**fingi**	tu	**finga**
lui/lei/Lei	**finge**	lui/lei/Lei	**finga**
noi	**fingiamo**	noi	**fingiamo**
voi	**fingete**	voi	**fingiate**
loro	**fingono**	loro	**fingano**

PERFECT		IMPERFECT	
io	**ho finto**	io	**fingevo**
tu	**hai finto**	tu	**fingevi**
lui/lei/Lei	**ha finto**	lui/lei/Lei	**fingeva**
noi	**abbiamo finto**	noi	**fingevamo**
voi	**avete finto**	voi	**fingevate**
loro	**hanno finto**	loro	**fingevano**

GERUND
fingendo

PAST PARTICIPLE
finto

EXAMPLE PHRASES

Ha finto di non conoscermi. *He pretended he didn't recognize me.*

Si **è finto** ubriaco. *He pretended he was drunk.*

Fingevano sempre di avere capito tutto. *They always pretended they'd understood everything.*

Non risposi, **fingendo** di non ricordare. *I didn't answer, pretending I couldn't remember.*

Remember that subject pronouns are not used very often in Italian.

fingere

FUTURE

io	**fingerò**
tu	**fingerai**
lui/lei/Lei	**fingerà**
noi	**fingeremo**
voi	**fingerete**
loro	**fingeranno**

CONDITIONAL

io	**fingerei**
tu	**fingeresti**
lui/lei/Lei	**fingerebbe**
noi	**fingeremmo**
voi	**fingereste**
loro	**fingerebbero**

PAST HISTORIC

io	**finsi**
tu	**fingesti**
lui/lei/Lei	**finse**
noi	**fingemmo**
voi	**fingeste**
loro	**finsero**

PLUPERFECT

io	**avevo finto**
tu	**avevi finto**
lui/lei/Lei	**aveva finto**
noi	**avevamo finto**
voi	**avevate finto**
loro	**avevano finto**

IMPERATIVE

fingi
fingiamo
fingete

EXAMPLE PHRASES

Fingeremo di avere molto da fare. *We'll pretend we've got a lot to do.*

La spia **finse** di essere un turista. *The spy pretended to be a tourist.*

Non devi **fingere** sentimenti che non provi. *You mustn't pretend you have feelings that you don't have.*

Fingiamo di dormire. *Let's pretend we're asleep.*

Italic letters in Italian words show where stress does not follow the usual rules.

fuggire (to run away)

PRESENT

io	**fuggo**
tu	**fuggi**
lui/lei/Lei	**fugge**
noi	**fuggiamo**
voi	**fuggite**
loro	**fuggono**

PRESENT SUBJUNCTIVE

io	**fugga**
tu	**fugga**
lui/lei/Lei	**fugga**
noi	**fuggiamo**
voi	**fuggiate**
loro	**fuggano**

PERFECT

io	**sono fuggito/a**
tu	**sei fuggito/a**
lui/lei/Lei	**è fuggito/a**
noi	**siamo fuggiti/e**
voi	**siete fuggiti/e**
loro	**sono fuggiti/e**

IMPERFECT

io	**fuggivo**
tu	**fuggivi**
lui/lei/Lei	**fuggiva**
noi	**fuggivamo**
voi	**fuggivate**
loro	**fuggivano**

GERUND

fuggendo

PAST PARTICIPLE

fuggito

EXAMPLE PHRASES

È fuggita di casa. *She ran away from home.*

Non è **fuggendo** che si risolvono i problemi. *You won't solve problems by running away from them.*

Il ladro stava **fuggendo** su un'auto sportiva. *The robber was escaping in a sports car.*

Remember that subject pronouns are not used very often in Italian.

fuggire

FUTURE

io	**fuggirò**
tu	**fuggirai**
lui/lei/Lei	**fuggirà**
noi	**fuggiremo**
voi	**fuggirete**
loro	**fuggiranno**

CONDITIONAL

io	**fuggirei**
tu	**fuggiresti**
lui/lei/Lei	**fuggirebbe**
noi	**fuggiremmo**
voi	**fuggireste**
loro	**fuggirebbero**

PAST HISTORIC

io	**fuggii**
tu	**fuggisti**
lui/lei/Lei	**fuggì**
noi	**fuggimmo**
voi	**fuggiste**
loro	**fuggirono**

PLUPERFECT

io	**ero fuggito/a**
tu	**eri fuggito/a**
lui/lei/Lei	**era fuggito/a**
noi	**eravamo fuggiti/e**
voi	**eravate fuggiti/e**
loro	**erano fuggiti/e**

IMPERATIVE

fuggi
fuggiamo
fuggite

EXAMPLE PHRASES

Non c'è bisogno che tu leghi il cane alla sedia: non, **fuggirà**. *There is no need for you to tie your dog to the chair: it won't run off.*

Se ci scopriranno, **fuggiremo**. *If they find us we'll run for it.*

Fuggirono di prigione. *They escaped from prison.*

La polizia! **Fuggiamo**! *It's the police! Run for it!*

Italic letters in Italian words show where stress does not follow the usual rules.

immergere (to immerse)

PRESENT

io	**immergo**
tu	**immergi**
lui/lei/Lei	**immerge**
noi	**immergiamo**
voi	**immergete**
loro	**immergono**

PRESENT SUBJUNCTIVE

io	**immerga**
tu	**immerga**
lui/lei/Lei	**immerga**
noi	**immergiamo**
voi	**immergiate**
loro	**immergano**

PERFECT

io	**ho immerso**
tu	**hai immerso**
lui/lei/Lei	**ha immerso**
noi	**abbiamo immerso**
voi	**avete immerso**
loro	**hanno immerso**

IMPERFECT

io	**immergevo**
tu	**immergevi**
lui/lei/Lei	**immergeva**
noi	**immergevamo**
voi	**immergevate**
loro	**immergevano**

GERUND
immergendo

PAST PARTICIPLE
immerso

EXAMPLE PHRASES

Ha immerso il metallo incandescente nell'acqua. *He plunged the red-hot metal into the water.*

Non la disturbare: **è immersa** nel lavoro. *Don't disturb her: she's deep in her work.*

Si **immergevano** nello studio ogni sera. *They immersed themselves in their studies every night.*

Ha scoperto il relitto **immergendosi** poco lontano. *He discovered the wreck when he was diving not far away.*

Remember that subject pronouns are not used very often in Italian.

immergere

FUTURE

io	**immergerò**
tu	**immergerai**
lui/lei/Lei	**immergerà**
noi	**immergeremo**
voi	**immergerete**
loro	**immergeranno**

CONDITIONAL

io	**immergerei**
tu	**immergeresti**
lui/lei/Lei	**immergerebbe**
noi	**immergeremmo**
voi	**immergereste**
loro	**immergerebbero**

PAST HISTORIC

io	**immersi**
tu	**immergesti**
lui/lei/Lei	**immerse**
noi	**immergemmo**
voi	**immergeste**
loro	**immersero**

PLUPERFECT

io	**avevo immerso**
tu	**avevi immerso**
lui/lei/Lei	**aveva immerso**
noi	**avevamo immerso**
voi	**avevate immerso**
loro	**avevano immerso**

IMPERATIVE

immergi
immergiamo
immergete

EXAMPLE PHRASES

Ci **immergeremo** nelle acque dell'Adriatico. *We'll dive in the waters of the Adriatic.*

Il sottomarino si **immerse**. *The submarine submerged.*

Italic letters in Italian words show where stress does not follow the usual rules.

intendere (to understand)

PRESENT

io	**intendo**
tu	**intendi**
lui/lei/Lei	**intende**
noi	**intendiamo**
voi	**intendete**
loro	**intendono**

PRESENT SUBJUNCTIVE

io	**intenda**
tu	**intenda**
lui/lei/Lei	**intenda**
noi	**intendiamo**
voi	**intendiate**
loro	**intendano**

PERFECT

io	**ho inteso**
tu	**hai inteso**
lui/lei/Lei	**ha inteso**
noi	**abbiamo inteso**
voi	**avete inteso**
loro	**hanno inteso**

IMPERFECT

io	**intendevo**
tu	**intendevi**
lui/lei/Lei	**intendeva**
noi	**intendevamo**
voi	**intendevate**
loro	**intendevano**

GERUND
intendendo

PAST PARTICIPLE
inteso

EXAMPLE PHRASES

Dipende da cosa **intendi** per "giustizia". *It depends what you mean by "justice".*

Si **intende** di fotografia. *She knows about photography.*

Non riusciamo a capire che cosa **intendano**. *We don't know what they mean.*

Siamo sicuri che si **intenda** di automobili? *Can we be sure he knows about cars?*

Ci **siamo intesi**? *Is that clear?*

Cosa **intendevi**? *What did you mean?*

Remember that subject pronouns are not used very often in Italian.

intendere

FUTURE

io	**intenderò**
tu	**intenderai**
lui/lei/Lei	**intenderà**
noi	**intenderemo**
voi	**intenderete**
loro	**intenderanno**

CONDITIONAL

io	**intenderei**
tu	**intenderesti**
lui/lei/Lei	**intenderebbe**
noi	**intenderemmo**
voi	**intendereste**
loro	**intenderebbero**

PAST HISTORIC

io	**intesi**
tu	**intendesti**
lui/lei/Lei	**intese**
noi	**intendemmo**
voi	**intendeste**
loro	**intesero**

PLUPERFECT

io	**avevo inteso**
tu	**avevi inteso**
lui/lei/Lei	**aveva inteso**
noi	**avevamo inteso**
voi	**avevate inteso**
loro	**avevano inteso**

IMPERATIVE

intendi
intendiamo
intendete

EXAMPLE PHRASES

Noi due non ci **intenderemo** mai. *We two will never agree.*
Intenderesti dire che ho sbagliato? *Are you saying I made a mistake?*

Italic letters in Italian words show where stress does not follow the usual rules.

invadere (to invade)

PRESENT

io	**invado**
tu	**invadi**
lui/lei/Lei	**invade**
noi	**invadiamo**
voi	**invadete**
loro	**invadono**

PRESENT SUBJUNCTIVE

io	**invada**
tu	**invada**
lui/lei/Lei	**invada**
noi	**invadiamo**
voi	**invadiate**
loro	**invadano**

PERFECT

io	**ho invaso**
tu	**hai invaso**
lui/lei/Lei	**ha invaso**
noi	**abbiamo invaso**
voi	**avete invaso**
loro	**hanno invaso**

IMPERFECT

io	**invadevo**
tu	**invadevi**
lui/lei/Lei	**invadeva**
noi	**invadevamo**
voi	**invadevate**
loro	**invadevano**

GERUND
invadendo

PAST PARTICIPLE
invaso

EXAMPLE PHRASES

La folla **invade** la piazza. *The crowd is streaming into the square.*

I tifosi **hanno invaso** il campo. *The fans invaded the pitch.*

L'esercito stava **invadendo** la città. *The army was taking possession of the city.*

invadere

FUTURE

io	**invaderò**
tu	**invaderai**
lui/lei/Lei	**invaderà**
noi	**invaderemo**
voi	**invaderete**
loro	**invaderanno**

CONDITIONAL

io	**invaderei**
tu	**invaderesti**
lui/lei/Lei	**invaderebbe**
noi	**invaderemmo**
voi	**invadereste**
loro	**invaderebbero**

PAST HISTORIC

io	**invasi**
tu	**invadesti**
lui/lei/Lei	**invase**
noi	**invademmo**
voi	**invadeste**
loro	**invasero**

PLUPERFECT

io	**avevo invaso**
tu	**avevi invaso**
lui/lei/Lei	**aveva invaso**
noi	**avevamo invaso**
voi	**avevate invaso**
loro	**avevano invaso**

IMPERATIVE

invadi
invadiamo
invadete

EXAMPLE PHRASES

Senza steccati le pecore **invaderebbero** i campi. *Without fences the sheep would overrun the fields.*

Il virus **invase** il mio computer. *The virus infected my computer.*

Italic letters in Italian words show where stress does not follow the usual rules.

invecchiare (to get old)

PRESENT		PRESENT SUBJUNCTIVE	
io	**invecchio**	io	**invecchi**
tu	**invecchi**	tu	**invecchi**
lui/lei/Lei	**invecchia**	lui/lei/Lei	**invecchi**
noi	**invecchiamo**	noi	**invecchiamo**
voi	**invecchiate**	voi	**invecchiate**
loro	**invecchiano**	loro	**invecchino**

PERFECT		IMPERFECT	
io	**sono invecchiato/a**	io	**invecchiavo**
tu	**sei invecchiato/a**	tu	**invecchiavi**
lui/lei/Lei	**è invecchiato/a**	lui/lei/Lei	**invecchiava**
noi	**siamo invecchiati/e**	noi	**invecchiavamo**
voi	**siete invecchiati/e**	voi	**invecchiavate**
loro	**sono invecchiati/e**	loro	**invecchiavano**

GERUND	PAST PARTICIPLE
invecchiando	**invecchiato**

EXAMPLE PHRASES

La barba ti **invecchia**. *The beard makes you look older.*

Tutti **invecchiano** prima o poi. *Everyone gets old sooner or later.*

Questo vino **è invecchiato** in botti di rovere. *This wine is aged in oak casks.*

Invecchiava a vista d'occhio. *He was visibly ageing.*

Il vino migliora **invecchiando**. *Wine gets better with age.*

Molti hanno paura di **invecchiare**. *A lot of people are afraid of getting old.*

Remember that subject pronouns are not used very often in Italian.

invecchiare

FUTURE

io	**invecchierò**
tu	**invecchierai**
lui/lei/Lei	**invecchierà**
noi	**invecchieremo**
voi	**invecchierete**
loro	**invecchieranno**

CONDITIONAL

io	**invecchierei**
tu	**invecchieresti**
lui/lei/Lei	**invecchierebbe**
noi	**invecchieremmo**
voi	**invecchiereste**
loro	**invecchierebbero**

PAST HISTORIC

io	**invecchiai**
tu	**invecchiasti**
lui/lei/Lei	**invecchiò**
noi	**invecchiammo**
voi	**invecchiaste**
loro	**invecchiarono**

PLUPERFECT

io	**ero invecchiato/a**
tu	**eri invecchiato/a**
lui/lei/Lei	**era invecchiato/a**
noi	**eravamo invecchiati/e**
voi	**eravate invecchiati/e**
loro	**erano invecchiati/e**

IMPERATIVE
invecchia
invecchiamo
invecchiate

EXAMPLE PHRASES

Quando la rividi **era** molto **invecchiata**. *When I saw her again she'd aged a lot.*

Italic letters in Italian words show where stress does not follow the usual rules.

inviare (to send)

PRESENT

io	**invio**
tu	**invii**
lui/lei/Lei	**invia**
noi	**inviamo**
voi	**inviate**
loro	**inviano**

PRESENT SUBJUNCTIVE

io	**invii**
tu	**invii**
lui/lei/Lei	**invii**
noi	**inviamo**
voi	**inviate**
loro	**inviino**

PERFECT

io	**ho inviato**
tu	**hai inviato**
lui/lei/Lei	**ha inviato**
noi	**abbiamo inviato**
voi	**avete inviato**
loro	**hanno inviato**

IMPERFECT

io	**inviavo**
tu	**inviavi**
lui/lei/Lei	**inviava**
noi	**inviavamo**
voi	**inviavate**
loro	**inviavano**

GERUND

inviando

PAST PARTICIPLE

inviato

EXAMPLE PHRASES

Per prenotare è necessario che tu **invii** una mail. *You have to send an email to book.*

Non **ho** ancora **inviato** la domanda di iscrizione. *I haven't sent the enrolment form off yet.*

Il figlio le **inviava** un sms tutte le sere. *Her son texted her every evening.*

Potete partecipare **inviando** il video. *You can take part by sending a videoclip.*

Remember that subject pronouns are not used very often in Italian.

inviare

FUTURE

io	**invierò**
tu	**invierai**
lui/lei/Lei	**invierà**
noi	**invieremo**
voi	**invierete**
loro	**invieranno**

CONDITIONAL

io	**invierei**
tu	**invieresti**
lui/lei/Lei	**invierebbe**
noi	**invieremmo**
voi	**inviereste**
loro	**invierebbero**

PAST HISTORIC

io	**inviai**
tu	**inviasti**
lui/lei/Lei	**inviò**
noi	**inviammo**
voi	**inviaste**
loro	**inviarono**

PLUPERFECT

io	**avevo inviato**
tu	**avevi inviato**
lui/lei/Lei	**aveva inviato**
noi	**avevamo inviato**
voi	**avevate inviato**
loro	**avevano inviato**

IMPERATIVE

invia
inviamo
inviate

EXAMPLE PHRASES

Vi **invieremo** ulteriori dettagli in seguito. *We will send you further details later.*

Ti **invierei** le informazioni, ma non ho la tua mail. *I'd send you the information, but I haven't got your email address.*

Quando arrivi, **inviami** un sms. *Text me when you arrive.*

Italic letters in Italian words show where stress does not follow the usual rules.

lasciare (to leave)

PRESENT		PRESENT SUBJUNCTIVE	
io	**lascio**	io	**lasci**
tu	**lasci**	tu	**lasci**
lui/lei/Lei	**lascia**	lui/lei/Lei	**lasci**
noi	**lasciamo**	noi	**lasciamo**
voi	**lasciate**	voi	**lasciate**
loro	**lasciano**	loro	**lascino**

PERFECT		IMPERFECT	
io	**ho lasciato**	io	**lasciavo**
tu	**hai lasciato**	tu	**lasciavi**
lui/lei/Lei	**ha lasciato**	lui/lei/Lei	**lasciava**
noi	**abbiamo lasciato**	noi	**lasciavamo**
voi	**avete lasciato**	voi	**lasciavate**
loro	**hanno lasciato**	loro	**lasciavano**

GERUND
lasciando

PAST PARTICIPLE
lasciato

EXAMPLE PHRASES

Mio padre non mi **lascia** uscire fino a tardi. *My father doesn't let me stay out late.*

È meglio che tu **lasci** acceso il vivavoce. *You'd better leave the loudspeaker on.*

I miei si **sono lasciati** un anno fa. *My parents split up a year ago.*

La madre non lo **lasciava** mai solo un minuto. *His mother never left him alone for a single minute.*

lasciare

FUTURE

io	lascerò
tu	lascerai
lui/lei/Lei	lascerà
noi	lasceremo
voi	lascerete
loro	lasceranno

CONDITIONAL

io	lascerei
tu	lasceresti
lui/lei/Lei	lascerebbe
noi	lasceremmo
voi	lascereste
loro	lascerebbero

PAST HISTORIC

io	lasciai
tu	lasciasti
lui/lei/Lei	lasciò
noi	lasciammo
voi	lasciaste
loro	lasciarono

PLUPERFECT

io	avevo lasciato
tu	avevi lasciato
lui/lei/Lei	aveva lasciato
noi	avevamo lasciato
voi	avevate lasciato
loro	avevano lasciato

IMPERATIVE

lascia
lasciamo
lasciate

EXAMPLE PHRASES

Fa caldo, **lascerò** a casa il maglione. *It's hot, so I'll leave my jumper at home.*

Il marito la **lasciò** per un'altra. *Her husband left her for another woman.*

Lascia fare a me. *Let me do it.*

Lasciamo stare, non vale la pena arrabbiarsi. *Let's forget it, it's not worth getting angry about.*

Italic letters in Italian words show where stress does not follow the usual rules.

leggere (to read)

PRESENT		PRESENT SUBJUNCTIVE	
io	**leggo**	io	**legga**
tu	**leggi**	tu	**legga**
lui/lei/Lei	**legge**	lui/lei/Lei	**legga**
noi	**leggiamo**	noi	**leggiamo**
voi	**leggete**	voi	**leggiate**
loro	**leggono**	loro	**leggano**

PERFECT		IMPERFECT	
io	**ho letto**	io	**leggevo**
tu	**hai letto**	tu	**leggevi**
lui/lei/Lei	**ha letto**	lui/lei/Lei	**leggeva**
noi	**abbiamo letto**	noi	**leggevamo**
voi	**avete letto**	voi	**leggevate**
loro	**hanno letto**	loro	**leggevano**

GERUND	PAST PARTICIPLE
leggendo	**letto**

EXAMPLE PHRASES

Legge il giornale tutti i giorni. *She reads the paper every day.*

Non **ho** ancora **letto** quel libro. *I haven't read that book yet.*

Leggevo molto prima di iniziare a lavorare. *I read a lot before I started working.*

Non li disturbiamo: stanno **leggendo**. *Don't let's disturb them, they're reading.*

Le piace molto **leggere**. *She loves reading.*

Remember that subject pronouns are not used very often in Italian.

leggere

FUTURE

io	**leggerò**
tu	**leggerai**
lui/lei/Lei	**leggerà**
noi	**leggeremo**
voi	**leggerete**
loro	**leggeranno**

CONDITIONAL

io	**leggerei**
tu	**leggeresti**
lui/lei/Lei	**leggerebbe**
noi	**leggeremmo**
voi	**leggereste**
loro	**leggerebbero**

PAST HISTORIC

io	**lessi**
tu	**leggesti**
lui/lei/Lei	**lesse**
noi	**leggemmo**
voi	**leggeste**
loro	**lessero**

PLUPERFECT

io	**avevo letto**
tu	**avevi letto**
lui/lei/Lei	**aveva letto**
noi	**avevamo letto**
voi	**avevate letto**
loro	**avevano letto**

IMPERATIVE

leggi
leggiamo
leggete

EXAMPLE PHRASES

Durante le vacanze **leggerò** un romanzo. *I'll read a novel during the holidays.*

Mi **leggeresti** le istruzioni? Sono senza occhiali. *Could you read me the instructions? I haven't got my glasses.*

Leggete a voce alta, per favore. *Read aloud please.*

Italic letters in Italian words show where stress does not follow the usual rules.

mangiare (to eat)

PRESENT

io	**mangio**
tu	**mangi**
lui/lei/Lei	**mangia**
noi	**mangiamo**
voi	**mangiate**
loro	**mangiano**

PRESENT SUBJUNCTIVE

io	**mangi**
tu	**mangi**
lui/lei/Lei	**mangi**
noi	**mangiamo**
voi	**mangiate**
loro	**mangino**

PERFECT

io	**ho mangiato**
tu	**hai mangiato**
lui/lei/Lei	**ha mangiato**
noi	**abbiamo mangiato**
voi	**avete mangiato**
loro	**hanno mangiato**

IMPERFECT

io	**mangiavo**
tu	**mangiavi**
lui/lei/Lei	**mangiava**
noi	**mangiavamo**
voi	**mangiavate**
loro	**mangiavano**

GERUND
mangiando

PAST PARTICIPLE
mangiato

EXAMPLE PHRASES

Non **mangio** carne. *I don't eat meat.*

Si **mangia** bene in quel ristorante. *The food is good in that restaurant.*

Chi **ha mangiato** l'ultima fetta di torta? *Who ate the last slice of cake?*

Ultimamente sto **mangiando** troppo. *I've been eating too much lately.*

Remember that subject pronouns are not used very often in Italian.

mangiare

FUTURE

io	**mangerò**
tu	**mangerai**
lui/lei/Lei	**mangerà**
noi	**mangeremo**
voi	**mangerete**
loro	**mangeranno**

CONDITIONAL

io	**mangerei**
tu	**mangeresti**
lui/lei/Lei	**mangerebbe**
noi	**mangeremmo**
voi	**mangereste**
loro	**mangerebbero**

PAST HISTORIC

io	**mangiai**
tu	**mangiasti**
lui/lei/Lei	**mangiò**
noi	**mangiammo**
voi	**mangiaste**
loro	**mangiarono**

PLUPERFECT

io	**avevo mangiato**
tu	**avevi mangiato**
lui/lei/Lei	**aveva mangiato**
noi	**avevamo mangiato**
voi	**avevate mangiato**
loro	**avevano mangiato**

IMPERATIVE

mangia
mangiamo
mangiate

EXAMPLE PHRASES

Domani **mangeremo** pesce. *We'll have fish tomorrow.*

Mangerei volentieri del gelato. *I'd like some ice cream.*

Mangiarono troppo e fecero indigestione. *They ate too much and got indigestion.*

Mangia che la minestra si raffredda. *Eat your soup, it's getting cold.*

Italic letters in Italian words show where stress does not follow the usual rules.

mettere (to put)

PRESENT

io	**metto**
tu	**metti**
lui/lei/Lei	**mette**
noi	**mettiamo**
voi	**mettete**
loro	**mettono**

PRESENT SUBJUNCTIVE

io	**metta**
tu	**metta**
lui/lei/Lei	**metta**
noi	**mettiamo**
voi	**mettiate**
loro	**mettano**

PERFECT

io	**ho messo**
tu	**hai messo**
lui/lei/Lei	**ha messo**
noi	**abbiamo messo**
voi	**avete messo**
loro	**hanno messo**

IMPERFECT

io	**mettevo**
tu	**mettevi**
lui/lei/Lei	**metteva**
noi	**mettevamo**
voi	**mettevate**
loro	**mettevano**

GERUND

mettendo

PAST PARTICIPLE

messo

EXAMPLE PHRASES

Non **metto** più quelle scarpe. *I don't wear those shoes any more.*

È meglio che tu **metta** la sveglia. *You'd better set the alarm.*

Hai messo i bambini a letto? *Have you put the children to bed?*

Quanto tempo ci **hai messo**? *How long did it take you?*

Si **metteva** sempre un vecchio maglione blu. *She always wore an old blue jumper.*

Remember that subject pronouns are not used very often in Italian.

mettere

FUTURE

io	**metterò**
tu	**metterai**
lui/lei/Lei	**metterà**
noi	**metteremo**
voi	**metterete**
loro	**metteranno**

CONDITIONAL

io	**metterei**
tu	**metteresti**
lui/lei/Lei	**metterebbe**
noi	**metteremmo**
voi	**mettereste**
loro	**metterebbero**

PAST HISTORIC

io	**misi**
tu	**mettesti**
lui/lei/Lei	**mise**
noi	**mettemmo**
voi	**metteste**
loro	**misero**

PLUPERFECT

io	**avevo messo**
tu	**avevi messo**
lui/lei/Lei	**aveva messo**
noi	**avevamo messo**
voi	**avevate messo**
loro	**avevano messo**

IMPERATIVE

metti
mettiamo
mettete

EXAMPLE PHRASES

Metterò un annuncio sul giornale. *I'll put an advert in the paper.*

Quanto ci **metteresti** lavorando giorno e notte? *How long would it take you if you worked day and night?*

Si **misero** a sedere e aspettarono. *They sat down and waited.*

Mettiti là e aspetta. *Wait there.*

Italic letters in Italian words show where stress does not follow the usual rules.

morire (to die)

PRESENT

io	**muoio**
tu	**muori**
lui/lei/Lei	**muore**
noi	**moriamo**
voi	**morite**
loro	**muoiono**

PRESENT SUBJUNCTIVE

io	**muoia**
tu	**muoia**
lui/lei/Lei	**muoia**
noi	**moriamo**
voi	**moriate**
loro	**muoiano**

PERFECT

io	**sono morto/a**
tu	**sei morto/a**
lui/lei/Lei	**è morto/a**
noi	**siamo morti/e**
voi	**siete morti/e**
loro	**sono morti/e**

IMPERFECT

io	**morivo**
tu	**morivi**
lui/lei/Lei	**moriva**
noi	**morivamo**
voi	**morivate**
loro	**morivano**

GERUND
morendo

PAST PARTICIPLE
morto

EXAMPLE PHRASES

Muoio di sete. *I'm parched.*

Sono morti in un incidente. *They were killed in an accident.*

Sta **morendo** di fame. *She's starving.*

Moriva dalla voglia di raccontarle tutto. *He was dying to tell her everything.*

Remember that subject pronouns are not used very often in Italian.

morire

FUTURE

io	**morirò**
tu	**morirai**
lui/lei/Lei	**morirà**
noi	**moriremo**
voi	**morirete**
loro	**moriranno**

CONDITIONAL

io	**morirei**
tu	**moriresti**
lui/lei/Lei	**morirebbe**
noi	**moriremmo**
voi	**morireste**
loro	**morirebbero**

PAST HISTORIC

io	**morii**
tu	**moristi**
lui/lei/Lei	**morì**
noi	**morimmo**
voi	**moriste**
loro	**morirono**

PLUPERFECT

io	**ero morto/a**
tu	**eri morto/a**
lui/lei/Lei	**era morto/a**
noi	**eravamo morti/e**
voi	**eravate morti/e**
loro	**erano morti/e**

IMPERATIVE

muori
moriamo
morite

EXAMPLE PHRASES

Morirei di paura, ma lo farei. *I'd be scared to death, but I'd do it.*

Morì nel 1857. *He died in 1857.*

Il padre **era morto** in un incidente stradale. *His father had been killed in a car crash.*

Italic letters in Italian words show where stress does not follow the usual rules.

muovere (to move)

PRESENT

io	**muovo**
tu	**muovi**
lui/lei/Lei	**muove**
noi	**muoviamo**
voi	**muovete**
loro	**muovono**

PRESENT SUBJUNCTIVE

io	**muova**
tu	**muova**
lui/lei/Lei	**muova**
noi	**muoviamo**
voi	**muoviate**
loro	**muovano**

PERFECT

io	**ho mosso**
tu	**hai mosso**
lui/lei/Lei	**ha mosso**
noi	**abbiamo mosso**
voi	**avete mosso**
loro	**hanno mosso**

IMPERFECT

io	**muovevo**
tu	**muovevi**
lui/lei/Lei	**muoveva**
noi	**muovevamo**
voi	**muovevate**
loro	**muovevano**

GERUND

muovendo

PAST PARTICIPLE

mosso

EXAMPLE PHRASES

Non si **muove**. *It won't move.*

Ho mosso l'alfiere per dare scacco al re. *I moved the bishop to check the king.*

Ti **sei mosso** e la foto è sfocata. *You moved and the photo is out of focus.*

Non **muovevo** più la gamba per il dolore. *I could no longer move my leg because of the pain.*

Il meccanismo si aziona **muovendo** la leva. *You work the mechanism by moving the lever.*

Remember that subject pronouns are not used very often in Italian.

muovere

FUTURE

io	**muoverò**
tu	**muoverai**
lui/lei/Lei	**muoverà**
noi	**muoveremo**
voi	**muoverete**
loro	**muoveranno**

CONDITIONAL

io	**muoverei**
tu	**muoveresti**
lui/lei/Lei	**muoverebbe**
noi	**muoveremmo**
voi	**muovereste**
loro	**muoverebbero**

PAST HISTORIC

io	**mossi**
tu	**muovesti**
lui/lei/Lei	**mosse**
noi	**muovemmo**
voi	**muoveste**
loro	**mossero**

PLUPERFECT

io	**avevo mosso**
tu	**avevi mosso**
lui/lei/Lei	**aveva mosso**
noi	**avevamo mosso**
voi	**avevate mosso**
loro	**avevano mosso**

IMPERATIVE

muovi
muoviamo
muovete

EXAMPLE PHRASES

Non ti **muovere**! *Don't move!*

Muoviti, o perdiamo il treno! *Hurry up, or we'll miss the train!*

Italic letters in Italian words show where stress does not follow the usual rules.

nascere (to be born)

PRESENT

io	**nasco**
tu	**nasci**
lui/lei/Lei	**nasce**
noi	**nasciamo**
voi	**nascete**
loro	**nascono**

PRESENT SUBJUNCTIVE

io	**nasca**
tu	**nasca**
lui/lei/Lei	**nasca**
noi	**nasciamo**
voi	**nasciate**
loro	**nascano**

PERFECT

io	**sono nato/a**
tu	**sei nato/a**
lui/lei/Lei	**è nato/a**
noi	**siamo nati/e**
voi	**siete nati/e**
loro	**sono nati/e**

IMPERFECT

io	**nascevo**
tu	**nascevi**
lui/lei/Lei	**nasceva**
noi	**nascevamo**
voi	**nascevate**
loro	**nascevano**

GERUND
nascendo

PAST PARTICIPLE
nato

EXAMPLE PHRASES

Speriamo che il bambino **nasca** dopo il trasloco. *We're hoping the baby will be born after the move.*

Sono nata il 28 aprile. *I was born on the 28th of April.*

È nato nel 1998. *He was born in 1998.*

Remember that subject pronouns are not used very often in Italian.

nascere

FUTURE

io	**nascerò**
tu	**nascerai**
lui/lei/Lei	**nascerà**
noi	**nasceremo**
voi	**nascerete**
loro	**nasceranno**

CONDITIONAL

io	**nascerei**
tu	**nasceresti**
lui/lei/Lei	**nascerebbe**
noi	**nasceremmo**
voi	**nascereste**
loro	**nascerebbero**

PAST HISTORIC

io	**nacqui**
tu	**nascesti**
lui/lei/Lei	**nacque**
noi	**nascemmo**
voi	**nasceste**
loro	**nacquero**

PLUPERFECT

io	**ero nato/a**
tu	**eri nato/a**
lui/lei/Lei	**era nato/a**
noi	**eravamo nati/e**
voi	**eravate nati/e**
loro	**erano nati/e**

IMPERATIVE

nasci
nasciamo
nascete

EXAMPLE PHRASES

Il bambino **nascerà** tra due settimane. *The baby is due in two weeks.*

Franz Kafka **nacque** nel 1883. *Franz Kafka was born in 1883.*

Lasciò molto presto la casa dove **era nato**. *Very soon he left the house where he was born.*

Italic letters in Italian words show where stress does not follow the usual rules.

nuocere (to harm)

PRESENT		PRESENT SUBJUNCTIVE	
io	**nuoccio**	io	**nuoccia**
tu	**nuoci**	tu	**nuoccia**
lui/lei/Lei	**nuoce**	lui/lei/Lei	**nuoccia**
noi	**nuociamo**	noi	**nuociamo**
voi	**nuocete**	voi	**nuociate**
loro	**nuocciono**	loro	**nuocciano**

PERFECT		IMPERFECT	
io	**ho nuociuto**	io	**nuocevo**
tu	**hai nuociuto**	tu	**nuocevi**
lui/lei/Lei	**ha nuociuto**	lui/lei/Lei	**nuoceva**
noi	**abbiamo nuociuto**	noi	**nuocevamo**
voi	**avete nuociuto**	voi	**nuocevate**
loro	**hanno nuociuto**	loro	**nuocevano**

GERUND
nuocendo

PAST PARTICIPLE
nuociuto

EXAMPLE PHRASES

Il fumo **nuoce** alla salute. *Smoking is bad for your health.*

Si pensa che **nuoccia** all'ambiente. *It is thought to be bad for the environment.*

Le cattive conoscenze **hanno nuociuto** alla sua reputazione. *His disreputable associates have damaged his reputation.*

Anche se gli **nuoceva**, continuava a bere. *Despite the harm it was doing him, he went on drinking.*

Remember that subject pronouns are not used very often in Italian.

nuocere

FUTURE

io	**nuocerò**
tu	**nuocerai**
lui/lei/Lei	**nuocerà**
noi	**nuoceremo**
voi	**nuocerete**
loro	**nuoceranno**

CONDITIONAL

io	**nuocerei**
tu	**nuoceresti**
lui/lei/Lei	**nuocerebbe**
noi	**nuoceremmo**
voi	**nuocereste**
loro	**nuocerebbero**

PAST HISTORIC

io	**nocqui**
tu	**nuocesti**
lui/lei/Lei	**nocque**
noi	**nuocemmo**
voi	**nuoceste**
loro	**nocquero**

PLUPERFECT

io	**avevo nuociuto**
tu	**avevi nuociuto**
lui/lei/Lei	**aveva nuociuto**
noi	**avevamo nuociuto**
voi	**avevate nuociuto**
loro	**avevano nuociuto**

IMPERATIVE

nuoci
nuociamo
nuocete

EXAMPLE PHRASES

Un po' di vino non ti **nuocerà**. *A drop of wine won't do you any harm.*

Una settimana al mare non mi **nuocerebbe**. *A week at the seaside would do me no harm.*

Italic letters in Italian words show where stress does not follow the usual rules.

offendere (to offend)

PRESENT

io	**offendo**
tu	**offendi**
lui/lei/Lei	**offende**
noi	**offendiamo**
voi	**offendete**
loro	**offendono**

PRESENT SUBJUNCTIVE

io	**offenda**
tu	**offenda**
lui/lei/Lei	**offenda**
noi	**offendiamo**
voi	**offendiate**
loro	**offendano**

PERFECT

io	**ho offeso**
tu	**hai offeso**
lui/lei/Lei	**ha offeso**
noi	**abbiamo offeso**
voi	**avete offeso**
loro	**hanno offeso**

IMPERFECT

io	**offendevo**
tu	**offendevi**
lui/lei/Lei	**offendeva**
noi	**offendevamo**
voi	**offendevate**
loro	**offendevano**

GERUND

offendendo

PAST PARTICIPLE

offeso

EXAMPLE PHRASES

Se non vieni mi **offendo**. *I'll be offended if you don't come.*

Si è **offeso** per non essere stato invitato. *He took offence because they didn't invite him.*

Da piccolo si **offendeva** per un nonnulla. *When he was a little boy he got upset over the slightest thing.*

Cambia tono: mi stai **offendendo**! *Don't talk like that: I find it offensive.*

Non avevo intenzione di **offenderti**. *I didn't mean to insult you.*

Remember that subject pronouns are not used very often in Italian.

offendere

FUTURE

io	**offenderò**
tu	**offenderai**
lui/lei/Lei	**offenderà**
noi	**offenderemo**
voi	**offenderete**
loro	**offenderanno**

CONDITIONAL

io	**offenderei**
tu	**offenderesti**
lui/lei/Lei	**offenderebbe**
noi	**offenderemmo**
voi	**offendereste**
loro	**offenderebbero**

PAST HISTORIC

io	**offesi**
tu	**offendesti**
lui/lei/Lei	**offese**
noi	**offendemmo**
voi	**offendeste**
loro	**offesero**

PLUPERFECT

io	**avevo offeso**
tu	**avevi offeso**
lui/lei/Lei	**aveva offeso**
noi	**avevamo offeso**
voi	**avevate offeso**
loro	**avevano offeso**

IMPERATIVE

offendi
offendiamo
offendete

EXAMPLE PHRASES

Dimmi tutto: prometto che non mi **offenderò**. *Tell me everything: I promise I won't be offended.*

Se glielo dicessi, si **offenderebbe**. *If I told him that he'd be offended.*

L'**avevamo offeso** e non ci parlava più. *We'd offended him and he wouldn't speak to us any more.*

Italic letters in Italian words show where stress does not follow the usual rules.

offrire (to offer)

PRESENT		PRESENT SUBJUNCTIVE	
io	offro	io	offra
tu	offri	tu	offra
lui/lei/Lei	offre	lui/lei/Lei	offra
noi	offriamo	noi	offriamo
voi	offrite	voi	offriate
loro	offrono	loro	offrano

PERFECT		IMPERFECT	
io	ho offerto	io	offrivo
tu	hai offerto	tu	offrivi
lui/lei/Lei	ha offerto	lui/lei/Lei	offriva
noi	abbiamo offerto	noi	offrivamo
voi	avete offerto	voi	offrivate
loro	hanno offerto	loro	offrivano

GERUND
offrendo

PAST PARTICIPLE
offerto

EXAMPLE PHRASES

Offro io, questa volta! *I'll pay this time!*

Spero si **offrano** di aiutarci. *I hope they'll offer to help us.*

Mi **ha offerto** un passaggio. *He offered me a lift.*

Nessuno si **è offerto** volontario. *Nobody volunteered.*

Offriva sempre il suo aiuto a tutti. *She always offered help to everyone.*

Remember that subject pronouns are not used very often in Italian.

offrire

FUTURE

io	**offrirò**
tu	**offrirai**
lui/lei/Lei	**offrirà**
noi	**offriremo**
voi	**offrirete**
loro	**offriranno**

CONDITIONAL

io	**offrirei**
tu	**offriresti**
lui/lei/Lei	**offrirebbe**
noi	**offriremmo**
voi	**offrireste**
loro	**offrirebbero**

PAST HISTORIC

io	**offrii**
tu	**offristi**
lui/lei/Lei	**offrì**
noi	**offrimmo**
voi	**offriste**
loro	**offrirono**

PLUPERFECT

io	**avevo offerto**
tu	**avevi offerto**
lui/lei/Lei	**aveva offerto**
noi	**avevamo offerto**
voi	**avevate offerto**
loro	**avevano offerto**

IMPERATIVE

offri
offriamo
offrite

EXAMPLE PHRASES

L'università **offrirà** consulenza e orientamento. *The university will provide guidance and advice.*

Mi **offriresti** una sigaretta? *Could you let me have a cigarette?*

Le **offrirono** un lavoro. *They offered her a job.*

Offri da bere agli amici! *Offer our friends a drink!*

Italic letters in Italian words show where stress does not follow the usual rules.

pagare (to pay)

PRESENT		PRESENT SUBJUNCTIVE	
io	**pago**	io	**paghi**
tu	**paghi**	tu	**paghi**
lui/lei/Lei	**paga**	lui/lei/Lei	**paghi**
noi	**paghiamo**	noi	**paghiamo**
voi	**pagate**	voi	**paghiate**
loro	**pagano**	loro	**paghino**

PERFECT		IMPERFECT	
io	**ho pagato**	io	**pagavo**
tu	**hai pagato**	tu	**pagavi**
lui/lei/Lei	**ha pagato**	lui/lei/Lei	**pagava**
noi	**abbiamo pagato**	noi	**pagavamo**
voi	**avete pagato**	voi	**pagavate**
loro	**hanno pagato**	loro	**pagavano**

GERUND	PAST PARTICIPLE
pagando	pagato

EXAMPLE PHRASES

Pago io. *I'll pay.*

Hai pagato il conto? *Have you paid the bill?*

Quando uscivamo insieme **pagava** sempre lui. *When we went out together he always paid.*

Pagando si ottiene tutto. *You can get anything if you pay for it.*

Avevo finito di **pagare** la macchina il giorno dell'incidente. *I'd finished paying for the car on the day of the accident.*

Remember that subject pronouns are not used very often in Italian.

pagare

FUTURE

io	**pagherò**
tu	**pagherai**
lui/lei/Lei	**pagherà**
noi	**pagheremo**
voi	**pagherete**
loro	**pagheranno**

CONDITIONAL

io	**pagherei**
tu	**pagheresti**
lui/lei/Lei	**pagherebbe**
noi	**pagheremmo**
voi	**paghereste**
loro	**pagherebbero**

PAST HISTORIC

io	**pagai**
tu	**pagasti**
lui/lei/Lei	**pagò**
noi	**pagammo**
voi	**pagaste**
loro	**pagarono**

PLUPERFECT

io	**avevo pagato**
tu	**avevi pagato**
lui/lei/Lei	**aveva pagato**
noi	**avevamo pagato**
voi	**avevate pagato**
loro	**avevano pagato**

IMPERATIVE

paga
paghiamo
pagate

EXAMPLE PHRASES

La **pagherai**! *You'll pay for this!*

Pagherei io, ma non accettano carte di credito. *I'd pay, but they don't accept credit cards.*

Pagò un conto salatissimo. *She paid an enormous bill.*

Paga tu stavolta! *You pay this time!*

Italic letters in Italian words show where stress does not follow the usual rules.

parere (to appear)

PRESENT		PRESENT SUBJUNCTIVE	
io	paio	io	paia
tu	pari	tu	paia
lui/lei/Lei	pare	lui/lei/Lei	paia
noi	pariamo	noi	paiamo
voi	parete	voi	paiate
loro	paiono	loro	paiano

PERFECT		IMPERFECT	
io	sono parso/a	io	parevo
tu	sei parso/a	tu	parevi
lui/lei/Lei	è parso/a	lui/lei/Lei	pareva
noi	siamo parsi/e	noi	parevamo
voi	siete parsi/e	voi	parevate
loro	sono parsi/e	loro	parevano

GERUND
parendo

PAST PARTICIPLE
parso

EXAMPLE PHRASES

Mi **pare** che sia già arrivato. *I think he's already here.*

Ci **è parso** che foste stanchi. *We thought you were tired.*

Faceva solo ciò che gli **pareva**. *He did just what he liked.*

parere

FUTURE

io	**parrò**
tu	**parrai**
lui/lei/Lei	**parrà**
noi	**parremo**
voi	**parrete**
loro	**parranno**

CONDITIONAL

io	**parrei**
tu	**parresti**
lui/lei/Lei	**parrebbe**
noi	**parremmo**
voi	**parreste**
loro	**parrebbero**

PAST HISTORIC

io	**parvi**
tu	**paresti**
lui/lei/Lei	**parve**
noi	**paremmo**
voi	**pareste**
loro	**parvero**

PLUPERFECT

io	**ero parso/a**
tu	**eri parso/a**
lui/lei/Lei	**era parso/a**
noi	**eravamo parsi/e**
voi	**eravate parsi/e**
loro	**erano parsi/e**

IMPERATIVE

pari
pariamo
parete

EXAMPLE PHRASES

Mi **parrebbe** di disturbare. *I wouldn't want to be a nuisance.*

Gli **parve** che non lo volessero con loro. *He thought they didn't want him with them.*

Quella sera mi **parvero** tutti ubriachi. *They all seemed drunk that night.*

Mi **era parso** che volessi da bere. *I'd thought you wanted something to drink.*

Italic letters in Italian words show where stress does not follow the usual rules.

parlare (to speak)

PRESENT

io	**parlo**
tu	**parli**
lui/lei/Lei	**parla**
noi	**parliamo**
voi	**parlate**
loro	**parlano**

PRESENT SUBJUNCTIVE

io	**parli**
tu	**parli**
lui/lei/Lei	**parli**
noi	**parliamo**
voi	**parliate**
loro	**parlino**

PERFECT

io	**ho parlato**
tu	**hai parlato**
lui/lei/Lei	**ha parlato**
noi	**abbiamo parlato**
voi	**avete parlato**
loro	**hanno parlato**

IMPERFECT

io	**parlavo**
tu	**parlavi**
lui/lei/Lei	**parlava**
noi	**parlavamo**
voi	**parlavate**
loro	**parlavano**

GERUND
parlando

PAST PARTICIPLE
parlato

EXAMPLE PHRASES

Pronto, chi **parla**? *Hello, who's speaking?*

Di cosa **parla** quel libro? *What is that book about?*

Lascia che gli **parli** io. *Let me talk to him.*

Abbiamo parlato per ore. *We talked for hours.*

Passammo il pomeriggio **parlando** del più e del meno. *We spent the afternoon talking about this and that.*

Remember that subject pronouns are not used very often in Italian.

parlare

FUTURE

io	**parlerò**
tu	**parlerai**
lui/lei/Lei	**parlerà**
noi	**parleremo**
voi	**parlerete**
loro	**parleranno**

CONDITIONAL

io	**parlerei**
tu	**parleresti**
lui/lei/Lei	**parlerebbe**
noi	**parleremmo**
voi	**parlereste**
loro	**parlerebbero**

PAST HISTORIC

io	**parlai**
tu	**parlasti**
lui/lei/Lei	**parlò**
noi	**parlammo**
voi	**parlaste**
loro	**parlarono**

PLUPERFECT

io	**avevo parlato**
tu	**avevi parlato**
lui/lei/Lei	**aveva parlato**
noi	**avevamo parlato**
voi	**avevate parlato**
loro	**avevano parlato**

IMPERATIVE

parla
parliamo
parlate

EXAMPLE PHRASES

Gli **parlerò** di te. *I'll talk to him about you.*
Non **parlerei** mai male dei miei amici. *I'd never speak ill of my friends.*
Mi **avevano** già **parlato** di te. *They'd already talked to me about you.*
Non **parliamone** più. *Let's just forget about it.*

Italic letters in Italian words show where stress does not follow the usual rules.

pescare (to fish)

PRESENT		PRESENT SUBJUNCTIVE	
io	**pesco**	io	**peschi**
tu	**peschi**	tu	**peschi**
lui/lei/Lei	**pesca**	lui/lei/Lei	**peschi**
noi	**peschiamo**	noi	**peschiamo**
voi	**pescate**	voi	**peschiate**
loro	**pescano**	loro	**peschino**

PERFECT		IMPERFECT	
io	**ho pescato**	io	**pescavo**
tu	**hai pescato**	tu	**pescavi**
lui/lei/Lei	**ha pescato**	lui/lei/Lei	**pescava**
noi	**abbiamo pescato**	noi	**pescavamo**
voi	**avete pescato**	voi	**pescavate**
loro	**hanno pescato**	loro	**pescavano**

GERUND	PAST PARTICIPLE
pescando	pescato

EXAMPLE PHRASES

Ho pescato un pesce enorme. *I caught an enormous fish.*

Dove diavolo **hai pescato** quella giacca? *Where on earth did you get that jacket?*

Ti insegnerò a **pescare**. *I'll teach you how to fish.*

pescare

FUTURE

io	**pescherò**
tu	**pescherai**
lui/lei/Lei	**pescherà**
noi	**pescheremo**
voi	**pescherete**
loro	**pescheranno**

CONDITIONAL

io	**pescherei**
tu	**pescheresti**
lui/lei/Lei	**pescherebbe**
noi	**pescheremmo**
voi	**peschereste**
loro	**pescherebbero**

PAST HISTORIC

io	**pescai**
tu	**pescasti**
lui/lei/Lei	**pescò**
noi	**pescammo**
voi	**pescaste**
loro	**pescarono**

PLUPERFECT

io	**avevo pescato**
tu	**avevi pescato**
lui/lei/Lei	**aveva pescato**
noi	**avevamo pescato**
voi	**avevate pescato**
loro	**avevano pescato**

IMPERATIVE

pesca
peschiamo
pescate

EXAMPLE PHRASES

Io **pescherò** il pesce e tu lo cucinerai. *I'll catch the fish and you can cook it.*
Pescammo tutto il giorno. *We fished all day.*
Avevano pescato molto pesce per la cena. *They'd caught a lot of fish for dinner.*

Italic letters in Italian words show where stress does not follow the usual rules.

piacere (to be pleasing)

PRESENT

io	**piaccio**
tu	**piaci**
lui/lei/Lei	**piace**
noi	**piacciamo**
voi	**piacete**
loro	**piacciono**

PRESENT SUBJUNCTIVE

io	**piaccia**
tu	**piaccia**
lui/lei/Lei	**piaccia**
noi	**piacciamo**
voi	**piacciate**
loro	**piacciano**

PERFECT

io	**sono piaciuto/a**
tu	**sei piaciuto/a**
lui/lei/Lei	**è piaciuto/a**
noi	**siamo piaciuti/e**
voi	**siete piaciuti/e**
loro	**sono piaciuti/e**

IMPERFECT

io	**piacevo**
tu	**piacevi**
lui/lei/Lei	**piaceva**
noi	**piacevamo**
voi	**piacevate**
loro	**piacevano**

GERUND
piacendo

PAST PARTICIPLE
piaciuto

EXAMPLE PHRASES

Questa musica non mi **piace**. *I don't like this music.*

Spero che il regalo vi **piaccia**. *I hope you like the present.*

La birra non le **è** mai **piaciuta**. *She's never liked beer.*

Da piccola non mi **piacevano** i ragni. *I didn't like spiders when I was little.*

Remember that subject pronouns are not used very often in Italian.

piacere

FUTURE

io	**piacerò**
tu	**piacerai**
lui/lei/Lei	**piacerà**
noi	**piaceremo**
voi	**piacerete**
loro	**piaceranno**

CONDITIONAL

io	**piacerei**
tu	**piaceresti**
lui/lei/Lei	**piacerebbe**
noi	**piaceremmo**
voi	**piacereste**
loro	**piacerebbero**

PAST HISTORIC

io	**piacqui**
tu	**piacesti**
lui/lei/Lei	**piacque**
noi	**piacemmo**
voi	**piaceste**
loro	**piacquero**

PLUPERFECT

io	**ero piaciuto/a**
tu	**eri piaciuto/a**
lui/lei/Lei	**era piaciuto/a**
noi	**eravamo piaciuti/e**
voi	**eravate piaciuti/e**
loro	**erano piaciuti/e**

IMPERATIVE

piaci
piacciamo
piacete

EXAMPLE PHRASES

La nuova casa ti **piacerà**, vedrai. *You'll like the new house, you'll see.*

Cosa ti **piacerebbe** fare? *What would you like to do?*

Mi **piacque** appena la vidi. *I liked her as soon as I saw her.*

Vi **era piaciuto** il film? *Did you like the film?*

Italic letters in Italian words show where stress does not follow the usual rules.

piovere (to rain)

PRESENT
piove

PRESENT SUBJUNCTIVE
piova

PERFECT
ha *or* è piovuto

IMPERFECT
pioveva

GERUND
piovendo

PAST PARTICIPLE
piovuto

EXAMPLE PHRASES
Piove. *It's raining.*
Speriamo che non **piova**. *Let's hope it doesn't rain.*
Ha piovuto tutto il giorno. *It's rained all day.*
Quando sono uscita **pioveva**. *When I went out it was raining.*
Sta **piovendo**: prendi l'ombrello. *It's raining – take your umbrella.*

Remember that subject pronouns are not used very often in Italian.

piovere

FUTURE
piover*à*

CONDITIONAL
pioverebbe

PAST HISTORIC
piovve

PLUPERFECT
era *or* **aveva piovuto**

IMPERATIVE

-

EXAMPLE PHRASES

Guarda che nubi: **piover*à*** di certo. *Look at those clouds – it's going to rain for sure.*

Piovve tutta la notte. *It rained all night.*

Aveva piovuto e le strade erano bagnate. *It had been raining and the roads were wet.*

Italic letters in Italian words show where stress does not follow the usual rules.

potere (to be able)

PRESENT		PRESENT SUBJUNCTIVE	
io	**posso**	io	**possa**
tu	**puoi**	tu	**possa**
lui/lei/Lei	**può**	lui/lei/Lei	**possa**
noi	**possiamo**	noi	**possiamo**
voi	**potete**	voi	**possiate**
loro	**possono**	loro	**possano**

PERFECT		IMPERFECT	
io	**ho potuto**	io	**potevo**
tu	**hai potuto**	tu	**potevi**
lui/lei/Lei	**ha potuto**	lui/lei/Lei	**poteva**
noi	**abbiamo potuto**	noi	**potevamo**
voi	**avete potuto**	voi	**potevate**
loro	**hanno potuto**	loro	**potevano**

GERUND	PAST PARTICIPLE
potendo	potuto

EXAMPLE PHRASES

Si **può** visitare il castello tutti i giorni dell'anno. *You can visit the castle any day of the year.*

Può aver avuto un incidente. *She may have had an accident.*

Speriamo che voi **possiate** aiutarci. *We hope you can help us.*

Non è **potuto** venire. *He couldn't come.*

Non sono venuti perché non **potevano**. *They didn't come because they weren't able to.*

Potendo, eviterei di partire domani. *I'd avoid setting off tomorrow if I could.*

Remember that subject pronouns are not used very often in Italian.

potere

FUTURE

io	**potrò**
tu	**potrai**
lui/lei/Lei	**potrà**
noi	**potremo**
voi	**potrete**
loro	**potranno**

CONDITIONAL

io	**potrei**
tu	**potresti**
lui/lei/Lei	**potrebbe**
noi	**potremmo**
voi	**potreste**
loro	**potrebbero**

PAST HISTORIC

io	**potei**
tu	**potesti**
lui/lei/Lei	**poté**
noi	**potemmo**
voi	**poteste**
loro	**poterono**

PLUPERFECT

io	**avevo potuto**
tu	**avevi potuto**
lui/lei/Lei	**aveva potuto**
noi	**avevamo potuto**
voi	**avevate potuto**
loro	**avevano potuto**

IMPERATIVE

–

EXAMPLE PHRASES

Non **potrò** venire domani. *I won't be able to come tomorrow.*

Potresti aprire la finestra? *Could you open the window?*

Potrebbe essere vero. *It could be true.*

Era dispiaciuto perché non **aveva potuto** aiutarci. *He was sorry he hadn't been able to help us.*

Italic letters in Italian words show where stress does not follow the usual rules.

prefiggersi (to set oneself)

PRESENT

io	**mi prefiggo**
tu	**ti prefiggi**
lui/lei/Lei	**si prefigge**
noi	**ci prefiggiamo**
voi	**vi prefiggete**
loro	**si prefiggono**

PRESENT SUBJUNCTIVE

io	**mi prefigga**
tu	**ti prefigga**
lui/lei/Lei	**si prefigga**
noi	**ci prefiggiamo**
voi	**vi prefiggiate**
loro	**si prefiggano**

PERFECT

io	**mi sono prefisso/a**
tu	**ti sei prefisso/a**
lui/lei/Lei	**si è prefisso/a**
noi	**ci siamo prefissi/e**
voi	**vi siete prefissi/e**
loro	**si sono prefissi/e**

IMPERFECT

io	**mi prefiggevo**
tu	**ti prefiggevi**
lui/lei/Lei	**si prefiggeva**
noi	**ci prefiggevamo**
voi	**vi prefiggevate**
loro	**si prefiggevano**

GERUND
prefiggendosi

PAST PARTICIPLE
prefisso

EXAMPLE PHRASES

Si **prefiggono** sempre obiettivi irrealizzabili. *They always set themselves goals they can't achieve.*

Voglio che tu ti **prefigga** un obiettivo. *I want you to set yourself a goal.*

Mi **prefiggevo** di finire il libro entro domenica. *I was aiming to finish the book by Sunday.*

Remember that subject pronouns are not used very often in Italian.

prefiggersi

FUTURE

io	**mi prefiggerò**
tu	**ti prefiggerai**
lui/lei/Lei	**si prefiggerà**
noi	**ci prefiggeremo**
voi	**vi prefiggerete**
loro	**si prefiggeranno**

CONDITIONAL

io	**mi prefiggerei**
tu	**ti prefiggeresti**
lui/lei/Lei	**si prefiggerebbe**
noi	**ci prefiggeremmo**
voi	**vi prefiggereste**
loro	**si prefiggerebbero**

PAST HISTORIC

io	**mi prefissi**
tu	**ti prefiggesti**
lui/lei/Lei	**si prefisse**
noi	**ci prefiggemmo**
voi	**vi prefiggeste**
loro	**si prefissero**

PLUPERFECT

io	**mi ero prefisso/a**
tu	**ti eri prefisso/a**
lui/lei/Lei	**si era prefisso/a**
noi	**ci eravamo prefissi/e**
voi	**vi eravate prefissi/e**
loro	**si erano prefissi/e**

IMPERATIVE

prefiggiti
prefiggiamoci
prefiggetevi

EXAMPLE PHRASES

Che cosa ti **prefiggerai** per il prossimo anno? *What are your aims for next year?*

Fossi in te, non mi **prefiggerei** una meta così ambiziosa. *If I were you I wouldn't set myself such an ambitious target.*

Hai raggiunto i risultati che ti **eri prefisso**? *Have you achieved the results you were aiming for?*

Questo era lo scopo che mi **ero prefissa**. *This was the goal that I had set myself.*

Italic letters in Italian words show where stress does not follow the usual rules.

prendere (to take)

PRESENT

io	**prendo**
tu	**prendi**
lui/lei/Lei	**prende**
noi	**prendiamo**
voi	**prendete**
loro	**prendono**

PRESENT SUBJUNCTIVE

io	**prenda**
tu	**prenda**
lui/lei/Lei	**prenda**
noi	**prendiamo**
voi	**prendiate**
loro	**prendano**

PERFECT

io	**ho preso**
tu	**hai preso**
lui/lei/Lei	**ha preso**
noi	**abbiamo preso**
voi	**avete preso**
loro	**hanno preso**

IMPERFECT

io	**prendevo**
tu	**prendevi**
lui/lei/Lei	**prendeva**
noi	**prendevamo**
voi	**prendevate**
loro	**prendevano**

GERUND

prendendo

PAST PARTICIPLE

preso

EXAMPLE PHRASES

Per chi mi **prendi**? *Who do you think I am?*

Prende qualcosa da bere? *Would you like something to drink?*

Non so quanto **prenda** per una traduzione. *I don't know how much she charges for a translation.*

Ho preso un bel voto. *I got a good mark.*

Remember that subject pronouns are not used very often in Italian.

prendere

FUTURE

io	**prenderò**
tu	**prenderai**
lui/lei/Lei	**prenderà**
noi	**prenderemo**
voi	**prenderete**
loro	**prenderanno**

CONDITIONAL

io	**prenderei**
tu	**prenderesti**
lui/lei/Lei	**prenderebbe**
noi	**prenderemmo**
voi	**prendereste**
loro	**prenderebbero**

PAST HISTORIC

io	**presi**
tu	**prendesti**
lui/lei/Lei	**prese**
noi	**prendemmo**
voi	**prendeste**
loro	**presero**

PLUPERFECT

io	**avevo preso**
tu	**avevi preso**
lui/lei/Lei	**aveva preso**
noi	**avevamo preso**
voi	**avevate preso**
loro	**avevano preso**

IMPERATIVE

prendi
prendiamo
prendete

EXAMPLE PHRASES

Copriti o **prenderai** il raffreddore. *Cover yourself up or you'll catch a cold.*
Quanto **prenderemo** per quel lavoro? *How much will we get for that job?*
Prenderei volentieri un caffè. *I'd love a coffee.*
Quella volta **prendemmo** una bella paura. *That time we got a real fright.*
Aveva preso un grosso pesce e lo cucinò. *He'd caught a big fish so he cooked it.*
Prendi quella borsa. *Take that bag.*

Italic letters in Italian words show where stress does not follow the usual rules.

prevedere (to foresee)

PRESENT		PRESENT SUBJUNCTIVE	
io	**prevedo**	io	**preveda**
tu	**prevedi**	tu	**preveda**
lui/lei/Lei	**prevede**	lui/lei/Lei	**preveda**
noi	**prevediamo**	noi	**prevediamo**
voi	**prevedete**	voi	**prevediate**
loro	**prevedono**	loro	**prevedano**

PERFECT		IMPERFECT	
io	**ho previsto**	io	**prevedevo**
tu	**hai previsto**	tu	**prevedevi**
lui/lei/Lei	**ha previsto**	lui/lei/Lei	**prevedeva**
noi	**abbiamo previsto**	noi	**prevedevamo**
voi	**avete previsto**	voi	**prevedevate**
loro	**hanno previsto**	loro	**prevedevano**

GERUND	PAST PARTICIPLE
prevedendo	previsto

EXAMPLE PHRASES

Si **prevede** maltempo per il fine settimana. *Bad weather is forecast for the weekend.*

Come **previsto**, arriveremo in orario. *As we planned, we'll get there on time.*

È **previsto** per martedì. *It's planned for Tuesday.*

Prevedevamo che arrivaste più tardi. *We thought the plan was for you to arrive later.*

Non possiamo **prevedere** cosa succederà. *We can't foresee what will happen.*

Remember that subject pronouns are not used very often in Italian.

prevedere

FUTURE

io	**prevederò**
tu	**prevederai**
lui/lei/Lei	**prevederà**
noi	**prevederemo**
voi	**prevederete**
loro	**prevederanno**

CONDITIONAL

io	**prevederei**
tu	**prevederesti**
lui/lei/Lei	**prevederebbe**
noi	**prevederemmo**
voi	**prevedereste**
loro	**prevederebbero**

PAST HISTORIC

io	**previdi**
tu	**prevedesti**
lui/lei/Lei	**previde**
noi	**prevedemmo**
voi	**prevedeste**
loro	**previdero**

PLUPERFECT

io	**avevo previsto**
tu	**avevi previsto**
lui/lei/Lei	**aveva previsto**
noi	**avevamo previsto**
voi	**avevate previsto**
loro	**avevano previsto**

IMPERATIVE

prevedi
prevediamo
prevedete

EXAMPLE PHRASES

Il mago **previde** il nostro incontro. *The clairvoyant foresaw that we'd meet.*

Non **avevano previsto** questi cambiamenti. *They hadn't foreseen these changes.*

È un ansioso che vuole **prevedere** tutto. *He's a worrier who wants to plan everything ahead.*

Italic letters in Italian words show where stress does not follow the usual rules.

procedere (to move along)

PRESENT

io	**procedo**
tu	**procedi**
lui/lei/Lei	**procede**
noi	**procediamo**
voi	**procedete**
loro	**procedono**

PRESENT SUBJUNCTIVE

io	**proceda**
tu	**proceda**
lui/lei/Lei	**proceda**
noi	**procediamo**
voi	**procediate**
loro	**procedano**

PERFECT

io	**sono proceduto/a**
tu	**sei proceduto/a**
lui/lei/Lei	**è proceduto/a**
noi	**siamo proceduti/e**
voi	**siete proceduti/e**
loro	**sono proceduti/e**

IMPERFECT

io	**procedevo**
tu	**procedevi**
lui/lei/Lei	**procedeva**
noi	**procedevamo**
voi	**procedevate**
loro	**procedevano**

GERUND
procedendo

PAST PARTICIPLE
proceduto

EXAMPLE PHRASES

Come **procede** il lavoro? *How's the work getting on?*

Gli affari **procedono** bene. *Business is going well.*

Voglio che tutto **proceda** senza intoppi. *I want everything to go ahead without any hitches.*

I miei studi **procedevano** con lentezza. *My studies were making slow progress.*

Il traffico sta **procedendo** lentamente. *The traffic is moving slowly.*

Remember that subject pronouns are not used very often in Italian.

procedere

FUTURE

io	**procederò**
tu	**procederai**
lui/lei/Lei	**procederà**
noi	**procederemo**
voi	**procederete**
loro	**procederanno**

CONDITIONAL

io	**procederei**
tu	**procederesti**
lui/lei/Lei	**procederebbe**
noi	**procederemmo**
voi	**procedereste**
loro	**procederebbero**

PAST HISTORIC

io	**procedetti**
tu	**procedesti**
lui/lei/Lei	**procedette**
noi	**procedemmo**
voi	**procedeste**
loro	**procedettero**

PLUPERFECT

io	**ero proceduto/a**
tu	**eri proceduto/a**
lui/lei/Lei	**era proceduto/a**
noi	**eravamo proceduti/e**
voi	**eravate proceduti/e**
loro	**erano proceduti/e**

IMPERATIVE
procedi
procediamo
procedete

EXAMPLE PHRASES

Procedettero lungo il corridoio. *They moved along the corridor.*

La strada è ghiacciata, **procedete** con cautela. *The road is icy, drive with caution.*

Italic letters in Italian words show where stress does not follow the usual rules.

produrre (to produce)

PRESENT		PRESENT SUBJUNCTIVE	
io	**produco**	io	**produca**
tu	**produci**	tu	**produca**
lui/lei/Lei	**produce**	lui/lei/Lei	**produca**
noi	**produciamo**	noi	**produciamo**
voi	**producete**	voi	**produciate**
loro	**producono**	loro	**producano**

PERFECT		IMPERFECT	
io	**ho prodotto**	io	**producevo**
tu	**hai prodotto**	tu	**producevi**
lui/lei/Lei	**ha prodotto**	lui/lei/Lei	**produceva**
noi	**abbiamo prodotto**	noi	**producevamo**
voi	**avete prodotto**	voi	**producevate**
loro	**hanno prodotto**	loro	**producevano**

GERUND
producendo

PAST PARTICIPLE
prodotto

EXAMPLE PHRASES

La ditta **produce** scarpe. *The company produces shoes.*

Questa soluzione non **ha prodotto** buoni risultati. *This solution did not produce good results.*

Questi macchinari **sono prodotti** in Giappone. *This machinery is produced in Japan.*

L'Italia **produceva** molto grano. *Italy used to produce a lot of wheat.*

Si sono arricchiti **producendo** maglie. *They got rich by manufacturing knitwear.*

Remember that subject pronouns are not used very often in Italian.

produrre

FUTURE

io	**produrrò**
tu	**produrrai**
lui/lei/Lei	**produrrà**
noi	**produrremo**
voi	**produrrete**
loro	**produrranno**

CONDITIONAL

io	**produrrei**
tu	**produrresti**
lui/lei/Lei	**produrrebbe**
noi	**produrremmo**
voi	**produrreste**
loro	**produrrebbero**

PAST HISTORIC

io	**produssi**
tu	**producesti**
lui/lei/Lei	**produsse**
noi	**producemmo**
voi	**produceste**
loro	**produssero**

PLUPERFECT

io	**avevo prodotto**
tu	**avevi prodotto**
lui/lei/Lei	**aveva prodotto**
noi	**avevamo prodotto**
voi	**avevate prodotto**
loro	**avevano prodotto**

IMPERATIVE
produci
produciamo
producete

EXAMPLE PHRASES

Se lavorerai sodo, **produrrai** di più. *If you work hard you'll produce more.*
Avevamo prodotto articoli di grande successo. *We'd manufactured very successful products.*

Italic letters in Italian words show where stress does not follow the usual rules.

proporre (to suggest)

PRESENT		PRESENT SUBJUNCTIVE	
io	**propongo**	io	**proponga**
tu	**proponi**	tu	**proponga**
lui/lei/Lei	**propone**	lui/lei/Lei	**proponga**
noi	**proponiamo**	noi	**proponiamo**
voi	**proponete**	voi	**proponiate**
loro	**propongono**	loro	**propongano**

PERFECT		IMPERFECT	
io	**ho proposto**	io	**proponevo**
tu	**hai proposto**	tu	**proponevi**
lui/lei/Lei	**ha proposto**	lui/lei/Lei	**proponeva**
noi	**abbiamo proposto**	noi	**proponevamo**
voi	**avete proposto**	voi	**proponevate**
loro	**hanno proposto**	loro	**proponevano**

GERUND
proponendo

PAST PARTICIPLE
proposto

EXAMPLE PHRASES

Che cosa **propone** lo chef? *What does the chef recommend?*

Ho proposto di andare al cinema. *I suggested going to the cinema.*

Maria **proponeva** una pizza, ma non ne ho voglia. *Maria suggested a pizza, but I don't feel like one.*

proporre

FUTURE

io	**proporrò**
tu	**proporrai**
lui/lei/Lei	**proporrà**
noi	**proporremo**
voi	**proporrete**
loro	**proporranno**

CONDITIONAL

io	**proporrei**
tu	**proporresti**
lui/lei/Lei	**proporrebbe**
noi	**proporremmo**
voi	**proporreste**
loro	**proporrebbero**

PAST HISTORIC

io	**proposi**
tu	**proponesti**
lui/lei/Lei	**propose**
noi	**proponemmo**
voi	**proponeste**
loro	**proposero**

PLUPERFECT

io	**avevo proposto**
tu	**avevi proposto**
lui/lei/Lei	**aveva proposto**
noi	**avevamo proposto**
voi	**avevate proposto**
loro	**avevano proposto**

IMPERATIVE

proponi
proponiamo
proponete

EXAMPLE PHRASES

Non **proporrei** mai una cosa del genere. *I'd never suggest something like that.*

Propose un brindisi alla salute dell'invitato. *He proposed a toast to the guest.*

Avevano proposto di fermarci, ma continuammo. *They'd suggested we should stop, but we continued.*

Forza, **proponete** qualcosa di nuovo per stasera. *Go on, suggest something new for this evening.*

Italic letters in Italian words show where stress does not follow the usual rules.

raggiungere (to reach)

PRESENT

io	**raggiungo**
tu	**raggiungi**
lui/lei/Lei	**raggiunge**
noi	**raggiungiamo**
voi	**raggiungete**
loro	**raggiungono**

PRESENT SUBJUNCTIVE

io	**raggiunga**
tu	**raggiunga**
lui/lei/Lei	**raggiunga**
noi	**raggiungiamo**
voi	**raggiungiate**
loro	**raggiungano**

PERFECT

io	**ho raggiunto**
tu	**hai raggiunto**
lui/lei/Lei	**ha raggiunto**
noi	**abbiamo raggiunto**
voi	**avete raggiunto**
loro	**hanno raggiunto**

IMPERFECT

io	**raggiungevo**
tu	**raggiungevi**
lui/lei/Lei	**raggiungeva**
noi	**raggiungevamo**
voi	**raggiungevate**
loro	**raggiungevano**

GERUND

raggiungendo

PAST PARTICIPLE

raggiunto

EXAMPLE PHRASES

La temperatura può **raggiungere** i quaranta gradi. *The temperature can reach forty degrees.*

Vi **raggiungo** più tardi. *I'll join you later.*

Non **ho** ancora **raggiunto** il mio scopo. *I haven't yet achieved my aim.*

raggiungere

FUTURE

io	**raggiungerò**
tu	**raggiungerai**
lui/lei/Lei	**raggiungerà**
noi	**raggiungeremo**
voi	**raggiungerete**
loro	**raggiungeranno**

CONDITIONAL

io	**raggiungerei**
tu	**raggiungeresti**
lui/lei/Lei	**raggiungerebbe**
noi	**raggiungeremmo**
voi	**raggiungereste**
loro	**raggiungerebbero**

PAST HISTORIC

io	**raggiunsi**
tu	**raggiungesti**
lui/lei/Lei	**raggiunse**
noi	**raggiungemmo**
voi	**raggiungeste**
loro	**raggiunsero**

PLUPERFECT

io	**avevo raggiunto**
tu	**avevi raggiunto**
lui/lei/Lei	**aveva raggiunto**
noi	**avevamo raggiunto**
voi	**avevate raggiunto**
loro	**avevano raggiunto**

IMPERATIVE

raggiungi
raggiungiamo
raggiungete

EXAMPLE PHRASES

Vi **raggiungeremo** in albergo. *We'll meet you in the hotel.*

Ci rincorsero e ci **raggiunsero**. *They ran after us and caught us up.*

Il fiume **aveva raggiunto** il livello di guardia. *The river had reached the high-water mark.*

I tuoi amici ti aspettano: **raggiungili**. *Your friends are waiting for you: go and join them.*

Italic letters in Italian words show where stress does not follow the usual rules.

rendere (to make)

PRESENT		PRESENT SUBJUNCTIVE	
io	**rendo**	io	**renda**
tu	**rendi**	tu	**renda**
lui/lei/Lei	**rende**	lui/lei/Lei	**renda**
noi	**rendiamo**	noi	**rendiamo**
voi	**rendete**	voi	**rendiate**
loro	**rendono**	loro	**rendano**

PERFECT		IMPERFECT	
io	**ho reso**	io	**rendevo**
tu	**hai reso**	tu	**rendevi**
lui/lei/Lei	**ha reso**	lui/lei/Lei	**rendeva**
noi	**abbiamo reso**	noi	**rendevamo**
voi	**avete reso**	voi	**rendevate**
loro	**hanno reso**	loro	**rendevano**

GERUND
rendendo

PAST PARTICIPLE
reso

EXAMPLE PHRASES

Forse non ti **rendi** conto di quanto sia pericoloso. *Maybe you don't realize how dangerous it is.*

Scusa, non mi **ero reso** conto di averti offeso. *I'm sorry, I didn't realize I'd upset you.*

Non si **è** mai **resa** conto dei suoi limiti. *She's never recognized her limitations.*

Potresti **rendermi** la penna? *Could you give me back my pen?*

Remember that subject pronouns are not used very often in Italian.

rendere

FUTURE

io	**renderò**
tu	**renderai**
lui/lei/Lei	**renderà**
noi	**renderemo**
voi	**renderete**
loro	**renderanno**

CONDITIONAL

io	**renderei**
tu	**renderesti**
lui/lei/Lei	**renderebbe**
noi	**renderemmo**
voi	**rendereste**
loro	**renderebbero**

PAST HISTORIC

io	**resi**
tu	**rendesti**
lui/lei/Lei	**rese**
noi	**rendemmo**
voi	**rendeste**
loro	**resero**

PLUPERFECT

io	**avevo reso**
tu	**avevi reso**
lui/lei/Lei	**aveva reso**
noi	**avevamo reso**
voi	**avevate reso**
loro	**avevano reso**

IMPERATIVE

rendi
rendiamo
rendete

EXAMPLE PHRASES

Questa crema **renderà** i capelli luminosi. *This cream will make your hair shiny.*

Un po' di diplomazia **renderebbe** tutto più facile. *A bit of diplomacy would make everything easier.*

Il ladro **rese** la refurtiva. *The burglar returned the stolen goods.*

Fai qualcosa! **Renditi** utile! *Do something! Make yourself useful!*

Italic letters in Italian words show where stress does not follow the usual rules.

restare (to stay)

	PRESENT		PRESENT SUBJUNCTIVE
io	**resto**	io	**resti**
tu	**resti**	tu	**resti**
lui/lei/Lei	**resta**	lui/lei/Lei	**resti**
noi	**restiamo**	noi	**restiamo**
voi	**restate**	voi	**restiate**
loro	**restano**	loro	**restino**

	PERFECT		IMPERFECT
io	**sono restato/a**	io	**restavo**
tu	**sei restato/a**	tu	**restavi**
lui/lei/Lei	**è restato/a**	lui/lei/Lei	**restava**
noi	**siamo restati/e**	noi	**restavamo**
voi	**siete restati/e**	voi	**restavate**
loro	**sono restati/e**	loro	**restavano**

GERUND
restando

PAST PARTICIPLE
restato

EXAMPLE PHRASES

Ne **restano** solo due. *There are only two left.*

Sono restato a casa tutto il giorno. *I stayed at home all day.*

Restava solo da pulire la cucina. *The only thing left to do was cleaning the kitchen.*

Remember that subject pronouns are not used very often in Italian.

restare

FUTURE

io	**resterò**
tu	**resterai**
lui/lei/Lei	**resterà**
noi	**resteremo**
voi	**resterete**
loro	**resteranno**

CONDITIONAL

io	**resterei**
tu	**resteresti**
lui/lei/Lei	**resterebbe**
noi	**resteremmo**
voi	**restereste**
loro	**resterebbero**

PAST HISTORIC

io	**restai**
tu	**restasti**
lui/lei/Lei	**restò**
noi	**restammo**
voi	**restaste**
loro	**restarono**

PLUPERFECT

io	**ero restato/a**
tu	**eri restato/a**
lui/lei/Lei	**era restato/a**
noi	**eravamo restati/e**
voi	**eravate restati/e**
loro	**erano restati/e**

IMPERATIVE

resta

restiamo

restate

EXAMPLE PHRASES

Resterò in Italia per tutta l'estate. *I'll stay in Italy for the whole summer.*

Resterei, ma ho da fare. *I'd stay, but I've got things to do.*

Mi **restarono** solo cinquanta sterline. *I only had fifty pounds left.*

Era restato da solo tutta la sera. *He'd been alone all evening.*

Dai, **resta** ancora un po'. *Go on, stay a bit longer.*

Italic letters in Italian words show where stress does not follow the usual rules.

ridere (to laugh)

PRESENT

io	**rido**
tu	**ridi**
lui/lei/Lei	**ride**
noi	**ridiamo**
voi	**ridete**
loro	**ridono**

PRESENT SUBJUNCTIVE

io	**rida**
tu	**rida**
lui/lei/Lei	**rida**
noi	**ridiamo**
voi	**ridiate**
loro	**ridano**

PERFECT

io	**ho riso**
tu	**hai riso**
lui/lei/Lei	**ha riso**
noi	**abbiamo riso**
voi	**avete riso**
loro	**hanno riso**

IMPERFECT

io	**ridevo**
tu	**ridevi**
lui/lei/Lei	**rideva**
noi	**ridevamo**
voi	**ridevate**
loro	**ridevano**

GERUND

ridendo

PAST PARTICIPLE

riso

EXAMPLE PHRASES

Perché **ridi**? *Why are you laughing?*

Abbiamo riso per tutto lo spettacolo. *We laughed all through the show.*

State **ridendo** di me? *Are you laughing at me?*

Tutti sono scoppiati a **ridere**. *They all burst out laughing.*

Non c'è niente da **ridere**. *It's not funny.*

Remember that subject pronouns are not used very often in Italian.

ridere

FUTURE

io	**riderò**
tu	**riderai**
lui/lei/Lei	**riderà**
noi	**rideremo**
voi	**riderete**
loro	**rideranno**

CONDITIONAL

io	**riderei**
tu	**rideresti**
lui/lei/Lei	**riderebbe**
noi	**rideremmo**
voi	**ridereste**
loro	**riderebbero**

PAST HISTORIC

io	**risi**
tu	**ridesti**
lui/lei/Lei	**rise**
noi	**ridemmo**
voi	**rideste**
loro	**risero**

PLUPERFECT

io	**avevo riso**
tu	**avevi riso**
lui/lei/Lei	**aveva riso**
noi	**avevamo riso**
voi	**avevate riso**
loro	**avevano riso**

IMPERATIVE

ridi
ridiamo
ridete

EXAMPLE PHRASES

Rideresti meno se sapessi la verità. *You wouldn't laugh so much if you knew the truth.*

Non **avevo** mai **riso** tanto in vita mia. *I'd never laughed so much in all my life.*

Italic letters in Italian words show where stress does not follow the usual rules.

riempire (to fill)

PRESENT

io	**riempio**
tu	**riempi**
lui/lei/Lei	**riempie**
noi	**riempiamo**
voi	**riempite**
loro	**riempiono**

PRESENT SUBJUNCTIVE

io	**riempia**
tu	**riempia**
lui/lei/Lei	**riempia**
noi	**riempiamo**
voi	**riempiate**
loro	**riempiano**

PERFECT

io	**ho riempito**
tu	**hai riempito**
lui/lei/Lei	**ha riempito**
noi	**abbiamo riempito**
voi	**avete riempito**
loro	**hanno riempito**

IMPERFECT

io	**riempivo**
tu	**riempivi**
lui/lei/Lei	**riempiva**
noi	**riempivamo**
voi	**riempivate**
loro	**riempivano**

GERUND
riempiendo

PAST PARTICIPLE
riempito

EXAMPLE PHRASES

Vedervi ci **riempie** di gioia. *It's always a joy to see you.*

È meglio che tu **riempia** la borraccia prima di partire. *You'd better fill your water bottle before you set off.*

Tieni, **ho riempito** il termos di caffè, va bene? *Here, I've filled the flask with coffee, okay?*

Remember that subject pronouns are not used very often in Italian.

riempire

FUTURE

io	**riempirò**
tu	**riempirai**
lui/lei/Lei	**riempirà**
noi	**riempiremo**
voi	**riempirete**
loro	**riempiranno**

CONDITIONAL

io	**riempirei**
tu	**riempiresti**
lui/lei/Lei	**riempirebbe**
noi	**riempiremmo**
voi	**riempireste**
loro	**riempirebbero**

PAST HISTORIC

io	**riempii**
tu	**riempisti**
lui/lei/Lei	**riempì**
noi	**riempimmo**
voi	**riempiste**
loro	**riempirono**

PLUPERFECT

io	**avevo riempito**
tu	**avevi riempito**
lui/lei/Lei	**aveva riempito**
noi	**avevamo riempito**
voi	**avevate riempito**
loro	**avevano riempito**

IMPERATIVE

riempi
riempiamo
riempite

EXAMPLE PHRASES

Riempiremo tutte le bottiglie col vino del nonno. *We're going to fill all the bottles with granddad's wine.*

Mi **riempì** la testa di sciocchezze. *She filled my head with nonsense.*

Riempi il modulo, per favore. *Fill in the form, please.*

Italic letters in Italian words show where stress does not follow the usual rules.

riflettere (to think)

PRESENT		PRESENT SUBJUNCTIVE	
io	**rifletto**	io	**rifletta**
tu	**rifletti**	tu	**rifletta**
lui/lei/Lei	**riflette**	lui/lei/Lei	**rifletta**
noi	**riflettiamo**	noi	**riflettiamo**
voi	**riflettete**	voi	**riflettiate**
loro	**riflettono**	loro	**riflettano**

PERFECT		IMPERFECT	
io	**ho riflettuto**	io	**riflettevo**
tu	**hai riflettuto**	tu	**riflettevi**
lui/lei/Lei	**ha riflettuto**	lui/lei/Lei	**rifletteva**
noi	**abbiamo riflettuto**	noi	**riflettevamo**
voi	**avete riflettuto**	voi	**riflettevate**
loro	**hanno riflettuto**	loro	**riflettevano**

GERUND	PAST PARTICIPLE
riflettendo	**riflettuto**

EXAMPLE PHRASES

È una persona cauta: **riflette** molto prima di agire. *He's a cautious person: he thinks a lot before he does anything.*

Ci **ho riflettuto** su e ho deciso di accettare. *I've thought about it and have decided to accept.*

Guardavo la TV mentre **riflettevo** sul da farsi. *I watched TV while I thought about what should be done.*

Riflettendo un po', troveremo la soluzione. *If we think a bit we'll find a solution.*

Agisce senza **riflettere**. *He does things without thinking.*

Remember that subject pronouns are not used very often in Italian.

riflettere

FUTURE

io	**rifletterò**
tu	**rifletterai**
lui/lei/Lei	**rifletterà**
noi	**rifletteremo**
voi	**rifletterete**
loro	**rifletteranno**

CONDITIONAL

io	**rifletterei**
tu	**rifletteresti**
lui/lei/Lei	**rifletterebbe**
noi	**rifletteremmo**
voi	**riflettereste**
loro	**rifletterebbero**

PAST HISTORIC

io	**riflettei**
tu	**riflettesti**
lui/lei/Lei	**rifletté**
noi	**riflettemmo**
voi	**rifletteste**
loro	**rifletterono**

PLUPERFECT

io	**avevo riflettuto**
tu	**avevi riflettuto**
lui/lei/Lei	**aveva riflettuto**
noi	**avevamo riflettuto**
voi	**avevate riflettuto**
loro	**avevano riflettuto**

IMPERATIVE

rifletti
riflettiamo
riflettete

EXAMPLE PHRASES

Io **rifletterei** un po' prima di fare una simile scelta. *I'd think a bit before I made a choice like that.*
Rifletti prima di parlare! *Think before you speak!*

Italic letters in Italian words show where stress does not follow the usual rules.

rimanere (to stay)

PRESENT

io	**rimango**
tu	**rimani**
lui/lei/Lei	**rimane**
noi	**rimaniamo**
voi	**rimanete**
loro	**rimangono**

PRESENT SUBJUNCTIVE

io	**rimanga**
tu	**rimanga**
lui/lei/Lei	**rimanga**
noi	**rimaniamo**
voi	**rimaniate**
loro	**rimangano**

PERFECT

io	**sono rimasto/a**
tu	**sei rimasto/a**
lui/lei/Lei	**è rimasto/a**
noi	**siamo rimasti/e**
voi	**siete rimasti/e**
loro	**sono rimasti/e**

IMPERFECT

io	**rimanevo**
tu	**rimanevi**
lui/lei/Lei	**rimaneva**
noi	**rimanevamo**
voi	**rimanevate**
loro	**rimanevano**

GERUND

rimanendo

PAST PARTICIPLE

rimasto

EXAMPLE PHRASES

Temo che **rimanga** poco tempo. *I'm afraid she won't stay long.*
Sono rimasto a casa tutto il giorno. *I stayed at home all day.*
Rimanevano sempre indietro. *They were always behind.*
Mi piacerebbe **rimanere** qualche altro giorno. *I'd like to stay a few more days.*

Remember that subject pronouns are not used very often in Italian.

rimanere

FUTURE

io	**rimarrò**
tu	**rimarrai**
lui/lei/Lei	**rimarrà**
noi	**rimarremo**
voi	**rimarrete**
loro	**rimarranno**

CONDITIONAL

io	**rimarrei**
tu	**rimarresti**
lui/lei/Lei	**rimarrebbe**
noi	**rimarremmo**
voi	**rimarreste**
loro	**rimarrebbero**

PAST HISTORIC

io	**rimasi**
tu	**rimanesti**
lui/lei/Lei	**rimase**
noi	**rimanemmo**
voi	**rimaneste**
loro	**rimasero**

PLUPERFECT

io	**ero rimasto/a**
tu	**eri rimasto/a**
lui/lei/Lei	**era rimasto/a**
noi	**eravamo rimasti/e**
voi	**eravate rimasti/e**
loro	**erano rimasti/e**

IMPERATIVE

rimani
rimaniamo
rimanete

EXAMPLE PHRASES

Rimarrete senza parole. *You'll be speechless.*

Ci **rimarrebbero** molto male. *They'd be very hurt.*

Ne **rimase** solo uno. *There was only one left.*

Eravamo rimasti senza pane, così andai a comprarlo. *We had no bread left, so I went to get some.*

Italic letters in Italian words show where stress does not follow the usual rules.

risolvere (to solve)

PRESENT

io	**risolvo**
tu	**risolvi**
lui/lei/Lei	**risolve**
noi	**risolviamo**
voi	**risolvete**
loro	**risolvono**

PRESENT SUBJUNCTIVE

io	**risolva**
tu	**risolva**
lui/lei/Lei	**risolva**
noi	**risolviamo**
voi	**risolviate**
loro	**risolvano**

PERFECT

io	**ho risolto**
tu	**hai risolto**
lui/lei/Lei	**ha risolto**
noi	**abbiamo risolto**
voi	**avete risolto**
loro	**hanno risolto**

IMPERFECT

io	**risolvevo**
tu	**risolvevi**
lui/lei/Lei	**risolveva**
noi	**risolvevamo**
voi	**risolvevate**
loro	**risolvevano**

GERUND
risolvendo

PAST PARTICIPLE
risolto

EXAMPLE PHRASES

Così non **risolvi** nulla. *You won't solve the problems that way.*
Ho risolto l'indovinello! *I've worked out the riddle!*

Remember that subject pronouns are not used very often in Italian.

risolvere

FUTURE

io	**risolverò**
tu	**risolverai**
lui/lei/Lei	**risolverà**
noi	**risolveremo**
voi	**risolverete**
loro	**risolveranno**

CONDITIONAL

io	**risolverei**
tu	**risolveresti**
lui/lei/Lei	**risolverebbe**
noi	**risolveremmo**
voi	**risolvereste**
loro	**risolverebbero**

PAST HISTORIC

io	**risolsi**
tu	**risolvesti**
lui/lei/Lei	**risolse**
noi	**risolvemmo**
voi	**risolveste**
loro	**risolsero**

PLUPERFECT

io	**avevo risolto**
tu	**avevi risolto**
lui/lei/Lei	**aveva risolto**
noi	**avevamo risolto**
voi	**avevate risolto**
loro	**avevano risolto**

IMPERATIVE
risolvi
risolviamo
risolvete

EXAMPLE PHRASES

Solo se ti calmerai **risolverai** i tuoi problemi. *You'll only solve your problems if you calm down.*

Una tua parola **risolverebbe** molte questioni. *If you said something it would resolve many issues.*

Il suo intervento **risolse** la controversia. *His intervention settled the dispute.*

Aveva risolto un'equazione difficilissima. *He'd worked out a very difficult equation.*

Italic letters in Italian words show where stress does not follow the usual rules.

rispondere (to answer)

PRESENT

io	**rispondo**
tu	**rispondi**
lui/lei/Lei	**risponde**
noi	**rispondiamo**
voi	**rispondete**
loro	**rispondono**

PRESENT SUBJUNCTIVE

io	**risponda**
tu	**risponda**
lui/lei/Lei	**risponda**
noi	**rispondiamo**
voi	**rispondiate**
loro	**rispondano**

PERFECT

io	**ho risposto**
tu	**hai risposto**
lui/lei/Lei	**ha risposto**
noi	**abbiamo risposto**
voi	**avete risposto**
loro	**hanno risposto**

IMPERFECT

io	**rispondevo**
tu	**rispondevi**
lui/lei/Lei	**rispondeva**
noi	**rispondevamo**
voi	**rispondevate**
loro	**rispondevano**

GERUND
rispondendo

PAST PARTICIPLE
risposto

EXAMPLE PHRASES

Cosa vuoi che ti **risponda**? *What do you want me to say?*

Ho telefonato ma non **ha risposto** nessuno. *I phoned, but nobody answered.*

Rispondeva sempre di sì a tutti. *She always said yes to everyone.*

Remember that subject pronouns are not used very often in Italian.

rispondere

FUTURE

io	**risponder***ò*
tu	**risponderai**
lui/lei/Lei	**risponder***à*
noi	**risponderemo**
voi	**risponderete**
loro	**risponderanno**

CONDITIONAL

io	**risponderei**
tu	**risponderesti**
lui/lei/Lei	**risponderebbe**
noi	**risponderemmo**
voi	**rispondereste**
loro	**rispondereb***b*ero

PAST HISTORIC

io	**risposi**
tu	**rispondesti**
lui/lei/Lei	**rispose**
noi	**rispondemmo**
voi	**rispondeste**
loro	**rispo***s*ero

PLUPERFECT

io	**avevo risposto**
tu	**avevi risposto**
lui/lei/Lei	**aveva risposto**
noi	**avevamo risposto**
voi	**avevate risposto**
loro	**avevano risposto**

IMPERATIVE
rispondi
rispondiamo
rispondete

EXAMPLE PHRASES

Risponderai di tutti i tuoi crimini. *You will answer for all your crimes.*
Cosa **rispondereste** a una domanda simile? *How would you answer a question like that?*
Rispose di no. *He said no.*
Avevate risposto alle sue lettere? *Had you replied to her letters?*
Rispondi alla mia domanda. *Answer my question.*

Italic letters in Italian words show where stress does not follow the usual rules.

rivolgere (to turn)

PRESENT		PRESENT SUBJUNCTIVE	
io	**rivolgo**	io	**rivolga**
tu	**rivolgi**	tu	**rivolga**
lui/lei/Lei	**rivolge**	lui/lei/Lei	**rivolga**
noi	**rivolgiamo**	noi	**rivolgiamo**
voi	**rivolgete**	voi	**rivolgiate**
loro	**rivolgono**	loro	**rivolgano**

PERFECT		IMPERFECT	
io	**ho rivolto**	io	**rivolgevo**
tu	**hai rivolto**	tu	**rivolgevi**
lui/lei/Lei	**ha rivolto**	lui/lei/Lei	**rivolgeva**
noi	**abbiamo rivolto**	noi	**rivolgevamo**
voi	**avete rivolto**	voi	**rivolgevate**
loro	**hanno rivolto**	loro	**rivolgevano**

GERUND	PAST PARTICIPLE
rivolgendo	**rivolto**

EXAMPLE PHRASES

Sono due giorni che non mi **rivolge** la parola. *She hasn't spoken to me for two days.*

È meglio che si **rivolga** all'impiegato laggiù. *You'd better go and ask the man over there.*

Si **è rivolta** a me per un consiglio. *She came to me for advice.*

Remember that subject pronouns are not used very often in Italian.

rivolgere

FUTURE

io	**rivolgerò**
tu	**rivolgerai**
lui/lei/Lei	**rivolgerà**
noi	**rivolgeremo**
voi	**rivolgerete**
loro	**rivolgeranno**

CONDITIONAL

io	**rivolgerei**
tu	**rivolgeresti**
lui/lei/Lei	**rivolgerebbe**
noi	**rivolgeremmo**
voi	**rivolgereste**
loro	**rivolgerebbero**

PAST HISTORIC

io	**rivolsi**
tu	**rivolgesti**
lui/lei/Lei	**rivolse**
noi	**rivolgemmo**
voi	**rivolgeste**
loro	**rivolsero**

PLUPERFECT

io	**avevo rivolto**
tu	**avevi rivolto**
lui/lei/Lei	**aveva rivolto**
noi	**avevamo rivolto**
voi	**avevate rivolto**
loro	**avevano rivolto**

IMPERATIVE

rivolgi
rivolgiamo
rivolgete

EXAMPLE PHRASES

Ci **rivolgeremo** alle autorità. *We'll go to the authorities*

In caso di problemi, ci **rivolgevamo** a lui. *If there was a problem we went to him.*

Non mi **rivolgerei** mai a te per avere aiuto. *I'd never come to you for help.*

Si **rivolse** a me in tono aggressivo. *She spoke to me aggressively.*

Rivolgetevi all'ufficio informazioni. *Go to the information office.*

Non so a chi **rivolgermi**. *I don't know who to go to.*

Italic letters in Italian words show where stress does not follow the usual rules.

rompere (to break)

PRESENT

io	**rompo**
tu	**rompi**
lui/lei/Lei	**rompe**
noi	**rompiamo**
voi	**rompete**
loro	**rompono**

PRESENT SUBJUNCTIVE

io	**rompa**
tu	**rompa**
lui/lei/Lei	**rompa**
noi	**rompiamo**
voi	**rompiate**
loro	**rompano**

PERFECT

io	**ho rotto**
tu	**hai rotto**
lui/lei/Lei	**ha rotto**
noi	**abbiamo rotto**
voi	**avete rotto**
loro	**hanno rotto**

IMPERFECT

io	**rompevo**
tu	**rompevi**
lui/lei/Lei	**rompeva**
noi	**rompevamo**
voi	**rompevate**
loro	**rompevano**

GERUND
rompendo

PAST PARTICIPLE
rotto

EXAMPLE PHRASES

Uffa quanto **rompi**! *What a pain you are!*

Ho rotto un bicchiere! *I've broken a glass!*

Il piatto si **è rotto**. *The plate broke.*

Da piccolo **rompeva** tutto quello che toccava. *When he was little he broke everything he touched.*

rompere

FUTURE

io	**romperò**
tu	**romperai**
lui/lei/Lei	**romperà**
noi	**romperemo**
voi	**romperete**
loro	**romperanno**

CONDITIONAL

io	**romperei**
tu	**romperesti**
lui/lei/Lei	**romperebbe**
noi	**romperemmo**
voi	**rompereste**
loro	**romperebbero**

PAST HISTORIC

io	**ruppi**
tu	**rompesti**
lui/lei/Lei	**ruppe**
noi	**rompemmo**
voi	**rompeste**
loro	**ruppero**

PLUPERFECT

io	**avevo rotto**
tu	**avevi rotto**
lui/lei/Lei	**aveva rotto**
noi	**avevamo rotto**
voi	**avevate rotto**
loro	**avevano rotto**

IMPERATIVE

rompi
rompiamo
rompete

EXAMPLE PHRASES

Rischia troppo: si **romperà** una gamba. *She takes too many risks: she'll break her leg.*

La corda si **romperebbe** se tirassi troppo. *The rope would break if I pulled too hard.*

La macchina si **ruppe** sull'autostrada. *The car broke down on the motorway.*

Italic letters in Italian words show where stress does not follow the usual rules.

salire (to go up)

PRESENT		PRESENT SUBJUNCTIVE	
io	**salgo**	io	**salga**
tu	**sali**	tu	**salga**
lui/lei/Lei	**sale**	lui/lei/Lei	**salga**
noi	**saliamo**	noi	**saliamo**
voi	**salite**	voi	**saliate**
loro	**salgono**	loro	**salgano**

PERFECT		IMPERFECT	
io	**sono salito/a**	io	**salivo**
tu	**sei salito/a**	tu	**salivi**
lui/lei/Lei	**è salito/a**	lui/lei/Lei	**saliva**
noi	**siamo saliti/e**	noi	**salivamo**
voi	**siete saliti/e**	voi	**salivate**
loro	**sono saliti/e**	loro	**salivano**

GERUND
salendo

PAST PARTICIPLE
salito

EXAMPLE PHRASES

Sali tu o scendo io? *Are you coming up or shall I come down?*

Non voglio che i tuoi amici **salgano** in casa. *I don't want your friends to come into the house.*

I prezzi **sono saliti**. *Prices have gone up.*

Mentre **saliva** verso la cima, si sentì senza forze. *As she climbed up to the summit she felt weak.*

Remember that subject pronouns are not used very often in Italian.

salire

FUTURE

io	**salirò**
tu	**salirai**
lui/lei/Lei	**salirà**
noi	**saliremo**
voi	**salirete**
loro	**saliranno**

CONDITIONAL

io	**salirei**
tu	**saliresti**
lui/lei/Lei	**salirebbe**
noi	**saliremmo**
voi	**salireste**
loro	**salirebbero**

PAST HISTORIC

io	**salii**
tu	**salisti**
lui/lei/Lei	**salì**
noi	**salimmo**
voi	**saliste**
loro	**salirono**

PLUPERFECT

io	**ero salito/a**
tu	**eri salito/a**
lui/lei/Lei	**era salito/a**
noi	**eravamo saliti/e**
voi	**eravate saliti/e**
loro	**erano saliti/e**

IMPERATIVE

sali
saliamo
salite

EXAMPLE PHRASES

Dopo cena **salirai** in camera tua. *After dinner you'll go up to your room.*

Non **salirei** mai su un aereo. *I'd never go on a plane.*

Salì sull'albero per raccogliere le ciliegie. *She climbed up the tree to pick the cherries.*

Sali in macchina e partiamo. *Get in the car and we'll be off.*

Italic letters in Italian words show where stress does not follow the usual rules.

sapere (to know)

PRESENT		PRESENT SUBJUNCTIVE	
io	**so**	io	**sappia**
tu	**sai**	tu	**sappia**
lui/lei/Lei	**sa**	lui/lei/Lei	**sappia**
noi	**sappiamo**	noi	**sappiamo**
voi	**sapete**	voi	**sappiate**
loro	**sanno**	loro	**sappiano**

PERFECT		IMPERFECT	
io	**ho saputo**	io	**sapevo**
tu	**hai saputo**	tu	**sapevi**
lui/lei/Lei	**ha saputo**	lui/lei/Lei	**sapeva**
noi	**abbiamo saputo**	noi	**sapevamo**
voi	**avete saputo**	voi	**sapevate**
loro	**hanno saputo**	loro	**sapevano**

GERUND
sapendo

PAST PARTICIPLE
saputo

EXAMPLE PHRASES

Sai dove abita? *Do you know where he lives?*

Non ne **so** nulla. *I don't know anything about it.*

Sa di fragola. *It tastes of strawberries.*

Sa di pesce. *It smells of fish.*

Non **abbiamo** più **saputo** nulla di lui. *We didn't hear anything more about him.*

Non **sapeva** andare in bicicletta. *He couldn't ride a bike.*

Remember that subject pronouns are not used very often in Italian.

sapere

FUTURE

io	**saprò**
tu	**saprai**
lui/lei/Lei	**saprà**
noi	**sapremo**
voi	**saprete**
loro	**sapranno**

CONDITIONAL

io	**saprei**
tu	**sapresti**
lui/lei/Lei	**saprebbe**
noi	**sapremmo**
voi	**sapreste**
loro	**saprebbero**

PAST HISTORIC

io	**seppi**
tu	**sapesti**
lui/lei/Lei	**seppe**
noi	**sapemmo**
voi	**sapeste**
loro	**seppero**

PLUPERFECT

io	**avevo saputo**
tu	**avevi saputo**
lui/lei/Lei	**aveva saputo**
noi	**avevamo saputo**
voi	**avevate saputo**
loro	**avevano saputo**

IMPERATIVE

sappi
sappiamo
sappiate

EXAMPLE PHRASES

Come **saprete**, abbiamo deciso di traslocare. *As you know, we've decided to move.*

Sapreste indicarmi la strada per la stazione? *Could you tell me the way to the station?*

Solo dopo molti anni **sapemmo** che era emigrato. *Only after many years did we hear that he'd emigrated.*

Sappi che non sono disposto a perdonarti. *I want you to know that I'm not prepared to forgive you.*

Italic letters in Italian words show where stress does not follow the usual rules.

sbagliare (to make a mistake)

PRESENT		PRESENT SUBJUNCTIVE	
io	**sbaglio**	io	**sbagli**
tu	**sbagli**	tu	**sbagli**
lui/lei/Lei	**sbaglia**	lui/lei/Lei	**sbagli**
noi	**sbagliamo**	noi	**sbagliamo**
voi	**sbagliate**	voi	**sbagliate**
loro	**sbagliano**	loro	**sbaglino**

PERFECT		IMPERFECT	
io	**ho sbagliato**	io	**sbagliavo**
tu	**hai sbagliato**	tu	**sbagliavi**
lui/lei/Lei	**ha sbagliato**	lui/lei/Lei	**sbagliava**
noi	**abbiamo sbagliato**	noi	**sbagliavamo**
voi	**avete sbagliato**	voi	**sbagliavate**
loro	**hanno sbagliato**	loro	**sbagliavano**

GERUND	PAST PARTICIPLE
sbagliando	sbagliato

EXAMPLE PHRASES

Mi dispiace, **avete sbagliato**. *I'm sorry, you've made a mistake.*

Scusi, **ho sbagliato** numero. *Sorry, I've got the wrong number.*

Pensavo fosse lei, ma mi **sono sbagliato**. *I thought it was her, but I was wrong.*

Ci eravamo persi e **sbagliavamo** sempre strada. *We were lost and kept taking the wrong road.*

Sbagliando s'impara. *You learn by your mistakes.*

Remember that subject pronouns are not used very often in Italian.

sbagliare

FUTURE

io	**sbaglierò**
tu	**sbaglierai**
lui/lei/Lei	**sbaglierà**
noi	**sbaglieremo**
voi	**sbaglierete**
loro	**sbaglieranno**

CONDITIONAL

io	**sbaglierei**
tu	**sbaglieresti**
lui/lei/Lei	**sbaglierebbe**
noi	**sbaglieremmo**
voi	**sbagliereste**
loro	**sbaglierebbero**

PAST HISTORIC

io	**sbagliai**
tu	**sbagliasti**
lui/lei/Lei	**sbagliò**
noi	**sbagliammo**
voi	**sbagliaste**
loro	**sbagliarono**

PLUPERFECT

io	**avevo sbagliato**
tu	**avevi sbagliato**
lui/lei/Lei	**aveva sbagliato**
noi	**avevamo sbagliato**
voi	**avevate sbagliato**
loro	**avevano sbagliato**

IMPERATIVE

sbaglia
sbagliamo
sbagliate

EXAMPLE PHRASES

Mi **sbaglierò**, ma per me questa è la risposta giusta. *I may be mistaken, but I think this is the right answer.*

Sbaglieresti, se pensassi che non mi importa. *You'd be wrong if you thought I didn't care.*

Aveva sbagliato e non voleva ammetterlo. *He'd been wrong but didn't want to admit it.*

Italic letters in Italian words show where stress does not follow the usual rules.

scegliere (to choose)

PRESENT		PRESENT SUBJUNCTIVE	
io	**scelgo**	io	**scelga**
tu	**scegli**	tu	**scelga**
lui/lei/Lei	**sceglie**	lui/lei/Lei	**scelga**
noi	**scegliamo**	noi	**scegliamo**
voi	**scegliete**	voi	**scegliate**
loro	**scelgono**	loro	**scelgano**

PERFECT		IMPERFECT	
io	**ho scelto**	io	**sceglievo**
tu	**hai scelto**	tu	**sceglievi**
lui/lei/Lei	**ha scelto**	lui/lei/Lei	**sceglieva**
noi	**abbiamo scelto**	noi	**sceglievamo**
voi	**avete scelto**	voi	**sceglievate**
loro	**hanno scelto**	loro	**sceglievano**

GERUND
scegliendo

PAST PARTICIPLE
scelto

EXAMPLE PHRASES

Chi **sceglie** il vino? *Who's going to choose the wine?*

Hai scelto il regalo per lei? *Have you chosen her present?*

Sceglievano sempre il vino più costoso. *They always chose the most expensive wine.*

Stavo **scegliendo** le pesche più mature. *I was choosing the ripest peaches.*

scegliere

FUTURE

io	**sceglierò**
tu	**sceglierai**
lui/lei/Lei	**sceglierà**
noi	**sceglieremo**
voi	**sceglierete**
loro	**sceglieranno**

CONDITIONAL

io	**sceglierei**
tu	**sceglieresti**
lui/lei/Lei	**sceglierebbe**
noi	**sceglieremmo**
voi	**scegliereste**
loro	**sceglierebbero**

PAST HISTORIC

io	**scelsi**
tu	**scegliesti**
lui/lei/Lei	**scelse**
noi	**scegliemmo**
voi	**sceglieste**
loro	**scelsero**

PLUPERFECT

io	**avevo scelto**
tu	**avevi scelto**
lui/lei/Lei	**aveva scelto**
noi	**avevamo scelto**
voi	**avevate scelto**
loro	**avevano scelto**

IMPERATIVE

scegli
scegliamo
scegliete

EXAMPLE PHRASES

Non sa ancora quale abito **sceglierà**. *She hasn't decided yet which dress she'll choose.*

Il cappello che **aveva scelto** con tanta cura ora non le piace più. *She no longer likes the hat she'd chosen with such care.*

Scegli la pizza che vuoi. *Choose which pizza you want.*

Italic letters in Italian words show where stress does not follow the usual rules.

scendere (to go down)

PRESENT		PRESENT SUBJUNCTIVE	
io	scendo	io	scenda
tu	scendi	tu	scenda
lui/lei/Lei	scende	lui/lei/Lei	scenda
noi	scendiamo	noi	scendiamo
voi	scendete	voi	scendiate
loro	scendono	loro	scendano

PERFECT		IMPERFECT	
io	sono sceso/a	io	scendevo
tu	sei sceso/a	tu	scendevi
lui/lei/Lei	è sceso/a	lui/lei/Lei	scendeva
noi	siamo scesi/e	noi	scendevamo
voi	siete scesi/e	voi	scendevate
loro	sono scesi/e	loro	scendevano

GERUND
scendendo

PAST PARTICIPLE
sceso

EXAMPLE PHRASES

Sali tu o **scendo** io? *Are you coming up or shall I come down?*

Scendo subito! *I'm coming!*

La temperatura **è scesa** di due gradi. *The temperature fell by two degrees.*

Scendevo le scale quando sono inciampata. *I tripped coming down the stairs.*

Si è storto una caviglia **scendendo** dalla macchina. *He twisted his ankle getting out of the car.*

Remember that subject pronouns are not used very often in Italian.

scendere

FUTURE

io	**scenderò**
tu	**scenderai**
lui/lei/Lei	**scenderà**
noi	**scenderemo**
voi	**scenderete**
loro	**scenderanno**

CONDITIONAL

io	**scenderei**
tu	**scenderesti**
lui/lei/Lei	**scenderebbe**
noi	**scenderemmo**
voi	**scendereste**
loro	**scenderebbero**

PAST HISTORIC

io	**scesi**
tu	**scendesti**
lui/lei/Lei	**scese**
noi	**scendemmo**
voi	**scendeste**
loro	**scesero**

PLUPERFECT

io	**ero sceso/a**
tu	**eri sceso/a**
lui/lei/Lei	**era sceso/a**
noi	**eravamo scesi/e**
voi	**eravate scesi/e**
loro	**erano scesi/e**

IMPERATIVE

scendi
scendiamo
scendete

EXAMPLE PHRASES

Dopo le feste i prezzi **scenderanno**. *After the holidays prices will come down.*

Sono arrivati. **Scendi** ad aprire la porta. *They're here. Go down and open the door.*

Italic letters in Italian words show where stress does not follow the usual rules.

sciare (to ski)

PRESENT

io	**scio**
tu	**scii**
lui/lei/Lei	**scia**
noi	**sciamo**
voi	**sciate**
loro	**sciano**

PRESENT SUBJUNCTIVE

io	**scii**
tu	**scii**
lui/lei/Lei	**scii**
noi	**sciamo**
voi	**sciate**
loro	**sciino**

PERFECT

io	**ho sciato**
tu	**hai sciato**
lui/lei/Lei	**ha sciato**
noi	**abbiamo sciato**
voi	**avete sciato**
loro	**hanno sciato**

IMPERFECT

io	**sciavo**
tu	**sciavi**
lui/lei/Lei	**sciava**
noi	**sciavamo**
voi	**sciavate**
loro	**sciavano**

GERUND

sciando

PAST PARTICIPLE

sciato

EXAMPLE PHRASES

Scia come un campione. *He skis like a champion.*

Sai **sciare**? *Can you ski?*

Abbiamo sciato tutto il giorno. *We skied all day.*

Si è rotto la gamba **sciando**. *He broke his leg when he was skiing.*

Remember that subject pronouns are not used very often in Italian.

sciare

FUTURE

io	**scierò**
tu	**scierai**
lui/lei/Lei	**scierà**
noi	**scieremo**
voi	**scierete**
loro	**scieranno**

CONDITIONAL

io	**scierei**
tu	**scieresti**
lui/lei/Lei	**scierebbe**
noi	**scieremmo**
voi	**sciereste**
loro	**scierebbero**

PAST HISTORIC

io	**sciai**
tu	**sciasti**
lui/lei/Lei	**sciò**
noi	**sciammo**
voi	**sciaste**
loro	**sciarono**

PLUPERFECT

io	**avevo sciato**
tu	**avevi sciato**
lui/lei/Lei	**aveva sciato**
noi	**avevamo sciato**
voi	**avevate sciato**
loro	**avevano sciato**

IMPERATIVE

scia
sciamo
sciate

EXAMPLE PHRASES

Se seguirai i miei consigli **scierai** meglio. *If you follow my advice you'll ski better.*

Adoro la montagna: **scierei** sempre. *I love the mountains: I'd like to spend all my time skiing.*

Sciò molto bene e vinse la gara. *She skied very well and won the competition.*

Avevamo sciato a lungo ed eravamo stanchi. *We'd been skiing for a long time and were tired.*

Italic letters in Italian words show where stress does not follow the usual rules.

sciogliere (to melt)

PRESENT		PRESENT SUBJUNCTIVE	
io	sciolgo	io	sciolga
tu	sciogli	tu	sciolga
lui/lei/Lei	scioglie	lui/lei/Lei	sciolga
noi	sciogliamo	noi	sciogliamo
voi	sciogliete	voi	sciogliate
loro	sciolgono	loro	sciolgano

PERFECT		IMPERFECT	
io	ho sciolto	io	scioglievo
tu	hai sciolto	tu	scioglievi
lui/lei/Lei	ha sciolto	lui/lei/Lei	scioglieva
noi	abbiamo sciolto	noi	scioglievamo
voi	avete sciolto	voi	scioglievate
loro	hanno sciolto	loro	scioglievano

GERUND	PAST PARTICIPLE
sciogliendo	sciolto

EXAMPLE PHRASES

Nell'acqua il sale si **scioglie**. *Salt dissolves in water.*

Fai attenzione che i nodi non si **sciolgano**. *Be careful that the knots don't come undone.*

Il sole **ha sciolto** la neve. *The sun has melted the snow.*

La neve si **è sciolta** al sole. *The snow melted in the sun.*

sciogliere

FUTURE

io	**scioglierò**
tu	**scioglierai**
lui/lei/Lei	**scioglierà**
noi	**scioglieremo**
voi	**scioglierete**
loro	**scioglieranno**

CONDITIONAL

io	**scioglierei**
tu	**scioglieresti**
lui/lei/Lei	**scioglierebbe**
noi	**scioglieremmo**
voi	**sciogliereste**
loro	**scioglierebbero**

PAST HISTORIC

io	**sciolsi**
tu	**sciogliesti**
lui/lei/Lei	**sciolse**
noi	**sciogliemmo**
voi	**scioglieste**
loro	**sciolsero**

PLUPERFECT

io	**avevo sciolto**
tu	**avevi sciolto**
lui/lei/Lei	**aveva sciolto**
noi	**avevamo sciolto**
voi	**avevate sciolto**
loro	**avevano sciolto**

IMPERATIVE

sciogli
sciogliamo
sciogliete

EXAMPLE PHRASES

Si **sciolse** i capelli. *She undid her hair.*

Sciogli la barca che salpiamo! *Untie the boat so we can move off.*

Facevamo esercizi per **sciogliere** i muscoli. *We did exercises to loosen up our muscles.*

Italic letters in Italian words show where stress does not follow the usual rules.

sconfiggere (to defeat)

PRESENT

io	**sconfiggo**
tu	**sconfiggi**
lui/lei/Lei	**sconfigge**
noi	**sconfiggiamo**
voi	**sconfiggete**
loro	**sconfiggono**

PRESENT SUBJUNCTIVE

io	**sconfigga**
tu	**sconfigga**
lui/lei/Lei	**sconfigga**
noi	**sconfiggiamo**
voi	**sconfiggiate**
loro	**sconfiggano**

PERFECT

io	**ho sconfitto**
tu	**hai sconfitto**
lui/lei/Lei	**ha sconfitto**
noi	**abbiamo sconfitto**
voi	**avete sconfitto**
loro	**hanno sconfitto**

IMPERFECT

io	**sconfiggevo**
tu	**sconfiggevi**
lui/lei/Lei	**sconfiggeva**
noi	**sconfiggevamo**
voi	**sconfiggevate**
loro	**sconfiggevano**

GERUND

sconfiggendo

PAST PARTICIPLE

sconfitto

EXAMPLE PHRASES

Hanno finalmente **sconfitto** la malattia. *They have at last conquered the disease.*

Li **hanno sconfitti** uno a zero. *They beat them one nil.*

La mia squadra **è** stata **sconfitta**. *My team was beaten.*

sconfiggere

FUTURE

io	**sconfiggerò**
tu	**sconfiggerai**
lui/lei/Lei	**sconfiggerà**
noi	**sconfiggeremo**
voi	**sconfiggerete**
loro	**sconfiggeranno**

CONDITIONAL

io	**sconfiggerei**
tu	**sconfiggeresti**
lui/lei/Lei	**sconfiggerebbe**
noi	**sconfiggeremmo**
voi	**sconfiggereste**
loro	**sconfiggerebbero**

PAST HISTORIC

io	**sconfissi**
tu	**sconfiggesti**
lui/lei/Lei	**sconfisse**
noi	**sconfiggemmo**
voi	**sconfiggeste**
loro	**sconfissero**

PLUPERFECT

io	**avevo sconfitto**
tu	**avevi sconfitto**
lui/lei/Lei	**aveva sconfitto**
noi	**avevamo sconfitto**
voi	**avevate sconfitto**
loro	**avevano sconfitto**

IMPERATIVE

sconfiggi
sconfiggiamo
sconfiggete

EXAMPLE PHRASES

Quel candidato **sconfiggerà** certamente tutti gli altri. *This candidate is sure to defeat all the others.*

Se fossi in forma non mi **sconfiggeresti** mai. *If I was fit you'd never beat me.*

L'esercito **sconfisse** i nemici. *The army defeated the enemy.*

Era triste perché lo **avevano sconfitto**. *He was unhappy because they'd beaten him.*

Attacchiamo e **sconfiggiamoli**! *Let's attack and defeat them!*

Italic letters in Italian words show where stress does not follow the usual rules.

scrivere (to write)

PRESENT

io	**scrivo**
tu	**scrivi**
lui/lei/Lei	**scrive**
noi	**scriviamo**
voi	**scrivete**
loro	**scrivono**

PRESENT SUBJUNCTIVE

io	**scriva**
tu	**scriva**
lui/lei/Lei	**scriva**
noi	**scriviamo**
voi	**scriviate**
loro	**scrivano**

PERFECT

io	**ho scritto**
tu	**hai scritto**
lui/lei/Lei	**ha scritto**
noi	**abbiamo scritto**
voi	**avete scritto**
loro	**hanno scritto**

IMPERFECT

io	**scrivevo**
tu	**scrivevi**
lui/lei/Lei	**scriveva**
noi	**scrivevamo**
voi	**scrivevate**
loro	**scrivevano**

GERUND

scrivendo

PAST PARTICIPLE

scritto

EXAMPLE PHRASES

Scrivo molti sms ai miei amici. *I write lots of text messages to my friends.*

Come si **scrive**? *How do you spell it?*

Ho scritto una mail a Luca. *I sent Luca an email.*

A Natale ci **scrivevano** sempre. *They always wrote to us at Christmas.*

Non so **scrivere** velocemente al computer. *I can't type fast on the computer.*

Sta **scrivendo** la tesi di laurea. *She's writing her thesis.*

Remember that subject pronouns are not used very often in Italian.

scrivere

FUTURE

io	**scriverò**
tu	**scriverai**
lui/lei/Lei	**scriverà**
noi	**scriveremo**
voi	**scriverete**
loro	**scriveranno**

CONDITIONAL

io	**scriverei**
tu	**scriveresti**
lui/lei/Lei	**scriverebbe**
noi	**scriveremmo**
voi	**scrivereste**
loro	**scriverebbero**

PAST HISTORIC

io	**scrissi**
tu	**scrivesti**
lui/lei/Lei	**scrisse**
noi	**scrivemmo**
voi	**scriveste**
loro	**scrissero**

PLUPERFECT

io	**avevo scritto**
tu	**avevi scritto**
lui/lei/Lei	**aveva scritto**
noi	**avevamo scritto**
voi	**avevate scritto**
loro	**avevano scritto**

IMPERATIVE

scrivi
scriviamo
scrivete

EXAMPLE PHRASES

Avevo scritto un appunto ma l'ho perso. *I'd written a note but lost it.*
Scrivimi presto. *Write to me soon.*

Italic letters in Italian words show where stress does not follow the usual rules.

scuotere (to shake)

PRESENT

io	**scuoto**
tu	**scuoti**
lui/lei/Lei	**scuote**
noi	**scuotiamo**
voi	**scuotete**
loro	**scuotono**

PRESENT SUBJUNCTIVE

io	**scuota**
tu	**scuota**
lui/lei/Lei	**scuota**
noi	**scuotiamo**
voi	**scuotiate**
loro	**scuotano**

PERFECT

io	**ho scosso**
tu	**hai scosso**
lui/lei/Lei	**ha scosso**
noi	**abbiamo scosso**
voi	**avete scosso**
loro	**hanno scosso**

IMPERFECT

io	**scuotevo**
tu	**scuotevi**
lui/lei/Lei	**scuoteva**
noi	**scuotevamo**
voi	**scuotevate**
loro	**scuotevano**

GERUND
scuotendo

PAST PARTICIPLE
scosso

EXAMPLE PHRASES

È sul terrazzo che **scuote** i tappeti. *She's on the balcony shaking the rugs.*

Ha scosso la testa. *He shook his head.*

Scuoteva la scatola per capire cosa conteneva. *He shook the box to see what was in it.*

Stava **scuotendo** la borsa per farne uscire il contenuto. *She was shaking the contents out of the bag.*

Se ne andò **scuotendo** la testa senza parlare. *She went off, shaking her head but saying nothing.*

Remember that subject pronouns are not used very often in Italian.

scuotere

FUTURE

io	**scuoterò**
tu	**scuoterai**
lui/lei/Lei	**scuoterà**
noi	**scuoteremo**
voi	**scuoterete**
loro	**scuoteranno**

CONDITIONAL

io	**scuoterei**
tu	**scuoteresti**
lui/lei/Lei	**scuoterebbe**
noi	**scuoteremmo**
voi	**scuotereste**
loro	**scuoterebbero**

PAST HISTORIC

io	**scossi**
tu	**scuotesti**
lui/lei/Lei	**scosse**
noi	**scuotemmo**
voi	**scuoteste**
loro	**scossero**

PLUPERFECT

io	**avevo scosso**
tu	**avevi scosso**
lui/lei/Lei	**aveva scosso**
noi	**avevamo scosso**
voi	**avevate scosso**
loro	**avevano scosso**

IMPERATIVE

scuoti
scuotiamo
scuotete

EXAMPLE PHRASES

Quel rumore mi **scosse** i nervi. *That noise drove me mad.*

Italic letters in Italian words show where stress does not follow the usual rules.

sedere (to sit)

PRESENT		PRESENT SUBJUNCTIVE	
io	**siedo**	io	**sieda**
tu	**siedi**	tu	**sieda**
lui/lei/Lei	**siede**	lui/lei/Lei	**sieda**
noi	**sediamo**	noi	**sediamo**
voi	**sedete**	voi	**sediate**
loro	**siedono**	loro	**siedano**

PERFECT		IMPERFECT	
io	**sono seduto/a**	io	**sedevo**
tu	**sei seduto/a**	tu	**sedevi**
lui/lei/Lei	**è seduto/a**	lui/lei/Lei	**sedeva**
noi	**siamo seduti/e**	noi	**sedevamo**
voi	**siete seduti/e**	voi	**sedevate**
loro	**sono seduti/e**	loro	**sedevano**

GERUND
sedendo

PAST PARTICIPLE
seduto

EXAMPLE PHRASES

Si **siede** sempre in ultima fila. *She always sits in the back row.*

Prego, si **sieda** qui accanto. *Please sit here beside me.*

Si **è seduto** per terra. *He sat on the floor.*

Sono stato **seduto** tutto il giorno. *I've been sitting down all day.*

Sedevano in silenzio e leggevano. *They were sitting in silence reading.*

Remember that subject pronouns are not used very often in Italian.

sedere

FUTURE

io	**sederò**
tu	**sederai**
lui/lei/Lei	**sederà**
noi	**sederemo**
voi	**sederete**
loro	**sederanno**

CONDITIONAL

io	**sederei**
tu	**sederesti**
lui/lei/Lei	**sederebbe**
noi	**sederemmo**
voi	**sedereste**
loro	**sederebbero**

PAST HISTORIC

io	**sedetti**
tu	**sedesti**
lui/lei/Lei	**sedette**
noi	**sedemmo**
voi	**sedeste**
loro	**sedettero**

PLUPERFECT

io	**ero seduto/a**
tu	**eri seduto/a**
lui/lei/Lei	**era seduto/a**
noi	**eravamo seduti/e**
voi	**eravate seduti/e**
loro	**erano seduti/e**

IMPERATIVE
siedi
sediamo
sedete

EXAMPLE PHRASES

Si **sedettero** a tavola e iniziarono la cena. *They sat down at the table and started dinner.*

Era seduta accanto a me. *She was sitting beside me.*

Siediti qui! *Sit here!*

Italic letters in Italian words show where stress does not follow the usual rules.

soddisfare (to satisfy)

PRESENT		PRESENT SUBJUNCTIVE	
io	**soddisfo**	io	**soddisfi**
tu	**soddisfi**	tu	**soddisfi**
lui/lei/Lei	**soddisfa**	lui/lei/Lei	**soddisfi**
noi	**soddisfiamo**	noi	**soddisfiamo**
voi	**soddisfate**	voi	**soddisfiate**
loro	**soddisfano**	loro	**soddisfino**

PERFECT		IMPERFECT	
io	**ho soddisfatto**	io	**soddisfacevo**
tu	**hai soddisfatto**	tu	**soddisfacevi**
lui/lei/Lei	**ha soddisfatto**	lui/lei/Lei	**soddisfaceva**
noi	**abbiamo soddisfatto**	noi	**soddisfacevamo**
voi	**avete soddisfatto**	voi	**soddisfacevate**
loro	**hanno soddisfatto**	loro	**soddisfacevano**

GERUND
soddisfacendo

PAST PARTICIPLE
soddisfatto

EXAMPLE PHRASES

Il mio lavoro non mi **soddisfa**. *My job doesn't satisfy me.*

Soddisfaceva ogni desiderio della moglie. *He satisfied his wife's every wish.*

Remember that subject pronouns are not used very often in Italian.

soddisfare

FUTURE

io	**soddisferò**
tu	**soddisferai**
lui/lei/Lei	**soddisferà**
noi	**soddisferemo**
voi	**soddisferete**
loro	**soddisferanno**

CONDITIONAL

io	**soddisferei**
tu	**soddisferesti**
lui/lei/Lei	**soddisferebbe**
noi	**soddisferemmo**
voi	**soddisfereste**
loro	**soddisferebbero**

PAST HISTORIC

io	**soddisfeci**
tu	**soddisfacesti**
lui/lei/Lei	**soddisfece**
noi	**soddisfacemmo**
voi	**soddisfaceste**
loro	**soddisfecero**

PLUPERFECT

io	**avevo soddisfatto**
tu	**avevi soddisfatto**
lui/lei/Lei	**aveva soddisfatto**
noi	**avevamo soddisfatto**
voi	**avevate soddisfatto**
loro	**avevano soddisfatto**

IMPERATIVE

soddisfa
soddisfiamo
soddisfate

EXAMPLE PHRASES

Questo libro **soddisferà** i lettori più esigenti. *This book will please the most demanding readers.*

Questa soluzione non ci **soddisferebbe**. *We wouldn't be satisfied by this solution.*

La sua scelta non li **aveva soddisfatti**. *They hadn't been pleased with her choice.*

Italic letters in Italian words show where stress does not follow the usual rules.

sognare (to dream)

PRESENT

io	**sogno**
tu	**sogni**
lui/lei/Lei	**sogna**
noi	**sogniamo**
voi	**sognate**
loro	**sognano**

PRESENT SUBJUNCTIVE

io	**sogni**
tu	**sogni**
lui/lei/Lei	**sogni**
noi	**sogniamo**
voi	**sogniate**
loro	**sognino**

PERFECT

io	**ho sognato**
tu	**hai sognato**
lui/lei/Lei	**ha sognato**
noi	**abbiamo sognato**
voi	**avete sognato**
loro	**hanno sognato**

IMPERFECT

io	**sognavo**
tu	**sognavi**
lui/lei/Lei	**sognava**
noi	**sognavamo**
voi	**sognavate**
loro	**sognavano**

GERUND

sognando

PAST PARTICIPLE

sognato

EXAMPLE PHRASES

Stanotte ti **ho sognato**. *I dreamt about you last night.*

Tutte le notti **sognavo** la stessa cosa. *I had the same dream every night.*

Stavo **sognando** ad occhi aperti. *I was daydreaming.*

Remember that subject pronouns are not used very often in Italian.

sognare

FUTURE

io	**sognerò**
tu	**sognerai**
lui/lei/Lei	**sognerà**
noi	**sogneremo**
voi	**sognerete**
loro	**sogneranno**

CONDITIONAL

io	**sognerei**
tu	**sogneresti**
lui/lei/Lei	**sognerebbe**
noi	**sogneremmo**
voi	**sognereste**
loro	**sognerebbero**

PAST HISTORIC

io	**sognai**
tu	**sognasti**
lui/lei/Lei	**sognò**
noi	**sognammo**
voi	**sognaste**
loro	**sognarono**

PLUPERFECT

io	**avevo sognato**
tu	**avevi sognato**
lui/lei/Lei	**aveva sognato**
noi	**avevamo sognato**
voi	**avevate sognato**
loro	**avevano sognato**

IMPERATIVE

sogna
sogniamo
sognate

EXAMPLE PHRASES

Non ci **sogneremmo** mai di chiedere una cosa simile. *We'd never dream of asking for something like that.*
Sognai di essere sulla luna. *I dreamt I was on the moon.*
Avevo sempre **sognato** una casa così. *I'd always dreamt of a house like that.*
Smetti di **sognare** e sii realista. *Stop dreaming and be realistic.*
Ve lo **sognate**! *You can forget it!*

Italic letters in Italian words show where stress does not follow the usual rules.

sparire (to disappear)

PRESENT

io	**sparisco**
tu	**sparisci**
lui/lei/Lei	**sparisce**
noi	**spariamo**
voi	**sparite**
loro	**spariscono**

PRESENT SUBJUNCTIVE

io	**sparisca**
tu	**sparisca**
lui/lei/Lei	**sparisca**
noi	**spariamo**
voi	**spariate**
loro	**spariscano**

PERFECT

io	**sono sparito/a**
tu	**sei sparito/a**
lui/lei/Lei	**è sparito/a**
noi	**siamo spariti/e**
voi	**siete spariti/e**
loro	**sono spariti/e**

IMPERFECT

io	**sparivo**
tu	**sparivi**
lui/lei/Lei	**spariva**
noi	**sparivamo**
voi	**sparivate**
loro	**sparivano**

GERUND

sparendo

PAST PARTICIPLE

sparito

EXAMPLE PHRASES

Sparisce ogni volta che c'è bisogno di lui. *He disappears whenever he's needed.*

La nave **è sparita** all'orizzonte. *The ship disappeared over the horizon.*

Dov'**è sparita** la mia penna? *Where has my pen gone?*

sparire

FUTURE
io	**sparirò**
tu	**sparirai**
lui/lei/Lei	**sparirà**
noi	**spariremo**
voi	**sparirete**
loro	**spariranno**

CONDITIONAL
io	**sparirei**
tu	**spariresti**
lui/lei/Lei	**sparirebbe**
noi	**spariremmo**
voi	**sparireste**
loro	**sparirebbero**

PAST HISTORIC
io	**sparii**
tu	**sparisti**
lui/lei/Lei	**sparì**
noi	**sparimmo**
voi	**spariste**
loro	**sparirono**

PLUPERFECT
io	**ero sparito/a**
tu	**eri sparito/a**
lui/lei/Lei	**era sparito/a**
noi	**eravamo spariti/e**
voi	**eravate spariti/e**
loro	**erano spariti/e**

IMPERATIVE
sparisci
spariamo
sparite

EXAMPLE PHRASES
Spariranno dopo cena, come al solito. *They'll go off after dinner, as usual.*
Sparì senza salutare nessuno. *He went off without saying goodbye to anyone.*
Erano spariti senza lasciare traccia. *They had disappeared without trace.*
Sparisci e non farti più vedere! *Be off with you and don't show your face around here again!*

Italic letters in Italian words show where stress does not follow the usual rules.

spegnere (to put out)

PRESENT

io	**spengo**
tu	**spegni**
lui/lei/Lei	**spegne**
noi	**spegniamo**
voi	**spegnete**
loro	**spengono**

PRESENT SUBJUNCTIVE

io	**spenga**
tu	**spenga**
lui/lei/Lei	**spenga**
noi	**spegniamo**
voi	**spegniate**
loro	**spengano**

PERFECT

io	**ho spento**
tu	**hai spento**
lui/lei/Lei	**ha spento**
noi	**abbiamo spento**
voi	**avete spento**
loro	**hanno spento**

IMPERFECT

io	**spegnevo**
tu	**spegnevi**
lui/lei/Lei	**spegneva**
noi	**spegnevamo**
voi	**spegnevate**
loro	**spegnevano**

GERUND

spegnendo

PAST PARTICIPLE

spento

EXAMPLE PHRASES

L'ultimo **spenga** la luce e chiuda la porta. *Will the last person turn off the light and shut the door.*

Hai spento la sigaretta? *Have you put your cigarette out?*

La luce si **è spenta** all'improvviso. *The light went off suddenly.*

La candela si stava **spegnendo** lentamente. *The candle was slowly going out.*

spegnere

FUTURE

io	**spegnerò**
tu	**spegnerai**
lui/lei/Lei	**spegnerà**
noi	**spegneremo**
voi	**spegnerete**
loro	**spegneranno**

CONDITIONAL

io	**spegnerei**
tu	**spegneresti**
lui/lei/Lei	**spegnerebbe**
noi	**spegneremmo**
voi	**spegnereste**
loro	**spegnerebbero**

PAST HISTORIC

io	**spensi**
tu	**spegnesti**
lui/lei/Lei	**spense**
noi	**spegnemmo**
voi	**spegneste**
loro	**spensero**

PLUPERFECT

io	**avevo spento**
tu	**avevi spento**
lui/lei/Lei	**aveva spento**
noi	**avevamo spento**
voi	**avevate spento**
loro	**avevano spento**

IMPERATIVE

spegni
spegniamo
spegnete

EXAMPLE PHRASES

Senza ossigeno il fuoco si **spegnerebbe**. *Without oxygen the fire would go out.*

Il motore si **spense** al semaforo. *The engine stalled at the traffic lights.*

Spegnete le luci che guardiamo il film. *Turn off the lights and we'll watch the film.*

Italic letters in Italian words show where stress does not follow the usual rules.

spendere (to spend)

PRESENT

io	**spendo**
tu	**spendi**
lui/lei/Lei	**spende**
noi	**spendiamo**
voi	**spendete**
loro	**spendono**

PRESENT SUBJUNCTIVE

io	**spenda**
tu	**spenda**
lui/lei/Lei	**spenda**
noi	**spendiamo**
voi	**spendiate**
loro	**spendano**

PERFECT

io	**ho speso**
tu	**hai speso**
lui/lei/Lei	**ha speso**
noi	**abbiamo speso**
voi	**avete speso**
loro	**hanno speso**

IMPERFECT

io	**spendevo**
tu	**spendevi**
lui/lei/Lei	**spendeva**
noi	**spendevamo**
voi	**spendevate**
loro	**spendevano**

GERUND
spendendo

PAST PARTICIPLE
speso

EXAMPLE PHRASES

Si mangia bene e si **spende** poco. *The food's good and it doesn't cost much.*

Quanto **hai speso**? *How much did you spend?*

Spendeva tutto quello che guadagnava. *He spent all he earned.*

Ultimamente stiamo **spendendo** troppo. *We've been spending too much lately.*

Remember that subject pronouns are not used very often in Italian.

spendere

FUTURE

io	**spenderò**
tu	**spenderai**
lui/lei/Lei	**spenderà**
noi	**spenderemo**
voi	**spenderete**
loro	**spenderanno**

CONDITIONAL

io	**spenderei**
tu	**spenderesti**
lui/lei/Lei	**spenderebbe**
noi	**spenderemmo**
voi	**spendereste**
loro	**spenderebbero**

PAST HISTORIC

io	**spesi**
tu	**spendesti**
lui/lei/Lei	**spese**
noi	**spendemmo**
voi	**spendeste**
loro	**spesero**

PLUPERFECT

io	**avevo speso**
tu	**avevi speso**
lui/lei/Lei	**aveva speso**
noi	**avevamo speso**
voi	**avevate speso**
loro	**avevano speso**

IMPERATIVE

spendi
spendiamo
spendete

EXAMPLE PHRASES

Lì **spenderete** poco e starete bene. *You won't have to pay much there, and you'll be comfortable.*

Non **spenderei** mai una cifra simile. *I'd never spend as much as that.*

Entrò nel negozio e **spese** tutto ciò che aveva. *She went into the shop and spent all she had.*

Aveva speso tutto al gioco e si è indebitato. *He'd spent all his money gambling and was in debt.*

Italic letters in Italian words show where stress does not follow the usual rules.

sporgersi (to lean out)

PRESENT

io	**mi sporgo**
tu	**ti sporgi**
lui/lei/Lei	**si sporge**
noi	**ci sporgiamo**
voi	**vi sporgete**
loro	**si sporgono**

PRESENT SUBJUNCTIVE

io	**mi sporga**
tu	**ti sporga**
lui/lei/Lei	**si sporga**
noi	**ci sporgiamo**
voi	**vi sporgiate**
loro	**si sporgano**

PERFECT

io	**mi sono sporto/a**
tu	**ti sei sporto/a**
lui/lei/Lei	**si è sporto/a**
noi	**ci siamo sporti/e**
voi	**vi siete sporti/e**
loro	**si sono sporti/e**

IMPERFECT

io	**mi sporgevo**
tu	**ti sporgevi**
lui/lei/Lei	**si sporgeva**
noi	**ci sporgevamo**
voi	**vi sporgevate**
loro	**si sporgevano**

GERUND
sporgendosi

PAST PARTICIPLE
sporto

EXAMPLE PHRASES
Sporgendoti, vedrai meglio. *If you lean out you'll see better.*

sporgersi

FUTURE

io	**mi sporgerò**
tu	**ti sporgerai**
lui/lei/Lei	**si sporgerà**
noi	**ci sporgeremo**
voi	**vi sporgerete**
loro	**si sporgeranno**

CONDITIONAL

io	**mi sporgerei**
tu	**ti sporgeresti**
lui/lei/Lei	**si sporgerebbe**
noi	**ci sporgeremmo**
voi	**vi sporgereste**
loro	**si sporgerebbero**

PAST HISTORIC

io	**mi sporsi**
tu	**ti sporgesti**
lui/lei/Lei	**si sporse**
noi	**ci sporgemmo**
voi	**vi sporgeste**
loro	**si sporsero**

PLUPERFECT

io	**mi ero sporto/a**
tu	**ti eri sporto/a**
lui/lei/Lei	**si era sporto/a**
noi	**ci eravamo sporti/e**
voi	**vi eravate sporti/e**
loro	**si erano sporti/e**

IMPERATIVE

sporgiti
sporgiamoci
sporgetevi

EXAMPLE PHRASES

Si **sporsero** per guardare la sfilata. *They leaned out to watch the parade.*

Si **era sporto** per salutare. *He'd leant out to say hello.*

Non **sporgerti** dal finestrino. *Don't lean out of the window.*

Italic letters in Italian words show where stress does not follow the usual rules.

stare (to be)

PRESENT		PRESENT SUBJUNCTIVE	
io	**sto**	io	**stia**
tu	**stai**	tu	**stia**
lui/lei/Lei	**sta**	lui/lei/Lei	**stia**
noi	**stiamo**	noi	**stiamo**
voi	**state**	voi	**stiate**
loro	**stanno**	loro	**stiano**

PERFECT		IMPERFECT	
io	**sono stato/a**	io	**stavo**
tu	**sei stato/a**	tu	**stavi**
lui/lei/Lei	**è stato/a**	lui/lei/Lei	**stava**
noi	**siamo stati/e**	noi	**stavamo**
voi	**siete stati/e**	voi	**stavate**
loro	**sono stati/e**	loro	**stavano**

GERUND	PAST PARTICIPLE
stando	stato

EXAMPLE PHRASES

Come **stai**? *How are you?*

Sta a te decidere. *It's up to you to decide.*

Sei mai **stato** in Francia? *Have you ever been to France?*

Stavo per uscire quando ha squillato il telefono. *I was about to go out when the phone rang.*

Stavo andando a casa. *I was going home.*

Stando così le cose, non voglio aiutarti. *In this situation I don't want to help you.*

Remember that subject pronouns are not used very often in Italian.

stare

FUTURE

io	**starò**
tu	**starai**
lui/lei/Lei	**starà**
noi	**staremo**
voi	**starete**
loro	**staranno**

CONDITIONAL

io	**starei**
tu	**staresti**
lui/lei/Lei	**starebbe**
noi	**staremmo**
voi	**stareste**
loro	**starebbero**

PAST HISTORIC

io	**stetti**
tu	**stesti**
lui/lei/Lei	**stette**
noi	**stemmo**
voi	**steste**
loro	**stettero**

PLUPERFECT

io	**ero stato/a**
tu	**eri stato/a**
lui/lei/Lei	**era stato/a**
noi	**eravamo stati/e**
voi	**eravate stati/e**
loro	**erano stati/e**

IMPERATIVE

stai
stiamo
state

EXAMPLE PHRASES

A Londra **starò** da amici. *I'll be staying with friends in London.*
Ci **stareste** a fare uno scherzo a Monica? *Do you want to play a trick on Monica?*
Era stata zitta tutta la sera. *She'd been silent all evening.*
Stai ancora un po'! *Stay a bit longer!*

Italic letters in Italian words show where stress does not follow the usual rules.

storcere (to twist)

PRESENT		PRESENT SUBJUNCTIVE	
io	**storco**	io	**storca**
tu	**storci**	tu	**storca**
lui/lei/Lei	**storce**	lui/lei/Lei	**storca**
noi	**storciamo**	noi	**storciamo**
voi	**storcete**	voi	**storciate**
loro	**storcono**	loro	**storcano**

PERFECT		IMPERFECT	
io	**ho storto**	io	**storcevo**
tu	**hai storto**	tu	**storcevi**
lui/lei/Lei	**ha storto**	lui/lei/Lei	**storceva**
noi	**abbiamo storto**	noi	**storcevamo**
voi	**avete storto**	voi	**storcevate**
loro	**hanno storto**	loro	**storcevano**

GERUND
storcendo

PAST PARTICIPLE
storto

EXAMPLE PHRASES

Storce sempre il naso se c'è da lavorare. *He always turns up his nose if there's any work to be done.*

È inutile che tu **storca** il naso. *There's no point turning up your nose.*

Le **ha storto** un braccio. *He twisted her arm.*

Mi **sono storto** una caviglia. *I've twisted my ankle.*

Remember that subject pronouns are not used very often in Italian.

storcere

FUTURE

io	**storcerò**
tu	**storcerai**
lui/lei/Lei	**storcerà**
noi	**storceremo**
voi	**storcerete**
loro	**storceranno**

CONDITIONAL

io	**storcerei**
tu	**storceresti**
lui/lei/Lei	**storcerebbe**
noi	**storceremmo**
voi	**storcereste**
loro	**storcerebbero**

PAST HISTORIC

io	**storsi**
tu	**storcesti**
lui/lei/Lei	**storse**
noi	**storcemmo**
voi	**storceste**
loro	**storsero**

PLUPERFECT

io	**avevo storto**
tu	**avevi storto**
lui/lei/Lei	**aveva storto**
noi	**avevamo storto**
voi	**avevate storto**
loro	**avevano storto**

IMPERATIVE

storci
storciamo
storcete

EXAMPLE PHRASES

Non **storceresti** il naso se fossi meno schizzinoso. *You wouldn't turn up your nose if you weren't so fussy.*

Guardò il cibo e **storse** il naso. *He looked at the food and turned up his nose.*

Italic letters in Italian words show where stress does not follow the usual rules.

stringere (to tighten)

PRESENT		PRESENT SUBJUNCTIVE	
io	**stringo**	io	**stringa**
tu	**stringi**	tu	**stringa**
lui/lei/Lei	**stringe**	lui/lei/Lei	**stringa**
noi	**stringiamo**	noi	**stringiamo**
voi	**stringete**	voi	**stringiate**
loro	**stringono**	loro	**stringano**

PERFECT		IMPERFECT	
io	**ho stretto**	io	**stringevo**
tu	**hai stretto**	tu	**stringevi**
lui/lei/Lei	**ha stretto**	lui/lei/Lei	**stringeva**
noi	**abbiamo stretto**	noi	**stringevamo**
voi	**avete stretto**	voi	**stringevate**
loro	**hanno stretto**	loro	**stringevano**

GERUND
stringendo

PAST PARTICIPLE
stretto

EXAMPLE PHRASES

La gonna è larga: bisogna che la **stringa**. *The skirt is too loose: I'll have to take it in.*

Ho stretto la cintura perché sono dimagrita. *I've tightened my belt because I've lost weight.*

Ci **siamo stretti** la mano. *We shook hands.*

Le scarpe **stringevano** e ho dovuto cambiarle. *The shoes were too tight so I had to change them.*

Remember that subject pronouns are not used very often in Italian.

stringere

FUTURE

io	**stringerò**
tu	**stringerai**
lui/lei/Lei	**stringerà**
noi	**stringeremo**
voi	**stringerete**
loro	**stringeranno**

CONDITIONAL

io	**stringerei**
tu	**stringeresti**
lui/lei/Lei	**stringerebbe**
noi	**stringeremmo**
voi	**stringereste**
loro	**stringerebbero**

PAST HISTORIC

io	**strinsi**
tu	**stringesti**
lui/lei/Lei	**strinse**
noi	**stringemmo**
voi	**stringeste**
loro	**strinsero**

PLUPERFECT

io	**avevo stretto**
tu	**avevi stretto**
lui/lei/Lei	**aveva stretto**
noi	**avevamo stretto**
voi	**avevate stretto**
loro	**avevano stretto**

IMPERATIVE

stringi
stringiamo
stringete

EXAMPLE PHRASES

Se ci **stringeremo** ci staremo tutti. *If we squeeze up we'll all get in.*
Stringiamo i denti e continuiamo. *Let's grit our teeth and carry on.*

Italic letters in Italian words show where stress does not follow the usual rules.

succedere (to happen)

PRESENT

io	–
tu	–
lui/lei/Lei	**succede**
noi	–
voi	–
loro	**succedono**

PRESENT SUBJUNCTIVE

io	–
tu	–
lui/lei/Lei	**succeda**
noi	–
voi	–
loro	**succedano**

PERFECT

io	–
tu	–
lui/lei/Lei	**è successo/a**
noi	–
voi	–
loro	**sono successi/e**

IMPERFECT

io	–
tu	–
lui/lei/Lei	**succedeva**
noi	–
voi	–
loro	**succedevano**

GERUND
succedendo

PAST PARTICIPLE
successo

EXAMPLE PHRASES

Sono cose che **succedono**. *These things happen.*

Non capisco cosa **succeda**. *I don't know what might be happening.*

Cos'**è successo**? *What happened?*

Dev'essergli **successo** qualcosa. *Something must have happened to him.*

Remember that subject pronouns are not used very often in Italian.

succedere

FUTURE

io	–
tu	–
lui/lei/Lei	**succederà**
noi	–
voi	–
loro	**succederanno**

CONDITIONAL

io	–
tu	–
lui/lei/Lei	**succederebbe**
noi	–
voi	–
loro	**succederebbero**

PAST HISTORIC

io	–
tu	–
lui/lei/Lei	**successe**
noi	–
voi	–
loro	**successero**

PLUPERFECT

io	–
tu	–
lui/lei/Lei	**era successo/a**
noi	–
voi	–
loro	**erano successi/e**

IMPERATIVE

–

EXAMPLE PHRASES

Ho paura di ciò che **succederà**. *I'm afraid of what will happen.*

Cosa **succederebbe** se lui tornasse? *What would happen if he came back?*

Dalla sua partenza erano **successe** molte cose. *A lot of things happened as a consequence of his departure.*

Successe il finimondo. *All hell broke loose.*

Italic letters in Italian words show where stress does not follow the usual rules.

tacere (to be quiet)

PRESENT

io	**taccio**
tu	**taci**
lui/lei/Lei	**tace**
noi	**tacciamo**
voi	**tacete**
loro	**tacciono**

PRESENT SUBJUNCTIVE

io	**taccia**
tu	**taccia**
lui/lei/Lei	**taccia**
noi	**tacciamo**
voi	**tacciate**
loro	**tacciano**

PERFECT

io	**ho taciuto**
tu	**hai taciuto**
lui/lei/Lei	**ha taciuto**
noi	**abbiamo taciuto**
voi	**avete taciuto**
loro	**hanno taciuto**

IMPERFECT

io	**tacevo**
tu	**tacevi**
lui/lei/Lei	**taceva**
noi	**tacevamo**
voi	**tacevate**
loro	**tacevano**

GERUND

tacendo

PAST PARTICIPLE

taciuto

EXAMPLE PHRASES

È meglio che **tacciate**. *It's best if you say nothing.*

Tacevano e si guardavano. *They said nothing and looked at each other.*

Pur **tacendo**, gli fece capire che sbagliava. *Even though she didn't say anything, she made him realize he was wrong.*

tacere

FUTURE

io	**tacerò**
tu	**tacerai**
lui/lei/Lei	**tacerà**
noi	**taceremo**
voi	**tacerete**
loro	**taceranno**

CONDITIONAL

io	**tacerei**
tu	**taceresti**
lui/lei/Lei	**tacerebbe**
noi	**taceremmo**
voi	**tacereste**
loro	**tacerebbero**

PAST HISTORIC

io	**tacqui**
tu	**tacesti**
lui/lei/Lei	**tacque**
noi	**tacemmo**
voi	**taceste**
loro	**tacquero**

PLUPERFECT

io	**avevo taciuto**
tu	**avevi taciuto**
lui/lei/Lei	**aveva taciuto**
noi	**avevamo taciuto**
voi	**avevate taciuto**
loro	**avevano taciuto**

IMPERATIVE

taci
tacciamo
tacete

EXAMPLE PHRASES

Improvvisamente **tacque** e sorrise. *He suddenly stopped talking and smiled.*

Avevo taciuto a lungo prima di parlare. *I'd been silent a long time before I spoke.*

Taci! *Be quiet!*

Italic letters in Italian words show where stress does not follow the usual rules.

tenere (to hold)

PRESENT		PRESENT SUBJUNCTIVE	
io	**tengo**	io	**tenga**
tu	**tieni**	tu	**tenga**
lui/lei/Lei	**tiene**	lui/lei/Lei	**tenga**
noi	**teniamo**	noi	**teniamo**
voi	**tenete**	voi	**teniate**
loro	**tengono**	loro	**tengano**

PERFECT		IMPERFECT	
io	**ho tenuto**	io	**tenevo**
tu	**hai tenuto**	tu	**tenevi**
lui/lei/Lei	**ha tenuto**	lui/lei/Lei	**teneva**
noi	**abbiamo tenuto**	noi	**tenevamo**
voi	**avete tenuto**	voi	**tenevate**
loro	**hanno tenuto**	loro	**tenevano**

GERUND	PAST PARTICIPLE
tenendo	**tenuto**

EXAMPLE PHRASES

Tiene la racchetta con la sinistra. *He holds the racket with his left hand.*

La mamma **tiene** in braccio il bambino. *The mother is holding the baby.*

Ecco i soldi, **tenga** pure il resto. *Here's the money, keep the change.*

Si **tenevano** per mano. *They were holding hands.*

tenere

FUTURE

io	**terrò**
tu	**terrai**
lui/lei/Lei	**terrà**
noi	**terremo**
voi	**terrete**
loro	**terranno**

CONDITIONAL

io	**terrei**
tu	**terresti**
lui/lei/Lei	**terrebbe**
noi	**terremmo**
voi	**terreste**
loro	**terrebbero**

PAST HISTORIC

io	**tenni**
tu	**tenesti**
lui/lei/Lei	**tenne**
noi	**tenemmo**
voi	**teneste**
loro	**tennero**

PLUPERFECT

io	**avevo tenuto**
tu	**avevi tenuto**
lui/lei/Lei	**aveva tenuto**
noi	**avevamo tenuto**
voi	**avevate tenuto**
loro	**avevano tenuto**

IMPERATIVE

tieni
teniamo
tenete

EXAMPLE PHRASES

Se non ti serve, lo **terrò** io. *If you don't need it I'll keep it.*

Mi **terresti** il posto? Torno subito. *Could you keep my place for me? I'll be right back.*

Ci dettero una parte dei soldi e **tennero** il resto per sé. *They gave us some of the money and kept the rest for themselves.*

Tieni, questo è per te. *Here, this is for you.*

Tieniti pronta per le cinque. *Be ready by five.*

Tieniti forte! *Hold on tight!*

Italic letters in Italian words show where stress does not follow the usual rules.

togliere (to take off)

PRESENT

io	**tolgo**
tu	**togli**
lui/lei/Lei	**toglie**
noi	**togliamo**
voi	**togliete**
loro	**tolgono**

PRESENT SUBJUNCTIVE

io	**tolga**
tu	**tolga**
lui/lei/Lei	**tolga**
noi	**togliamo**
voi	**togliate**
loro	**tolgano**

PERFECT

io	**ho tolto**
tu	**hai tolto**
lui/lei/Lei	**ha tolto**
noi	**abbiamo tolto**
voi	**avete tolto**
loro	**hanno tolto**

IMPERFECT

io	**toglievo**
tu	**toglievi**
lui/lei/Lei	**toglieva**
noi	**toglievamo**
voi	**toglievate**
loro	**toglievano**

GERUND
togliendo

PAST PARTICIPLE
tolto

EXAMPLE PHRASES

Avevo caldo e mi **sono tolto** la giacca. *I was hot and took my jacket off.*

Ho tolto il poster dalla parete. *I took the poster off the wall.*

Stavo **togliendo** i vestiti dall'armadio quando mi hanno chiamato. *I was taking clothes out of the cupboard when they phoned me.*

togliere

FUTURE

io	**toglierò**
tu	**toglierai**
lui/lei/Lei	**toglierà**
noi	**toglieremo**
voi	**toglierete**
loro	**toglieranno**

CONDITIONAL

io	**toglierei**
tu	**toglieresti**
lui/lei/Lei	**toglierebbe**
noi	**toglieremmo**
voi	**togliereste**
loro	**toglierebbero**

PAST HISTORIC

io	**tolsi**
tu	**togliesti**
lui/lei/Lei	**tolse**
noi	**togliemmo**
voi	**toglieste**
loro	**tolsero**

PLUPERFECT

io	**avevo tolto**
tu	**avevi tolto**
lui/lei/Lei	**aveva tolto**
noi	**avevamo tolto**
voi	**avevate tolto**
loro	**avevano tolto**

IMPERATIVE

togli
togliamo
togliete

EXAMPLE PHRASES

Mi **toglieranno** due denti. *I'm going to have two teeth out.*

Lo riconobbi solo quando si **tolse** il cappello. *I only recognized him when he took his hat off.*

Togliti il cappotto. *Take off your coat.*

Italic letters in Italian words show where stress does not follow the usual rules.

trarre (to draw)

PRESENT		PRESENT SUBJUNCTIVE	
io	**traggo**	io	**tragga**
tu	**trai**	tu	**tragga**
lui/lei/Lei	**trae**	lui/lei/Lei	**tragga**
noi	**traiamo**	noi	**traiamo**
voi	**traete**	voi	**traiate**
loro	**traggono**	loro	**traggano**

PERFECT		IMPERFECT	
io	**ho tratto**	io	**traevo**
tu	**hai tratto**	tu	**traevi**
lui/lei/Lei	**ha tratto**	lui/lei/Lei	**traeva**
noi	**abbiamo tratto**	noi	**traevamo**
voi	**avete tratto**	voi	**traevate**
loro	**hanno tratto**	loro	**traevano**

GERUND	PAST PARTICIPLE
traendo	**tratto**

EXAMPLE PHRASES

Il suo modo di fare **trae** in inganno. *His manner is misleading.*

Sono stati **tratti** in salvo dai vigili del fuoco. *They were rescued by the firefighters.*

Un film **tratto** da un romanzo di Agatha Christie. *A film based on a novel by Agatha Christie.*

Dalla ricerca **hanno tratto** conclusioni interessanti. *They've drawn some interesting conclusions from the research.*

Traeva tutti in inganno con la sua falsa modestia. *She deceived everyone with her false modesty.*

Remember that subject pronouns are not used very often in Italian.

trarre

FUTURE

io	**trarrò**
tu	**trarrai**
lui/lei/Lei	**trarrà**
noi	**trarremo**
voi	**trarrete**
loro	**trarranno**

CONDITIONAL

io	**trarrei**
tu	**trarresti**
lui/lei/Lei	**trarrebbe**
noi	**trarremmo**
voi	**trarreste**
loro	**trarrebbero**

PAST HISTORIC

io	**trassi**
tu	**traesti**
lui/lei/Lei	**trasse**
noi	**traemmo**
voi	**traeste**
loro	**trassero**

PLUPERFECT

io	**avevo tratto**
tu	**avevi tratto**
lui/lei/Lei	**aveva tratto**
noi	**avevamo tratto**
voi	**avevate tratto**
loro	**avevano tratto**

IMPERATIVE

trai

traiamo

traete

EXAMPLE PHRASES

Non **trarrei** delle conclusioni così affrettate. *I wouldn't draw such hasty conclusions.*

Trassero in salvo l'alpinista ferito. *They rescued the injured climber.*

Italic letters in Italian words show where stress does not follow the usual rules.

uscire (to go out)

PRESENT

io	**esco**
tu	**esci**
lui/lei/Lei	**esce**
noi	**usciamo**
voi	**uscite**
loro	**escono**

PRESENT SUBJUNCTIVE

io	**esca**
tu	**esca**
lui/lei/Lei	**esca**
noi	**usciamo**
voi	**usciate**
loro	**escano**

PERFECT

io	**sono uscito/a**
tu	**sei uscito/a**
lui/lei/Lei	**è uscito/a**
noi	**siamo usciti/e**
voi	**siete usciti/e**
loro	**sono usciti/e**

IMPERFECT

io	**uscivo**
tu	**uscivi**
lui/lei/Lei	**usciva**
noi	**uscivamo**
voi	**uscivate**
loro	**uscivano**

GERUND
uscendo

PAST PARTICIPLE
uscito

EXAMPLE PHRASES

La rivista **esce** di lunedì. *The magazine comes out on Mondays.*

I suoi non sono contenti che **esca** tutte le sere. *Her parents aren't happy with the fact she goes out every evening.*

È uscita a comprare il giornale. *She's gone out to buy a newspaper.*

Li ho incontrati **uscendo**. *I met them as I was going out.*

L'ho incontrata che **usciva** dalla farmacia. *I met her coming out of the chemist's.*

Remember that subject pronouns are not used very often in Italian.

uscire

FUTURE

io	**usci****rò**
tu	**uscirai**
lui/lei/Lei	**usci****rà**
noi	**usciremo**
voi	**uscirete**
loro	**usciranno**

CONDITIONAL

io	**uscirei**
tu	**usciresti**
lui/lei/Lei	**uscirebbe**
noi	**usciremmo**
voi	**uscireste**
loro	**uscirebbero**

PAST HISTORIC

io	**uscii**
tu	**uscisti**
lui/lei/Lei	**usc****ì**
noi	**uscimmo**
voi	**usciste**
loro	**usc****irono**

PLUPERFECT

io	**ero uscito/a**
tu	**eri uscito/a**
lui/lei/Lei	**era uscito/a**
noi	**eravamo usciti/e**
voi	**eravate usciti/e**
loro	**erano usciti/e**

IMPERATIVE

esci
usciamo
uscite

EXAMPLE PHRASES

Uscirà dall'ospedale domani. *He's coming out of hospital tomorrow.*
Usciresti con me stasera? *Would you go out with me this evening?*
La macchina **uscì** di strada. *The car came off the road.*
Quando siamo arrivati **era** appena **uscita**. *When we arrived she'd just left.*
Uscite di qui immediatamente! *Get out of here this minute!*

Italic letters in Italian words show where stress does not follow the usual rules.

valere (to be worth)

PRESENT		PRESENT SUBJUNCTIVE	
io	**valgo**	io	**valga**
tu	**vali**	tu	**valga**
lui/lei/Lei	**vale**	lui/lei/Lei	**valga**
noi	**valiamo**	noi	**valiamo**
voi	**valete**	voi	**valiate**
loro	**valgono**	loro	**valgano**

PERFECT		IMPERFECT	
io	**sono valso/a**	io	**valevo**
tu	**sei valso/a**	tu	**valevi**
lui/lei/Lei	**è valso/a**	lui/lei/Lei	**valeva**
noi	**siamo valsi/e**	noi	**valevamo**
voi	**siete valsi/e**	voi	**valevate**
loro	**sono valsi/e**	loro	**valevano**

GERUND
valendo

PAST PARTICIPLE
valso

EXAMPLE PHRASES

L'auto **vale** tremila euro. *The car is worth three thousand euros.*

Non ne **vale** la pena. *It's not worth it.*

È stato difficile, ma ne **è valsa** la pena. *It was difficult, but it was worth it.*

Non **valeva** la pena arrabbiarsi tanto. *It wasn't worth getting so angry.*

Valendo poco, questa moto è difficile da vendere. *Since it's worth so little, this bike is difficult to sell.*

valere

FUTURE

io	**varrò**
tu	**varrai**
lui/lei/Lei	**varrà**
noi	**varremo**
voi	**varrete**
loro	**varranno**

CONDITIONAL

io	**varrei**
tu	**varresti**
lui/lei/Lei	**varrebbe**
noi	**varremmo**
voi	**varreste**
loro	**varrebbero**

PAST HISTORIC

io	**valsi**
tu	**valesti**
lui/lei/Lei	**valse**
noi	**valemmo**
voi	**valeste**
loro	**valsero**

PLUPERFECT

io	**ero valso/a**
tu	**eri valso/a**
lui/lei/Lei	**era valso/a**
noi	**eravamo valsi/e**
voi	**eravate valsi/e**
loro	**erano valsi/e**

IMPERATIVE
vali
valiamo
valete

EXAMPLE PHRASES

Senza il giardino la casa non **varrebbe** niente. *Without the garden the house wouldn't be worth anything.*

Italic letters in Italian words show where stress does not follow the usual rules.

vedere (to see)

PRESENT

io	**vedo**
tu	**vedi**
lui/lei/Lei	**vede**
noi	**vediamo**
voi	**vedete**
loro	**vedono**

PRESENT SUBJUNCTIVE

io	**veda**
tu	**veda**
lui/lei/Lei	**veda**
noi	**vediamo**
voi	**vediate**
loro	**vedano**

PERFECT

io	**ho visto**
tu	**hai visto**
lui/lei/Lei	**ha visto**
noi	**abbiamo visto**
voi	**avete visto**
loro	**hanno visto**

IMPERFECT

io	**vedevo**
tu	**vedevi**
lui/lei/Lei	**vedeva**
noi	**vedevamo**
voi	**vedevate**
loro	**vedevano**

GERUND
vedendo

PAST PARTICIPLE
visto

EXAMPLE PHRASES

Non ci **vedo** senza occhiali. *I can't see without my glasses.*

Ci **vediamo** domani! *See you tomorrow!*

Non **vedevo** l'ora di conoscerla. *I couldn't wait to meet her.*

Avete visto Marco? *Have you seen Marco?*

Non **vedendovi** arrivare, ce ne siamo andati. *As we didn't see you arriving, we went away.*

Remember that subject pronouns are not used very often in Italian.

vedere

FUTURE

io	**vedrò**
tu	**vedrai**
lui/lei/Lei	**vedrà**
noi	**vedremo**
voi	**vedrete**
loro	**vedranno**

CONDITIONAL

io	**vedrei**
tu	**vedresti**
lui/lei/Lei	**vedrebbe**
noi	**vedremmo**
voi	**vedreste**
loro	**vedrebbero**

PAST HISTORIC

io	**vidi**
tu	**vedesti**
lui/lei/Lei	**vide**
noi	**vedemmo**
voi	**vedeste**
loro	**videro**

PLUPERFECT

io	**avevo visto**
tu	**avevi visto**
lui/lei/Lei	**aveva visto**
noi	**avevamo visto**
voi	**avevate visto**
loro	**avevano visto**

IMPERATIVE

vedi
vediamo
vedete

EXAMPLE PHRASES

Stasera **vedremo** un film in TV. *We're going to watch a film on TV this evening.*

Finalmente **vedemmo** una nave all'orizzonte. *At last we saw a ship on the horizon.*

Non **avevo** mai **visto** una cosa simile. *I'd never seen such a thing.*

Vediamo un po' il tuo tema. *Let's have a look at your essay.*

Italic letters in Italian words show where stress does not follow the usual rules.

venire (to come)

PRESENT

io	**vengo**
tu	**vieni**
lui/lei/Lei	**viene**
noi	**veniamo**
voi	**venite**
loro	**vengono**

PRESENT SUBJUNCTIVE

io	**venga**
tu	**venga**
lui/lei/Lei	**venga**
noi	**veniamo**
voi	**veniate**
loro	**vengano**

PERFECT

io	**sono venuto/a**
tu	**sei venuto/a**
lui/lei/Lei	**è venuto/a**
noi	**siamo venuti/e**
voi	**siete venuti/e**
loro	**sono venuti/e**

IMPERFECT

io	**venivo**
tu	**venivi**
lui/lei/Lei	**veniva**
noi	**venivamo**
voi	**venivate**
loro	**venivano**

GERUND

venendo

PAST PARTICIPLE

venuto

EXAMPLE PHRASES

Da dove **vieni**? *Where do you come from?*

Quanto **viene**? *How much is it?*

È **venuto** in macchina. *He came by car.*

Era depressa e le **veniva** sempre da piangere. *She was depressed and always felt like crying.*

La casa sta **venendo** bene. *The house is taking shape.*

Remember that subject pronouns are not used very often in Italian.

venire

FUTURE

io	**verrò**
tu	**verrai**
lui/lei/Lei	**verrà**
noi	**verremo**
voi	**verrete**
loro	**verranno**

CONDITIONAL

io	**verrei**
tu	**verresti**
lui/lei/Lei	**verrebbe**
noi	**verremmo**
voi	**verreste**
loro	**verrebbero**

PAST HISTORIC

io	**venni**
tu	**venisti**
lui/lei/Lei	**venne**
noi	**venimmo**
voi	**veniste**
loro	**vennero**

PLUPERFECT

io	**ero venuto/a**
tu	**eri venuto/a**
lui/lei/Lei	**era venuto/a**
noi	**eravamo venuti/e**
voi	**eravate venuti/e**
loro	**erano venuti/e**

IMPERATIVE

vieni
veniamo
venite

EXAMPLE PHRASES

A forza di bere gli **verrà** il mal di testa. *He'll get a headache if he drinks like that.*

Verresti a cena da me domani? *Would you come to dinner tomorrow?*

Mi **venne** un'idea. *I had an idea.*

Erano venuti per parlare con te, ma non c'eri. *They'd come to talk to you, but you weren't there.*

Vieni a trovarci. *Come and see us!*

Italic letters in Italian words show where stress does not follow the usual rules.

vincere (to defeat)

PRESENT

io	**vinco**
tu	**vinci**
lui/lei/Lei	**vince**
noi	**vinciamo**
voi	**vincete**
loro	**vincono**

PRESENT SUBJUNCTIVE

io	**vinca**
tu	**vinca**
lui/lei/Lei	**vinca**
noi	**vinciamo**
voi	**vinciate**
loro	**vincano**

PERFECT

io	**ho vinto**
tu	**hai vinto**
lui/lei/Lei	**ha vinto**
noi	**abbiamo vinto**
voi	**avete vinto**
loro	**hanno vinto**

IMPERFECT

io	**vincevo**
tu	**vincevi**
lui/lei/Lei	**vinceva**
noi	**vincevamo**
voi	**vincevate**
loro	**vincevano**

GERUND
vincendo

PAST PARTICIPLE
vinto

EXAMPLE PHRASES

Quando giochiamo **vince** sempre lui. *When we play he always wins.*

Che **vinca** il migliore! *May the best man win!*

Ieri **abbiamo vinto** la partita. *We won the match yesterday.*

Vincendo l'incontro, si sono aggiudicati il campionato. *By winning the match they won the championship.*

Remember that subject pronouns are not used very often in Italian.

vincere

FUTURE

io	**vincerò**
tu	**vincerai**
lui/lei/Lei	**vincerà**
noi	**vinceremo**
voi	**vincerete**
loro	**vinceranno**

CONDITIONAL

io	**vincerei**
tu	**vinceresti**
lui/lei/Lei	**vincerebbe**
noi	**vinceremmo**
voi	**vincereste**
loro	**vincerebbero**

PAST HISTORIC

io	**vinsi**
tu	**vincesti**
lui/lei/Lei	**vinse**
noi	**vincemmo**
voi	**vinceste**
loro	**vinsero**

PLUPERFECT

io	**avevo vinto**
tu	**avevi vinto**
lui/lei/Lei	**aveva vinto**
noi	**avevamo vinto**
voi	**avevate vinto**
loro	**avevano vinto**

IMPERATIVE

vinci
vinciamo
vincete

EXAMPLE PHRASES

Stavolta **vincerò** io. *I'm going to win this time.*

Non **vincerebbero** mai senza di lui in squadra. *They'd never win without him in the team.*

Vinsero la lotteria e cambiarono vita. *They won the lottery and changed their lives.*

Italic letters in Italian words show where stress does not follow the usual rules.

vivere (to live)

PRESENT

io	**vivo**
tu	**vivi**
lui/lei/Lei	**vive**
noi	**viviamo**
voi	**vivete**
loro	**vivono**

PRESENT SUBJUNCTIVE

io	**viva**
tu	**viva**
lui/lei/Lei	**viva**
noi	**viviamo**
voi	**viviate**
loro	**vivano**

PERFECT

io	**ho vissuto**
tu	**hai vissuto**
lui/lei/Lei	**ha vissuto**
noi	**abbiamo vissuto**
voi	**avete vissuto**
loro	**hanno vissuto**

IMPERFECT

io	**vivevo**
tu	**vivevi**
lui/lei/Lei	**viveva**
noi	**vivevamo**
voi	**vivevate**
loro	**vivevano**

GERUND

vivendo

PAST PARTICIPLE

vissuto

EXAMPLE PHRASES

Vivevano in una piccola casa di periferia. *They lived in a small house in the suburbs.*

Vivendo in città si respira molto smog. *If you live in a city you breathe a lot of smog.*

vivere

FUTURE

io	**vivrò**
tu	**vivrai**
lui/lei/Lei	**vivrà**
noi	**vivremo**
voi	**vivrete**
loro	**vivranno**

CONDITIONAL

io	**vivrei**
tu	**vivresti**
lui/lei/Lei	**vivrebbe**
noi	**vivremmo**
voi	**vivreste**
loro	**vivrebbero**

PAST HISTORIC

io	**vissi**
tu	**vivesti**
lui/lei/Lei	**visse**
noi	**vivemmo**
voi	**viveste**
loro	**vissero**

PLUPERFECT

io	**avevo vissuto**
tu	**avevi vissuto**
lui/lei/Lei	**aveva vissuto**
noi	**avevamo vissuto**
voi	**avevate vissuto**
loro	**avevano vissuto**

IMPERATIVE

vivi
viviamo
vivete

EXAMPLE PHRASES

Non **vivrei** mai in un Paese caldo. *I'd never live in a hot country.*
Vivemmo un'esperienza indimenticabile. *We had an unforgettable experience.*
Non **avevo** mai **vissuto** prima in campagna. *I'd never lived in the countryside before.*
Vivi la tua vita giorno per giorno. *Live your life day by day.*

Italic letters in Italian words show where stress does not follow the usual rules.

volere (to want)

PRESENT		PRESENT SUBJUNCTIVE	
io	**voglio**	io	**voglia**
tu	**vuoi**	tu	**voglia**
lui/lei/Lei	**vuole**	lui/lei/Lei	**voglia**
noi	**vogliamo**	noi	**vogliamo**
voi	**volete**	voi	**vogliate**
loro	**vogliono**	loro	**vogliano**

PERFECT		IMPERFECT	
io	**ho voluto**	io	**volevo**
tu	**hai voluto**	tu	**volevi**
lui/lei/Lei	**ha voluto**	lui/lei/Lei	**voleva**
noi	**abbiamo voluto**	noi	**volevamo**
voi	**avete voluto**	voi	**volevate**
loro	**hanno voluto**	loro	**volevano**

GERUND
volendo

PAST PARTICIPLE
voluto

EXAMPLE PHRASES

Voglio comprare una macchina nuova. *I want to buy a new car.*

Devo pagare subito o posso pagare domani? – Come **vuole**. *Do I have to pay now or can I pay tomorrow? – As you prefer.*

La campanella **voleva** dire che la lezione era finita. *The bell meant the lesson was finished.*

Anche **volendo** non posso invitarti: la festa è sua. *I'd like to, but I can't invite you: it's his party.*

Remember that subject pronouns are not used very often in Italian.

volere

FUTURE

io	**vorrò**
tu	**vorrai**
lui/lei/Lei	**vorrà**
noi	**vorremo**
voi	**vorrete**
loro	**vorranno**

CONDITIONAL

io	**vorrei**
tu	**vorresti**
lui/lei/Lei	**vorrebbe**
noi	**vorremmo**
voi	**vorreste**
loro	**vorrebbero**

PAST HISTORIC

io	**volli**
tu	**volesti**
lui/lei/Lei	**volle**
noi	**volemmo**
voi	**voleste**
loro	**vollero**

PLUPERFECT

io	**avevo voluto**
tu	**avevi voluto**
lui/lei/Lei	**aveva voluto**
noi	**avevamo voluto**
voi	**avevate voluto**
loro	**avevano voluto**

IMPERATIVE

–

EXAMPLE PHRASES

Quanto ci **vorrà** prima che finiate? *How long will it take you to finish?*

Ci **vorrà** una app per scaricare la musica. *You'll need an app to download music.*

Mi chiedo che cosa **vorrà** dire tutto ciò. *I wonder what it all will mean.*

Che cosa **vorresti** che faccia? *What would you like me to do?*

Volle pagare lui a tutti i costi. *He wanted to pay at all costs.*

Il figlio **aveva voluto** la macchina come regalo di laurea. *Their son had wanted a car as a graduation present.*

Italic letters in Italian words show where stress does not follow the usual rules.

How to use the verb index

The verbs in bold are the model verbs which you will find in the Verb Tables. All the other verbs follow one of these patterns, so the number next to each verb indicates which pattern fits this particular verb. For example, **divertire** (*to amuse*) follows the same pattern as **dormire** (*to sleep*), which is number 76 in the Verb Tables.

All the verbs are in alphabetical order. Superior numbers ([1], [2] etc) refer you to notes on page 247. These notes explain any differences between the verbs and their model.

With the exception of reflexive verbs which *always* take **essere**, all verbs have the same auxiliary (**essere** or **avere**) as their model verbs. There are a few exceptions which are indicated by superior numbers [1] to [4]. An asterisk (*) means that the verb takes **avere** when it is used with a direct object, and **essere** when it isn't.

*For more information on verbs that take either **avere** or **essere**, see pages 41–45.*

Verb Index

Notes

[1] Auxiliary = **avere**.

[2] Auxiliary = **essere**.

[3] Auxiliary = either **essere** or **avere**.

[4] Past participle of this verb is rare.